INVESTMENT BANKING
EXPLAINED

INVESTMENT BANKING
EXPLAINED

AN INSIDER'S GUIDE
TO THE INDUSTRY

MICHEL FLEURIET

New York   Chicago   San Francisco   Lisbon
London   Madrid   Mexico City   Milan   New Delhi
San Juan   Seoul   Singapore   Sydney   Toronto

0   QFR/QFR   0 1 4 3 2

ISBN 978–0–07–149733–6
MHID   0–07–149733–1

McGraw-Hill books are available at special quantity discounts to use as premiums and sales promotions, or for use in corporate training programs. To contact a representative please visit the Contact Us pages at www.mhprofessional.com.

This book is printed on acid-free paper.

Contents

Preface

Investment banking is a complicated industry of traders, analysts, brokers, managers, hedgers, "quant jocks," retirement planners, and, yes, even bankers! This business is as creative as it is mechanical, as qualitative as it is quantitative; its clients range from middle-American mom-and-pops to international billionaires, from newly created firms to multinational giants. Investment banks also work for governments.

The business of an investment bank is to deliver a broad range of products and services to both issuing and investing clients. Its offerings go from strategic advice to the management of risk. In the last century, the main purpose of an investment bank was to raise capital and to advise on mergers and acquisitions. Investment-banking services were defined as either *underwriting* or *financial advisory.* We tend to use a broader definition today. This is how JPMorgan describes it: "In the simplest terms, investment banking helps companies decide on their marketplace strategy. . . . Investment banking also provides access to public and private investment grade debt, high yield and bank markets for a wide range of high-profile clients from governments and multi-national companies to family-owned companies and individuals."[1] Investment banks also trade for their own account, and many are involved in managing third-party assets.

The largest investment banks have been around for more than one hundred years, some of them even for two hundred years. However, their business has changed tremendously in the last ten years, as investment banks have innovated at a furious pace. This is probably why they still exist today, "for as all organic beings are striving, it may be said, to seize on each place in the economy of nature, if any one species does not become modified and improved in a corresponding degree with its competitors, it will soon be exterminated."[2]

Forty years ago, if one could insure operational risks, investing on the stock market was rather like taking a bet. The stock market was the realm of speculators. In the 1960s, a new approach and new mathematical models, which could be run with recently invented computers, allowed financial service companies to develop revolutionary diversification techniques to manage the financial risks of investing. A good way for the investment banks to show their mettle in managing risks was to acquire asset managers.

Over the last decade, however, the approach to risk has changed. Investing in diversified assets is still a tenet of money management, but a new approach has transformed the financial markets. Instead of diversifying the risks among various assets, investment banks now slice them up and package them into bits that trade on markets. These bits, which we call *swaps, derivatives, CDOs*, and *credit-default swaps*, allow the transfer of risk from one party who cannot manage it to another party who wants it.

With this new approach to risk, investment banks have taken on more risk, and they have changed the mix of their business. They are now investing their own capital and trading more innovative products, and they have taken on more risk as they have moved away from the pure intermediary approach of their previous business model. This new way of doing business has, not surprisingly, created new kinds of conflicts of interest between the investment banks and their clients. In any of the big investment banks' 10-K filings with the Securities and Exchange Commission (SEC), there are tens of pages on pending legal claims from customers or regulators.

The late 1990s and early 2000s evoke many scandals in which investment banks were involved—think of Enron, Global Crossing, and WorldCom (the telecommunications giant that filed for Chapter 11 bankruptcy protection in 2002 with $30 billion in debt). Moreover, before that, there was the collapse of the two-hundred-year-old Barings Bank, one of the ancestors of today's modern investment banks, and the bankruptcy of Orange County.

In fact no current-day business segment of investment banking has gone unscathed:

- Research and the scandal involving Salomon Smith Barney and Merrill Lynch in 2001
- Trading and the collapse of Long-Term Capital Management (LTCM)
- Fixed income and the bankruptcy of Orange County or the special-purpose vehicles that Enron used to disguise its debt
- Equity issues and the IPO allocation scandal involving Frank Quattrone at CSFB
- The big mergers that turned sour, like DaimlerChrysler and AOL Time Warner
- The 2003 mutual fund scandals involving Janus Capital Group Inc., Strong Financial Corp., and Putnam Investments (owned by Marsh & McLennan)

The scandals have been exposed by dozens of books, and the investment banks have been easy targets for many scathing articles in the business press. Because investment banks are difficult institutions for outsiders to understand and there are few books that explain how they function, we know only the dark side of the picture without comprehending much else, let alone the "whole picture."

To begin with, do you know the difference between investment banking, investment banks, and merchant banking? Or:

everybody talks about globalization, but how do investment banks work outside of Wall Street? As a potential client, how do you choose a bank that is going to create value for you, not for itself? Or, on a professional level, if you want to work for an investment bank, what can you expect?

This book tells how investment banks work most of the time—i.e., very efficiently—and why they have survived. This book is a guide to investment banks. It explains the strategies of the global investment banks. It reviews how investment banks are organized and the interdependency among the various areas. I begin with the long-term history of investment banks (long before Wall Street) and then go on to describe the various businesses of investment banking, taking time to illustrate two different (but arguably equally successful) strategies—those of Merrill Lynch and Goldman Sachs. We then travel across the capital markets around the world, and I explain how the banks develop their international strategy. The various market mechanisms are described, and it is interesting to see how the investment banks have influenced the consolidation of exchanges and electronic venues. The book then analyzes the strategy in each of the main functional areas of an investment bank: *client-relationship management, equity research, equity capital markets, debt capital markets, M&A,* and *third-party asset management.*

Notes

1. sagrad.jpmorgan.com/content/content_9.htm.
2. Charles Darwin, *On the Origin of Species* (London: John Murray, 1859), chap. 4; pages.britishlibrary.net/charles.darwin2/texts.html.

INVESTMENT BANKING
EXPLAINED

1

The Origins of Investment Banking

The NYSE traces its origins to shortly after the American Revolutionary War, when a small group of New York brokers traded a handful of securities on Wall Street. In May 1792, 24 brokers and merchants signed the historic "Buttonwood Agreement," under which they agreed to trade securities on a commission basis. In 1865, the NYSE moved to its present location near Wall Street. In February 1971, the NYSE incorporated as a New York not-for-profit corporation and was owned by its broker-dealer users, known as members or "seat holders." The NYSE was demutualized and converted from a not-for-profit entity into a for-profit entity when it merged with Archipelago on March 7, 2006 and became a wholly owned subsidiary of NYSE Group."[1]

Investment banking tends to be seen as an American phenomenon. Ask anyone on Wall Street where investment banking came from. If the answer is the Banking Act of 1933, then you asked the wrong person, a lawyer! If it is May 17, 1792, and the birth of the New York Stock Exchange outside of 68 Wall Street under a buttonwood tree, then you spoke to an investment banker (and an educated one). If your interlocutor says that she does not know, then she is perfectly normal: nobody really knows where investment banking came from, let alone what it actually is.

In the traditional sense, *investment banking* is buying original issues of securities for resale to the public. But investment banks have many more activities than this, and many of these businesses are much older than the investment banks themselves.

1

Let's start with the financial products in which investment banks deal. Investment banks underwrite and trade government bonds. They finance themselves through repurchase agreements. They develop new instruments of structured finance, the first of which were mortgage-based securities. They participate in international bond syndications. They trade sophisticated options.

Well, these very complex financial products have been around for more than five hundred years—some of them for a few thousand years. And they were developed by the European ancestors of today's investment banks to provide financing in a society that had very little liquidity. Strangely enough, the basic components of financial capitalism—paper money, joint-stock corporations, and stock markets—are much more recent: two hundred to three hundred years old. Invented by European banks, they are the pillars of the industrialization of the economy.

Money, corporations, and stock exchanges are also at the origin of the investment bank, which involves, simply put, an investment by a bank: the purchase of new securities from their corporate issuers and their resale to the public with a listing on a stock exchange. It should be noted that American investment banks have played an important role here, often by promoting a strategic vision for their corporate clients. For many people, it is John Pierpont Morgan who invented (without using the word) investment banking in the early 1900s.

The Glass-Steagall Act of 1933 separated commercial banking from investment banking. It gave the big banks a year to choose between retail banking and issuing securities. They could not do both. Those that chose to specialize in financial markets and securities underwriting became known as investment banks. Protected by law from competition from commercial banks, American investment banks were able to concentrate on capital market activities and on financing the economy. However, while investment banking may have been refined in the United States after 1933, its origin goes back to many centuries before.

The Great Ancestors: The Merchant Banker and the Financier

Success, as is well known, has many fathers, but failure is an orphan. Investment banking has many fathers. The first father is the merchant bank, a type of outfit that operated in the eighteenth century in France and later in the United Kingdom. The term *merchant banker* is a contraction of "merchant and banker." It meant a merchant who extended his activities by offering credit to his clients, initially through the acceptance of commercial bills. The practice is very old: there were exchange bankers in Genoa in the twelfth century. The Genoese bankers received deposits and made *giro*, or international money transfers.[2] They were dealers in bills of exchange, and they operated with correspondents abroad and speculated on the rate of exchange. But they also invested a portion of their deposits and took equity shares as partners in commercial firms and shipping companies. Thereafter, some firms gave up acting as goods merchants and concentrated on trade finance and securities, while others specialized in equity investments.

Later, the Italian merchant bankers introduced into England not only the bill of exchange, but also the techniques used to finance international trade, like the acceptance of commercial bills. In England (and to a lesser extent in the United States afterward), chartered banks could not invest directly in commercial firms or underwrite new issues of corporate securities. The merchant banks also were loath to take a participation in industry or to deal in equity issues.[3] As a result, the financing of firms came through the provision of short-term credit and acceptances, and also from the markets through issuance of bonds.

The other ancestor of investment banks, the financier, was a lender to the prince. True, the Church prohibited usury, but not when lending to governments. For instance, the Order of Knights Templar lent money to the king of France, Louis VII, when he took part in the second crusade in 1146. Beginning in the early 1200s, Italian merchant bankers used their expertise in international finance for the financing of kings and princes. They became bankers to the Pope around 1250 and to Edward I of England a few years later. The Frescobaldi family of Florence, installed in London since 1276, serviced the king until 1311, when it was expelled by Edward II.

It was not easy to be bankers to kings. The Bardi and the Peruzzi of Florence, the two most powerful banking houses of the time, financed Edward III in 1336, the year the Hundred Years' War with the French began. Unfortunately, the English Crown was soon almost bankrupt; the Peruzzi went under in 1342 and the Bardi in 1346.

The Medici bank, created in 1397 and the principal banker to the Papacy, was the largest of its time. It was organized on the hub-and-spoke model, as a family partnership with equity holdings in subsidiaries in which associates could have minority participation. The Medici were toppled by a revolution when they sided with the invading French in 1494.

The next most powerful house was the Fugger family in Germany. Jacob Fugger (1459–1525) was banker to Maximilian I of Austria, Holy Roman Emperor. Fugger lent money to Maximilian to help fund a war with France and Italy. In the early 1500s, the Fuggers became accredited bankers to the Papacy, collecting taxes and selling indulgences, which infuriated Martin Luther. In 1519, Jacob Fugger headed the banking consortium that assembled the funds necessary to have Charles V (duke of Burgundy and king of Spain) elected emperor by the German electors against the other contender, François I of France.

Even while making kings and emperors, the financiers needed to refinance themselves. To do so, they first used the money markets at Antwerp and Lyon in the 1500s, when the usury laws were abandoned, and then the Amsterdam Stock Exchange, where they started mastering the techniques for raising capital.

The European Ancestors

It is conventional to contrast the role of banks in England, where they took no participation in industry, with a European continental model, in which links between banks and industry were legion. In both places, the financing of the Industrial Revolution in the nineteenth century came essentially from private equity and bank credit. During the first half of the century, the banking structure of European countries was dominated by private banks mixing business, family, and personal ties (though with very different national features in England, France, and Germany).[4]

In England, because of the lack of coins, the private banks served as an intermediary between the agricultural counties of the south and the industrial regions of the north and Midlands. As mentioned before, the British private banks took almost no equity participation in industry. After 1880, with a concomitant decline in private banks, the banking system in the United Kingdom concentrated on joint-stock banking.

The banking structure was basically oriented toward commerce and international finance, with a clear division between deposit and merchant banking. Joint-stock banks collected sight deposits and extended very short-term credit (called "discounting operations"). The merchant banks (Barings, Rothschild, and Hambros) financed international commerce through the acceptance and flotation of bonds.

The rapid expansion of financial markets caused merchant bankers to take little interest in industrial investment. Barings dominated the government (or public) debt business at the start of the 1800s. Sir Francis Baring had founded a firm acting as import and export agents for others in 1763; it became a merchant bank in 1776 under the name Baring Brothers. In the 1780s, Barings worked out an alliance with Hope & Co. of Amsterdam, the most powerful merchant bank in Europe's leading financial center. Initially, Barings raised the financing to support the British army fighting in North America during the

War of American Independence. Then it sustained the British war effort against the Napoleonic armies. From 1803 until the early 1870s, Barings was the bank for the United States in London. The bank made payments and purchases for the U.S. government and represented its financial interests. For example, it handled the financing of the purchase of Louisiane from France in 1803–1804.

Barings's main competitors were the Rothschilds. Nathan Rothschild's breakthrough came when he financed Wellington's army against Napoleon in 1814. After that, he financed the post-war stabilization of Europe's conservative powers. After 1815, what made the Rothschilds "the dominant force in international finance" was "the sheer scale—and sophistication—of their operations."[5] By issuing foreign bonds with fixed rates in relation to sterling, the Rothschilds did much to create the international bond market. In 1830 they launched the first bond of the newly created state of Belgium. But, it should be noted, their great strategic error was the lack of a major U.S. operation.

Although not strictly a British bank initially, one should mention the creation of Hong Kong Shanghai Banking Corp in 1865 to finance the growing trade between Europe, India, and China. In 1874, HSBC handled China's first public loan and thereafter issued most of China's government loans. The bank's offices in mainland China, with the exception of Shanghai, were closed between 1949 and 1955, at which point HSBC developed out of Hong Kong and then London, to become the largest European bank and the second largest in the world in the late 1990s.

In France, private banks in the 1800s were already closely tied to business under the name of *marchand banquier.*

> *The wars of the Revolution and Empire caused merchant bankers to refine their techniques of the financing of large concerns. Paris progressively emerged as a national and international payments centre. . . . Continental merchants turned to Parisian banks to manage their debt to Anglo-Saxon countries. Foreign banks had also set up offices in Paris, chiefly Swiss Protestants and Jewish financiers from the German states.[6]*

The Swiss Protestants were Mallet, Delessert, and Hottinguer. The most significant of the Jewish financiers was James Rothschild, who created the French branch of his family's operation in 1814. As a result, the "Haute Banque" came into being in Paris during the Bourbon Restoration; it was an informal but closed circle of twenty private banks, some of them established well before the Revolution:

> In France, the higher echelon of banking engaged much sooner than anywhere else in long-term credit operations, whether as participant investors or by making straight advances to industrial enterprise. Investment in railways encouraged banks to invest in mines, furnaces, iron and steel and metallurgy.[7]

The idea that a bank could invest in equities may have originated in France, but its implementation did not work for long: the French investment banks quickly went bankrupt.

The First Investment Banks

The French banker and politician Jacques Lafitte had, over the course of many years, had the project of creating a merchant bank specializing in long-term financing that would take equity holdings and make long-term loans and would have features of both investment banking (lending to foreign governments and trading on the stock exchange) and commercial banking (taking deposits). He had a political career instead, and it was only in 1837 that he created Caisse Générale du Commerce et de l'Industrie. The bank (also known by the name of its founder, Caisse Lafitte) transformed deposits into long-term industrial equity participations and railway investments. It went bankrupt in 1848. After that, the Crédit Mobilier, founded in 1852 by the Péreire Brothers to finance railways and metallurgy through the issue of short- and long-term CDs (short-term bonds issued by banks), lasted only fifteen years and went bankrupt in 1867. Rothschild had also participated in all the railways and industrial coalitions that opposed the Péreire enterprise. (Of course, Rothschild is still active today in Europe as an investment bank specializing in mergers and acquisitions [M&A].) Finally, the Union Générale was the last to go belly-up in 1882, at which point French banks stopped investing in equities.

In 1863, a law authorized the creation of joint-stock banks in France without prior authorization by the government. Crédit Lyonnais and Société Générale were both joint-stock banks aimed at financing a competitor of the Péreire. They disengaged themselves from universal banking in order to restrict themselves to deposit taking through their vast branch network and short-term credit transactions. Both banks still exist today (although Crédit Lyonnais has recently been merged into Crédit Agricole).

The French system did not work in France, but it did in Germany. According to Professor John Munro, investment banking came to play a far more important role in financing industrialization in Germany than anywhere else.[8]

Private German banks originated with big business and the financial activities of the "court Jews" in the late eighteenth century. The "court Jews" were financiers to the kings and princes of Central Europe between the 1600s and the early 1800s. These German banking dynasties were the Seligmans in Mannheim, who created the von Eichtal bank; the Bethmanns and the Rothschilds in Frankfurt; and the Oppenheims in Hanover. The Warburgs established a banking house in Hamburg in 1798, the same year that Meyer Amschel Rothschild sent his third son, Nathan, to England, where he set up in London six years later.

The formation of Cologne's Schaafhausenscher Bankverein in 1848 marked the beginning of true investment banking in Germany. The Darmstädter Bank für Handel und Industrie was created in Hesse in 1852 on the model of Crédit Mobilier. But it was not until a 1870 law allowing the creation of joint-stock banks that German banks became the paradigm of the universal bank model with the creation of Deutsche Bank and CommerzBank in 1870 and Dresdner Bank in 1872.

Deutsche Bank was founded in Berlin "to transact banking business of all kinds, in particular to promote and facilitate trade relations between Germany, other European countries and overseas markets." These banks created strong links with new industrial firms: witness Georg von Siemens, one of the first directors of Deutsche Bank, and his cousin Friedrich von Siemens, the industrialist. All these banks still exist today, and Deutsche Bank remains the house bank to Siemens.

The U.S. Ancestors

The National Bank Act of 1863, which established a national banking system in the United States for the first time, regulated chartered banks; the notes they issued had to be backed by U.S. government securities. As in England, chartered banks could not mix banking and commerce, but, unlike in England, private banks could. The Boston firm of John E. Thayer and Brother (a precursor to Kidder Peabody) was a private bank whose "principal activities included brokerage, and banking as well as investing in, and trading in, railroads, savings banks, insurance."[9]

The New York firm of Winslow, Lanier & Company specialized in railroad financing, beyond merely distributing the bonds and paying interest. Railway firms were highly leveraged, perhaps because the investing public was distrustful of stocks. The bank was merely following an approach that became so common that it had a nickname: "morganization" (after . . . guess who?). This basically meant that the bank would take several steps to improve the financial position of the firm and to assert some degree of control over it.[10] Isn't that what private equity firms do today? It reveals a strategic vision of the evolution of the clients, which is at the root of modern-day investment banking.

In 1838, an American businessman, George Peabody, opened a London merchant-banking firm. In 1864, Junius S. Morgan named it J.S. Morgan & Co. In 1895, five years after his father's death, John Pierpont Morgan consolidated the family's banking interests, assuming the role of senior partner in each of four related firms in New York, Philadelphia, London, and Paris. (The U.S. firms became J.P. Morgan.) During the Panic of 1893, President Cleveland appealed to Morgan for help. Morgan backed a $62 million gold bond to support the U.S. gold standard and thus prevented a financial collapse of the dollar.

J. P. Morgan also played a very important role in the financing and restructuring of industrial America. He contributed to the making of General Electric, and he set up U.S. Steel by purchasing Carnegie's steel business, thus creating a firm that produced 60 percent of the steel in America at the time. In the first years of the twentieth century, the established firms of the day—J.P. Morgan, Kuhn Loeb & Co., and Speyer & Co.—massively underwrote the securities issues of the utilities and the railroads.

Outside of the quasi monopoly in equity offerings established by J.P. Morgan, two investment banks specialized in the lesser IPOs: Goldman Sachs and Lehman Brothers. Marcus Goldman arrived from Germany in 1848 and founded Marcus Goldman & Co. in 1869 as a broker of IOUs in New York. In 1882 the firm became Goldman Sachs, which grew to be the largest dealer in commercial paper in the United States by the end of the century.

In the early 1900s, Goldman Sachs started co-underwriting all equity issues with Lehman Brothers. Initially they specialized in retail businesses because industrial and utilities issues were for the most part monopolized by J.P. Morgan. The first issue was Sears, Roebuck in 1906, a chain of department stores founded in 1893. For the next thirty years, Goldman Sachs and Lehman Brothers acted as co-underwriters for a total of 140 offerings for fifty-six different issuers!

Henry Lehman, an immigrant from Germany, opened his small shop (a commodities business) in the city of Montgomery, Alabama, in 1844. During the vigorous economic expansion of the second half of the nineteenth century, Lehman Brothers broadened its expertise beyond commodities brokerage to merchant banking. After building a securities trading business, it became a member of the New York Stock Exchange in 1887. After the stock market crash of 1929, the Depression placed tremendous pressure on the availability of capital. Lehman Brothers was one of the pioneers of innovative financing techniques such as private placements, which arranged loans between blue-chip borrowers and private lenders.

Other banks took different paths. Lazard Frères & Co. started as a dry goods business in New Orleans in 1848. Soon after the gold rush, the Lazard brothers moved to San Francisco, where they opened a business selling imported goods and exporting gold bullion. Like Lehman Brothers, they progressively became involved in the banking and foreign-exchange businesses, and by 1876 their businesses had become solely focused on providing financial services. Lazard opened offices in Europe, first in Paris in 1852 and then in London in 1870. Through the early and mid-twentieth century, the three Lazard "houses" in London, Paris, and New York continued to grow their respective operations independently of each other. During the early years of the twentieth century, David Weill ran the firm out of Paris together with Michel and André Lazard, sons of the first-generation Lazard brothers. The London operations were sold to Pearson in 1932.

During the Second World War, Pierre David-Weill fled from the Nazi invasion to New York along with one of the younger nonfamily Paris partners, Andre Meyer. After the war, Lazard Frères & Co. in New York came into its own and attained M&A supremacy. Meanwhile, Lazard Frères in Paris acquired a reputation as a preeminent financial advisor. In the twentieth century, Lazard secured key advisory roles in some of the most important, complex, and recognizable mergers and acquisitions of the time, as well as advising on some of the largest and highest-profile corporate restructurings around the world.

Charles Merrill chose a difficult year to create his brokerage firm: 1914. At that time, brokerage and investment were intertwined, and Merrill Lynch purchased control of Safeway, then a southern California grocery chain, in 1926. Merrill warned his clients about the risk of a crash as early as 1928; he sold the brokerage business to E. A. Pierce in 1930. He then developed Safeway and the idea of "bringing Wall Street to Main Street," i.e., selling securities to average Americans. In the three years between 1938 and 1941, Merrill, Lynch & Co. reentered the brokerage business through acquisitions and marriages. It became the world's largest securities house in 1941 . . . another difficult year. Chapter 3 tells the full story of Merrill Lynch's intelligent design.

The Birth of Modern-Day Investment Banking

The National Bank Act of 1863 had prohibited chartered commercial banks from engaging in corporate securities activities, such as the underwriting and distribution of corporate bonds and equities, but the largest banks found ways around this restriction by establishing state-chartered affiliates to do the underwriting.[11] It was nearly fifty years before the Federal Reserve Act of 1913 established the Federal Reserve System as the central banking system of the United States. Less than fifteen years later, the National Banking Laws and the Federal Reserve Act were amended by the McFadden Act of 1927, which prohibited interstate banking, but also explicitly authorized the national banks to deal in and underwrite investment securities through an internal securities department. Commercial banks had already been active in the securities business, either through an internal securities department like that of the German universal banks or through organizing state bank affiliates.

Peter F. Drucker made a very interesting point at a conference at Wharton in 1993: "The first textbook on banking was published in 1903. It began with two sentences: 'Banks prosper because of the incurable ignorance of the public. Banks make money from the margin between what they get on the money they pay out and what customers don't get on the money they pay in.'"[12] In the 1900s, banks were doing more than taking a margin on depositors' funds. They had also been investing their own assets in speculative securities despite the risk to their depositors. The railroads were initially the most important case of banker control, but as more corporations began to go public in the 1890s, such as General Electric in 1892, bank control extended to other industries. From 1910 to 1915, an investment banking syndicate controlled General Motors via a voting trust![13] Of course, the banks used rather loose lending policies with those companies in which they held shares. On top of that, banks were lending money to their customers to buy securities. The 1914 Clayton Act prohibited interlocking directors within the banking sector, but banks could still sit on the boards of non-bank corporations.

The stock market crashed on "Black Thursday," October 24, 1929, and there was a run on the banks. But that was only the beginning: between 1930 and 1933, nearly 10,000 banks failed. After October 1929, American banks called in loans made to Europe, thus accelerating the banking crises in Germany and in Austria, which saw the failure of Creditanstalt in May 1931. Founded in 1855 in Vienna by the Rothschild family, Creditanstalt was the largest bank in Austria. Austria and Germany had relied heavily on U.S. banks to refinance the consequences of the war. In 1931, German chancellor Brüning had to close all the banks for two days and to introduce foreign-exchange controls. In 1933, Hitler came to power and nationalized all the German banks.

President Roosevelt also closed all the national banks in the United States for a week in March 1933. Around this time, three very important acts were put in place: the Securities Act of 1933 (for primary markets), the Banking Act (the same year), and the Securities Exchange Act of 1934 (for secondary markets). The Banking Act of 1933, also known as the Glass-Steagall Act, separated commercial banking from investment banking and prohibited commercial banks in the Federal Reserve System from engaging in investment-banking activities (i.e., issuing, underwriting, selling, or distributing stock, bonds, or other securities).

It also prohibited any firm that was "principally engaged" in investment banking from owning member banks. The act established the Federal Deposit Insurance Corporation as a temporary agency to guarantee the deposits within commercial banks, and it forced the large banks to choose between investment-banking and deposit-taking activities. J.P. Morgan & Co., for example, chose to continue its commercial-banking business. Senior partners and staff members left the firm to form the securities firm Morgan Stanley & Co. But if the Banking Act separated commercial banking from investment banking, it also eliminated competition for investment banks.

The Banking Act of 1933 is partially to blame for the negligible equity stake banks have owned in nonfinancial companies. With respect to loans, banks cannot lend more than 15 percent of their capital to a single borrower (unlike banks in Japan and Germany, where the thresholds are, respectively, 30 percent and 50 percent). Large-scale issues of debt securities by high-credit-rating companies also help explain why their relationship with banks has been kept at arm's length. Banks' disposition to exert control over major corporations is additionally inhibited by the bankruptcy law, as it imputes legal responsibility to banks if they influence companies' decisions. No wonder American corporate governance has not relied on relationship banking as a mechanism for mitigating managerial moral hazard![14]

Meanwhile, nothing happened (to the banking industry, at least) in the United Kingdom and very little in France. In Germany, the banks were saved by the nationalization decreed by Hitler. The separation between commercial and investment banking was made mandatory in Belgium, Italy, Sweden, and Switzerland, following the U.S. model. In Belgium and in Italy, mixed banks had to split, with only deposit banks being allowed to use the title "bank." The two types of banking were merged again in Europe in the 1960s.

In the United States, even though the commercial banks had to be separated from the investment banks, the funny thing is that the word *bank* was not defined until very late. The Bank Holding Act of 1956 defined a "bank" as "any national banking association or any state bank, saving bank or trust company." (A bank is a bank is a bank.) One had to wait until 1966, when an amendment to the Bank Holding Act defined a "bank" as any institution accepting deposits, which the depositor has a legal right to withdraw on demand, and engaging in the business of making commercial loans.

The Evolution of Modern Banking: The Sixties and Beyond

The emergence of market alternatives to traditional bank loans in the 1960s and 1970s created strong competition for commercial banks. As Drucker noted at the same conference at Wharton: "These margins are gone. Customers switch to the bank with the best rates. Since we can no longer depend on interest differentials, we have to go to fee-based systems."

The McFadden Act and related laws limited commercial banks' ability to expand geographically, and the Glass-Steagall Act restricted the range of products that these banks could offer. The commercial banks were kept at bay. The investment banks, protected by the Glass-Steagall Act from competition from commercial banks, had the field of issuing, underwriting, selling, and distributing stocks, bonds, and other securities to themselves. The Glass-Steagall Act *did not*, however, prohibit the commercial banks from underwriting and dealing in securities outside of the United States.

In the 1960s, the development of a truly international Eurodollar market presented a great opportunity for European universal banks and American money-center banks alike to underwrite huge Eurobond issues. Twenty years later, concentration in the U.S. investment banking led to nonbank corporations trying to enter the business: Salomon Brothers sold itself to Phibro Corp. in 1981, Dean Witter to Sears (the same company that Goldman Sachs and Lehman Brothers had brought to market in 1906), and Lehman Brothers to Shearson American

Express in 1984, and Kidder Peabody was acquired by General Electric in 1986. None of these acquisitions worked out. The marriage of Salomon with Phibro ended in 1986; in 1997, Salomon combined with Smith Barney to form Salomon Smith Barney (which ultimately became Smith Barney again, under the umbrella of Citigroup). Lehman Brothers was spun off by American Express's shareholders in 1994, and today is one of the oldest independent investment banks in the United States. Paine Webber acquired Kidder Peabody from General Electric in 1995 before being merged into UBS in 2000.

Many American investment banks stayed independent, but they had to rely on the equity market. Bear Stearns became a public company in 1985 and Morgan Stanley in 1986, and, the same year, Goldman Sachs (then a private partnership) sold 12.5 percent of its capital to Sumitomo, then the third-largest bank in the world. Finally, Goldman Sachs also went public in 1999. The only remaining partnership is Brown Brothers Harriman, America's oldest private bank, tracing its origin to Brown Brothers, a merchant bank created in 1810 in Liverpool, which opened a branch in Philadelphia in 1818 and merged with Harriman in 1931.

The Banking Act had successfully eliminated competition for investment banks, but this ended in 1999, when its last vestiges were repealed by the Gramm-Leach-Bliley Act. Yet even before that fateful date, commercial banks had invaded the turf of investment banks. Corporations' dependence on bank loans had decreased with time, as they increasingly tapped the debt market. Commercial banks therefore entered the fixed-income business, and the investment banks' market share in this business slipped from 41 percent in 1996 to less than 30 percent in 2002. As a result, investment banks focused on higher-value-added products like structured debt, derivatives, and proprietary trading. They also entered the fund-management business: Merrill Lynch acquired the U.K.'s dominant Mercury Asset Management in 1997, and Morgan Stanley bought Dean Witter Discovery a year later.

The end of the Banking Act allowed commercial banks to become universal banks. In 1998, Citibank's merger with Travelers Group (the owner of Salomon Smith Barney) was a $70 billion endeavor. Chase Manhattan Corp. merged with J.P. Morgan & Co. Inc. to form JPMorgan Chase & Co. in early 2001. In July 2003, Wachovia Corp. acquired a majority of Prudential Financial's retail brokerage business.

Meanwhile, universal banks in Europe tried to resist the competition from the American behemoths, many of them by making acquisitions in the United States. Credit Suisse from Switzerland acquired First Boston Corporation in 1978 to create Credit Suisse First Boston. Another Swiss bank, Swiss Bank Corp. (SBC), acquired the London-based investment bank Warburg in 1994 and, in 1997, the New York–based Dillon Read, one of America's older investment banks. SBC merged with Union Bank of Switzerland in 1997 to form UBS, and Warburg Dillon Read is now the investment-banking arm of UBS. In 1999, Deutsche Bank bought Bankers Trust, which had acquired America's oldest investment bank, Alex. Brown, two years before.

Another strategy for European commercial banks is the one illustrated by Société Générale of France, which has leveraged the steady income from its French retail-banking network to build newer, high-growth and high-return businesses in emerging Europe and in investment banking. As a result, SG was the market leader in equity derivatives worldwide in 2006, a leading global player in traditional–structured-finance businesses such as project, trade, and export finance, and one of the leading underwriters of asset-backed deals denominated in euros.

But most European banks are still too dependent on their old nation-states, and U.S. banks are still very American. The universal bank model, invented in Europe, has yet to become truly global. . . . The trend has just started. So the question is: will investment banks develop a new strategy to keep their activities safe from this emerging model?

Notes

1. From the prospectus for the merger between the NYSE and Archipelago.
2. For instance, the Leccacorvo bank in the 1240s and 1250s.
3. "The London merchant banks did not possess the apparatus of investigation necessary for home industrial flotations, but were admirably placed for the handling of loans to foreign governments and corporations. . . . They were under no temptation to dabble in home industrial issues (except the very largest)." A. K. Cairncross, *Home and Foreign Investment, 1870–1913* (Cambridge: Cambridge University Press, 1953).
4. See R. Bogaert, G. Kurgan-Van Hentenryk, and H. Van der Wee, *A History of European Banking* (Antwerp: Fonds Mercator, 1994), pp. 279–296.
5. "The Richest Dynasty in History?" *Business Week*, December 7, 1998.
6. Bogaert et al., *History of European Banking*, p. 293.
7. Ibid.
8. John Munro, *The Economic History of Modern Europe to 1914* (University of Toronto lecture topic, February 27, 2007).
9. Joseph G. Haubrich and Joao A. C. Santos, *Alternative Forms of Mixing Banking with Commerce: Evidence from American History* (February 2003), ssrn.com/abstract=305281 or DOI: 10.2139/ssrn.305281.
10. Ibid.
11. Randall S. Kroszner and Raghuram G. Rajan, "Is the Glass-Steagall Act Justified?" *American Economic Review*, Vol. 84, no. 4 (September 1994), pp. 810–832.
12. "The New Organization," SEI Center for Advanced Studies in Management, The Wharton School, April 7, 1993.
13. Haubrich and Santos, *Alternative Forms of Mixing Banking with Commerce*.
14. Dante Mendes Aldrighi, *The Mechanisms of Corporate Governance in the United States: An Assessment* (Graduate School of Economics, Getulio Vargas Foundation [Brazil] in its journal *Revista Brasileira de Economia*, April 2003).

Today's repurchase agreements (or repos) are used quite differently, but the mechanics are the same: in a repo transaction, a person sells securities, or other instruments, for a price with the agreement that the seller will buy them back at a higher price on some future date. Repos enable investment banks to finance their inventory of securities. Commercial banks use a different system: they can meet short-term liquidity needs through the fed funds market, which allows a bank to borrow another bank's excess reserves held within the Federal Reserve System on an overnight basis. Since investment banks do not have access to the fed funds market, they created a repo market (also overnight). The repo market is larger than the fed funds market; in fact, it is the largest short-term money market in the world.

Mortgage-Backed Securities

A mortgage is a loan secured by real property. Of course, a straight loan was prohibited in the Middle Ages, even when secured by real property. In order to circumvent the prohibition, the lender would not charge any interest, but he would receive the usufruct from the securitized property as a disguised interest payment. There are examples of liens, or mortgage loans, on windmills, vineyards, fields, and salt mines, or sometimes even a chapel where a portion of the plate collection was paid as disguised interest!

Mortgage loans became very important in the United States to finance private homes. In 1968, the U.S. Congress sponsored the creation of the Government National Mortgage Association (GNMA, better known as Ginnie Mae) to provide liquidity to the secondary mortgage market. Liquidity is the ability to buy or sell a security immediately without materially affecting the market price. The securitization of mortgage loans, introduced in 1970 by Ginnie Mae, allows lenders to move mortgages off their balance sheets while retaining the servicing rights. Any lenders adhering to the GNMA mortgage standards can pool the mortgages, purchase a performance guarantee from GNMA, and then issue

2

The History of Some Key Financial Products

To most people unfamiliar with investment banking, instruments like government securities, repurchase agreements, mortgage-backed securities, and Eurobonds seem unnecessarily complex and sophisticated, invented solely for the benefit of traders and speculators.

In fact, these seemingly modern financial innovations were developed many centuries ago to circumvent the Church's prohibition against charging interest for the loan of money.[1] Until at least the fifteenth century, Church canon law held that usury—charging interest on loans—was contrary to the law of God. The Church forbade lending at interest and reinforced this interdiction regularly. Writing in the early fifth century, St. Augustine bluntly called usury a crime. As a recent illustrious banker and eminent Christian has pointed out:

> *Thomas Aquinas, the brilliant and widely influential systematizer of medieval thought, shared the view that taking interest in any form was morally wrong. The Protestant Luther also shared this view—in fact, if anything, he held it even more forcefully. For him, usury was so wrong that money-lenders deserved to be excommunicated and should be denied a Christian burial.[2]*

The Councils of Lyons in 1274, of Vienna in 1311, and of Vienna in 1392 instituted heavy penalties for usury. The prohibition lasted until the early 1500s, when the search for ways to overcome this interdiction gave rise to newer types of financial products, many of which are essential for modern financial markets.

If the sophisticated instruments of investment banking have been around for almost a millennium, many staples of our financial life today were invented only recently. Take paper money, the limited-liability corporation, and the stock exchange—all three are not even five hundred years old. And it is not a coincidence that they were invented just before the beginning of the Industrial Revolution.

The lesson of history is that governments have favored the growth of money markets and banks as ways to finance their own needs. Initially, banks were the instruments used by governments to finance their wars. States resorted to borrowing to finance the expenses of their maritime expeditions, or to invest in such things as canals and waterways. Then, in the early nineteenth century, these banks played a role in financing the needed infrastructure and the development of industry.

Treasury Bills

Today's Treasury bills are short-term securities issued by the U.S. Treasury to finance the national debt. Treasury bills are issued at a discount from their face value. For example, an investor might pay $960 for a $1,000 bill. When the bill matures, he would be paid its face value, $1,000. The interest is the face value minus the purchase price—in this example, $40 or 4 percent. Similar instruments exist throughout the world, because all governments are in the red! A note promising to repay more than the original credit at a later date was originally called a "bill of exchange." Its appearance is linked to the Champagne fairs, which developed in France (long before the bubbling drink) from the mid-twelfth century on and it could have been invented by Italians from Tuscany.

A bill of exchange was essentially an IOU, but more specifically it was a letter of credit given for the transfer of goods to a creditor for payment at the next fair, in a different location and in a foreign currency. Creditors escaped the interest-rate prohibition because the bill of exchange involved not only credit, but also an exchange of currency and a transfer of goods as part of the same transaction.

Once negotiability was established by imperial edict of Charles V in 1541, these bills were used exactly like transferable letters of credit in that they could be passed around or transferred from hand to hand. Netting was facilitated by the practice of the Antwerp Exchange of concentrating payments at certain set times of day.[3]

During the revolt of the Netherlands against the son of Charles V, Philippe II (1556–1598), bills of exchange were used for short-term public credit. The *asientos* were bills of exchange between the Spanish sovereign and merchant bankers. The merchant bankers provided cash in the Netherlands to pay the Spanish armies and were in turn paid back in Spain with arriving silver from South America that had a value greater than the loans. In some ways, the *asientos* were precursors of Treasury bills.

Repurchase Agreements

A repurchase agreement is a sale-and-buyback transaction, in which money is lent without interest being charged. In a repurchase agreement, a person sells goods for a price, and simultaneously it is agreed that the seller will buy those goods back at a higher price on some future date. For instance, someone buys a flock of sheep with an agreement to sell back the sheep six months later, but the buyer retains any lambs born in the interim. This is not a loan (apparently), and thus it does not break the law of the Church. In reality, the buyer lends money (the purchase price) and keeps the production (usufruct) as disguised interest. In the case of sheep, the lambs are the interest.

certificates in the pool. These certificates, which are sold to investors and represent pro rata claims on the pool, are known today as asset-backed securities.

Asset-backed securities were actually invented nearly five hundred years earlier. Starting in 1522, the city of Paris sold enormous quantities of perpetual, or life, securities—*Rentes sur l'Hotel de Ville*, or Rents of City Hall—secured by municipal revenues at the behest of King François I. None other than Karl Marx made reference to this in *Das Kapital*: according to the memoirs of the Count of Bussy-Rabutin, a celebrated seventeenth-century French gentleman and lover, he suggested to Cardinal Mazarin, the French prime minister, that the taxes collected from the Nivernois province be placed with investors. Mazarin is said to have answered that these future revenues already guaranteed the annuities of City Hall![4]

Today asset-backed securities are any securities backed by loans on assets and properties like cars, computers, and credit card receivables: a collateralized debt obligation (CDO) is a securitized pool of debts, a collateralized mortgage obligation (CMO) is a pool of mortgages, and so on. These are very important products for investment banks. For instance, the CDO industry had grown 180 percent since 1997 to stand at $80 billion in 2005.[5] The sub prime crisis of 2007 slowed down the process.

Bond Syndication

Needless to say, debt and equity security issues are central to investment banking. This practice originated at the beginning of the last millennium, when some governments began borrowing as an alternative to collecting taxes. In 1157, the Republic of Venice was among the first to issue a loan in order to finance the war against Constantinople. Unfortunately, no real stock exchange existed in Venice, and the city's action turned out to be an isolated experiment. Because of the prohibition on the trading of interest-bearing debt certificates, there was no secondary market—no gathering place that would have enabled investors to buy the loans contracted by the gondoliers when they wished to recover the funds that they had invested because they needed to repair their gondola.

Whenever the commune of Genoa in Italy needed to finance a major expenditure, such as a war or colonization, it formed a syndicate (*compera*) of investors to provide the capital. Each investor contributed, let's say, 100 florins, and received in exchange one bond (*luoghe*). To fund the interest and repayment, the commune vested in the *compera* the right to collect a tax, usually created for the purpose. The earliest known *compera*, from 1164, had eleven shareholders and was constituted for a period of eleven years.[6]

The sale of *rentes* by northern French cities in the 1220s seems the most likely precursor to perpetual bonds. The tenants of lands had to pay a rent charge, or *cens*, on land—a formal obligation to pay a stated annuity, in kind or in money. The sale of rents (*census*) was not considered usurious, however: the annuity was considered to be a payment for the irrevocable use of capital, not interest. Rents were perpetual, and the buyer had no expectation of repayment. Theoretically, these rents could have been traded, but the place to trade them came into being only much later.

The French king François I was one of the first kings in the world to issue bonds. His son Henri II tried to use this technique on a large scale. *Le Grand Parti*, in 1555, was the first known attempt to use a large bond issued to all to finance the Royal Treasury. Aside from the fact that the prohibition on lending at interest did not apply to kings and princes, this prohibition was starting to erode anyway. A mass of small subscribers was therefore able to invest their savings in government bonds at a 20 percent yearly rate over twenty years. Unfortunately, the king was defeated at Saint Quentin by the Spanish in 1557 and died two years later, ruining the private savings of many Frenchmen (and at the same time France's "evolution of financial capitalism").

Many financiers lent money to kings and princes. Beginning in the 1600s, the Amsterdam merchant bankers also lent directly to European sovereigns. After the first stock exchanges were created to provide liquidity for these securities, these merchant bankers could refinance the loans in the capital markets. If a loan was too large, they could raise money through the issue of government bonds.

Options

An Egyptian papyrus dating from the middle of the second century BC details a loan in which the lender agreed not to be reimbursed if the boat and its cargo were to be lost at sea, in return for 33 percent interest.[7] In today's financial analysis terms, we would say that the shipmaster had purchased an option to default, in exchange for a 33 percent premium.

Two French economists, Eric Briys and François de Varenne, discovered a similar loan dating from 1298.[8] A Genoese merchant named Benedetto Zaccaria wished to invest in a shipload of thirty tons of alum (used in dyeing and tanning) from Aigues Mortes, on the French Mediterranean coast, to Bruges—in other words, from southern to western Europe. Marine navigation was very protracted—it would take two months to haul the freight—and nothing could be taken for granted; the risk of disaster was always imminent. What Zaccaria did was to sell the alum to two Genoese financiers, Enrico Suppa and Baliano Grilli; he also promised to repurchase the goods on their safe arrival in Bruges at a price significantly higher than that of the preliminary spot transaction. If all went well, Suppa and Grilli would cash in; as for Zaccaria, having repurchased the alum, he would be in a position to sell it at a higher price on the Bruges market. Were the goods to be lost, Zaccaria would owe nothing. He would have effected his sale (albeit at a markedly lower price than he would have received in Bruges), so a heist or a shipwreck was by no means the end of the world. This is what we call today a "buy option." Zaccaria purchased a buy option, or "call," that endowed him with the right (but not the obligation) to repurchase the goods at a future date and at a predetermined price. And all this just before the year 1300!

Cash Is King

What is more ingrained in our daily life than the banknote? For Western civilization, paper money is a recent creation, going back to only the early 1700s in England (it had already been invented and used by the Chinese many centuries before). In 1694, the Bank of England was created as a private institution. Two years later, it started issuing promissory notes to finance the English floating debt. Lenders could either be reimbursed at will at the bank or else hand over their claim to another lender. The credit of the bank was so good, in fact, that most of the lenders used the notes to pay for large purchases.

As mentioned, China was the first country to use paper money over an extended period of time. The first issues might have been as early as the ninth century, but paper money definitely existed in 1107, when China issued a six-color bill.[9] For the next twenty years, these bills were printed out by the zillions (thereby causing at least double-digit inflation). This type of domestic bill disappeared only little by little, and paper money was one of the marvels recounted by Marco Polo.

In *Das Kapital*, Karl Marx explains how the Bank of England managed to create a true currency (nearly six hundred years later) by dint of the short-term loans it received from the public:

> *Lenders could either be reimbursed at will at the Bank or else hand over their claim to another lender. Gradually it became inevitably the receptacle of the metallic hoard of the country, and the centre of gravity of all commercial credit. What effect was produced on their contemporaries by the sudden uprising of this brood of bankocrats, financiers, rentiers, brokers, stock-jobbers, etc., is proved by the writings of that time.[10]*

Today's English ten-pound note still says, "I promise to pay the bearer on demand the sum of ten pounds," and carries the signature of the chief cashier of the Bank of England.

The word *cash* itself is a recent designation in English; its root, however, is the very ancient Tamil word *kasu* or *kcu* meaning coin, and pronounced *cash* to this very day in Tamil Nadu.[11] According to the *American Heritage Dictionary*, the word *cash* comes from the Portuguese *caixa*. *Caixa* is both a box and money. The main mint of the Portuguese empire was located at its headquarters in Goa. When Vasco da Gama arrived on the Malabar Coast in 1498, I can only imagine that the coins of small denomination called *cash* that were kept in a box, *caixa*, gave birth to the word *caixa*, and when the English arrived in southern India, they quickly adopted the word.

The Corporation

The corporation is a structure that is essential to economic growth; in fact, a corporation is considered a person the world over. Because it is a person with limited liability, it can raise capital by issuing shares to the investing public. But it took time to recognize this fact. The first serious issuers of financial instruments were states with their public debt (I already mentioned Venice in 1157). Only later did firms come to play a role as capitalism first took shape, most notably with the development of long-distance seaborne trade at the time of the Renaissance. These firms had to raise capital. In order for this to happen, however, limited liability had to be invented. In a limited-liability company, the shareholders are not liable for the debts of the firm.

The concept of liability being limited to contributions goes back to Roman jurisprudence; that said, over many centuries, associates basically took company debts to their own account. Only in Florence in the early sixteenth century was the notion of a *societa en accomandita* brought into being, in which the associates were not personally accountable for any joint debt; all they were liable to lose was the sums of money they had invested in the association. According to John F. Padgett and Paul D. McLean:

> *The limited liability or accomandite partnership was not legally established in Florence until 1408, well after the invention of partnership systems. Even after their authorization, limited-liability accomandite partnerships were not used heavily in Florence until the 1500s, perhaps because of the popularity of the functional substitute of partnership systems.*[12]

One of the first instances of a public stock issue may well have been that of a joint-stock company going by the mellifluous name of "The Mysterie and Compagnie of the Merchant Adventurers for the Discoverie of Regions, Dominions, Islands and Places Unknown" in 1553. Alexander Gorokhovsky points out that "the promoters raised a capital of £6,000 in shares of £25 each from 'every man willing to be of the societie' (Discovery of Muscovy by Richard Hakluyt 1589/1965), devoting this sum to the purchase of some goods and three ships."[13] The industrial project consisted of discovering the northeast passage to the Promised Land, Cathay (the ancient name for China). Instead, they found a seaway leading to Russia and opened up a maritime trade monopoly with the tsar (Ivan the Terrible). That said, this joint undertaking and others like it were necessarily chartered by a sovereign.

We should also recall the essential role taken on by the VOC (Vereenigde Oost-Indische Compagnie, or United East India Company), founded in Amsterdam in 1602, whose publicly diffused capital was quoted on the stock market at the start of the seventeenth century. Endowed with wide-ranging powers (it could go to war with Spain in India and pay the bills), the VOC paved the way for the Dutch colonial empire and secured it a monopoly in the spice trade. The same kind of company existed in England and was soon to exist in France. All these state-run companies were capital-based and benefited from special authorization from the sovereign to wage war in his or her stead. They were the only companies that were in a position to raise substantial funds because the authorization of the sovereign was crucial to going public.

The free creation of a firm with limited liability and without specific authorization is a much more recent development. The French commercial code of 1807 provided limited liability for joint-stock companies, but they still needed an authorization from the government. It wasn't until 1811 in New York that a new statute for manufacturing companies saw the light of day: open to one and all, the new company did not need any authorization from the state, and losses were limited to contributions. However, the other states did not follow this lead until the beginning of the twentieth century.

In the United Kingdom, the Joint Stock Companies Act of 1844 opened up access to the incorporation of joint-stock companies, but with maintenance of liability.

The tendency to build up business enterprises commanding considerable capital—what may be called the tendency toward capitalistic concentration (*concentration capitaliste*)—was reflected in the creation of innumerable joint-stock companies. Over six hundred such companies—insurance companies, waterworks, gas plants, mines, canals, ports, improvements, and railroads—were founded between 1822 and 1850.[14]

Limited liability was introduced in the United Kingdom by the Limited Liability Act of 1855.

The Stock Exchanges

It all started with the need for settlement of bills of exchange. Today, clearing and settlement is the process by which payment is collected from the buyer and transferred to the seller, while the securities are transferred from the latter to the former. In Genoa, the moneychangers took deposits and offered a transfer as a means of payment between accounts. The brokers for these bank transfers were called *banchieri*, an expression used by the notaries that is derived from the German term for a banker's bench used for money changing (hence the word *bank*).

Exchange brokers needed a place to transfer bills of exchange. Initially the brokers would clear and settle the bills at the next fair, wherever and whenever that was. Later, they began gathering on a regular basis and in the same place, like the Piazza di Rialto in Venice. In the 1340s in Belgium, traders met in Bruges in front of the Van der Beurse Inn—decorated with sculpted *bourses* (purses)—to clear and settle bills of exchange and to do a few commercial transactions involving commodities. This led to the creation of an exchange in Antwerp in 1460, essentially for commodities trading and for settlement purposes. The Antwerp Bourse erected its permanent residence in 1531 with the following statement emblazoned across the façade: "For the practice of merchants from all countries and languages." Antwerp soon became the international financial capital of Europe, especially as a secondary market in national *rentes* (bonds). However, no stocks were listed on this exchange.

In 1521, in the Netherlands, the Amsterdam Bourse still traded in wheat, herring, and spices—not a single security was listed. The essential innovation was the creation of the first public company in the world, the VOC, in 1602 . . . an exchange was needed to allow VOC shares to be transferred. Thus, Amsterdam became the first stock exchange in the world. When the king of England (James I) bestowed a new charter on the English East India Company in 1609 and granted it a monopoly concerning English trade with the Orient, the shares of this company were quoted on what was to become the London Stock Exchange.

Amsterdam became a real capital market in the eighteenth century, trading debt and equity in cash and even in futures markets. It was a truly global exchange, quoting foreign debt and listing foreign equity issuers such as the English East India Company, the French South Sea Company, and a few Swedish companies. The Amsterdam Bourse was by then the largest stock exchange in the world, and was the originator of the modern system of international bond issues. As early as 1725, nearly all large issues were offered in Amsterdam. The issuing syndicate was pretty much structured as it is now, with underwriters and managers of bond issues and a syndicate of selling brokers—almost identical to today's investment bank!

Notes

1. John H. Munro, "The Late-Medieval Origins of the Modern Financial Revolution: Overcoming Impediments from Church and State," University of Toronto, Working Paper Revised, April 17, 2003.
2. Stephen Green, *Serving God? Serving Mammon?* (London: Marshall Pickering, 1996).
3. Meir Kohn, "Bills of Exchange and the Money Market to 1600," 1999, http://www.dartmouth.edu/~mkohn/Papers/99–04.pdf.
4. Karl Marx, *Capital*, 1867, Book 1, Chap. 31.
5. Merrill Lynch annual report for 2005.
6. Meir Kohn, Department of Economics, Dartmouth College.
7. J. Liversidge, *Everyday Life in the Roman Empire* (New York: G. P. Putnam's Sons, 1976), cited in B. Jacobs, *Capital Ideas and Market Realities* (New York: Blackwell, 1999), p. 27.
8. Eric Briys and François de Varenne, *The Fisherman and the Rhinoceros: How International Finance Shapes Everyday Life* (London: Wiley, 2000).
9. Discussed by the great Swiss historian Paul Baroch in *Victoires et Deboires* (Paris: Gallimard, 1997), p. 332.
10. Karl Marx, *Capital*, Vol. I. Library of Economics and Liberty. Retrieved May 26, 2006 from the World Wide Web: www.econlib.org/LIBRARY/YPDBooks/Marx/mrxCpA31.html.
11. Tamil was the language of the traders in south India and Sri Lanka.
12. "Organizational Invention and Elite Transformation: The Birth of Partnership Systems in Renaissance Florence," *American Journal of Sociology*, January 2006.

13. "Trade and Diplomacy: The English Merchants in Sixteenth Century Russia," *Student Economic Review,* Vol. 18, 2004.

14. Henri Sée, *Modern Capitalism: Its Origin and Evolution* (Kitchener, Ontario: Batoche Books, 2004).

3

The Business of Investment Banks

What is investment banking?

In finance, *investment* means buying securities or other financial assets.

Simply put, investment banks . . . invest. They purchase new securities from corporate issuers and resell them to the public. But they also trade securities on capital markets.

In the Standard Industrial Classification (SIC) Code List,[1] the word *bank* is used for Commercial Banks (group 602) only. In the wake of the 1956 act's open-ended definition of a bank— "any national banking association or any State bank, savings bank, or trust company"—Congress has amended the statutory definition three times. Since 1970, the statute has specified that a bank is any institution that "(1) accepts deposits that the depositor has a legal right to withdraw on demand, and (2) engages in the business of making commercial loans."[2]

Investment banks are included in the Security and Commodity Brokers and Dealers groups (groups 621 and 622). These major groups include establishments engaged in the underwriting, purchase, sale, or brokerage of securities and other financial contracts on their own account or for the account of others.

Whereas commercial banks serve as intermediaries between customers who save money and customers who borrow it, investment banks facilitate companies' direct access to the capital markets.

If investment banks do not lend money (but sometimes do lend money), another question arises.

What Do Investment Banks Do?

To answer this question, here's a simple illustration. A corporation needs capital in order to grow. An investment bank will sell securities issued by that corporation to investors in order to *raise* the money that the corporation needs. By contrast, a commercial bank *lends* money to the corporation, rather than *raising* it.

The core functions of investment banking include the following:

- Raising capital
- Trading securities
- Advising on corporate mergers and acquisitions

More generally, an investment bank acts as an intermediary and matches sellers of securities with buyers of securities. But investment banks do more than just that: "The scope of investment banking include all major capital market activities such as underwriting, private placement, M&A, venture capital, market making, proprietary trading, financial engineering, clearing and settlement, and financing and money management."[3]

Take two leading U.S. investment banks, Merrill Lynch and Goldman Sachs. What are their *core competencies* (areas of expertise that provide customers benefits, are hard to imitate, and can be leveraged widely to many products and markets)? Both banks define themselves according to their service offering:

> *Merrill Lynch & Co. . . . provides capital markets services, investment banking and advisory services, wealth management, asset management, insurance, banking and related products and services on a global basis. . . . Merrill Lynch offers these products and services to a wide array of*

clients, including: individuals and institutional investors, business of all sizes, financial institutions, government and governmental agencies.[4]

Goldman Sachs is a leading global investment banking, securities and investment management firm that provides a wide range of services world-wide to a substantial and diversified client base that includes corporations, financial institutions, governments and high-net-worth individuals.[5]

Both investment banks offer a wide range of services, which include raising capital and providing strategic advice, to the same client base.

Now compare the values of Goldman Sachs and Merrill Lynch, respectively:

- Client focus, integrity, meritocracy, excellence, entrepreneurial spirit, and teamwork
- Client focus, respect for the individual, teamwork, responsible citizenship, and integrity

As you can see, their values are very similar. Basically, these two investment banks offer the same scope of services to the same clients, and they abide by the same values.

The Scope of Investment-Banking Operations

At heart, an investment bank acts as an intermediary,[6] matching sellers of securities with buyers of securities. It acts as an intermediary for its clients (i.e., corporations, governments, institutions, and individuals). These clients can be either investors or issuers. In spite of the name, the former do not always invest—they can be either buyers or sellers. The latter are issuers of securities and are firmly on the sell side.

An investment bank therefore acts as an intermediary either between investors (buyers and sellers) or between investors and issuers. They can work either on the buy side or on the sell side. They can also act in an advisory capacity for their clients. An investment bank acts in three ways: services to clients, available products, and financial role.

Services to Clients

Both Goldman and Merrill stress their presence and intelligence as the key to their servicing all financial needs:

> We [at Goldman Sachs] seek to be the advisor of choice for our clients, and draw on our worldwide presence and industry leadership to develop a portfolio of offerings designed to serve the full spectrum of financial needs.

> We [at Merrill Lynch] leverage our global resources and market intelligence to deliver innovative, comprehensive solutions to our clients.

So not only do both firms cater to the needs of their clients, focus on solutions, and render many services, but they are also damn smart (ipse dixit)!

The range of activities that Goldman and Merrill provide depends on the type of clients:

- For *issuers of securities*—like investment institutions, corporations, governments, and agencies—the bank offers its capital market services. These services continue the investment banks' ancestral role of financier, but modern-day banks' activities go beyond that. The banks keep inventing (and underwriting) new financing structures to adjust the issuers' cash flow to the appetite of investors.
- For *investors*, the bank proposes its selling capabilities to advise on the attractiveness of a financial product. Its brokers (private-client representatives) talk to individual investors. Its institutional sales force provides investors with opportunities to diversify their portfolios, manage risk, and enhance returns.
- For *buyers and sellers of securities*—like money management firms, insurance companies, and the various types of funds—the bank proposes its trading expertise to execute transactions in equities, bonds, currencies (referred to as Forex or FX), options, and futures. The bank's traders then lock horns with other traders at commercial banks, investment banks, and large institutional investors.

- For *clients dealing in commodities*, whether as industrial companies hedging their risks or as speculators taking a position in the market, the bank makes a market in this product. When making a market, the investment bank acts as a principal that takes the other side of customer trades.
- The research departments of investment banks *convey information to investors* about monetary or economic matters. They also provide recommendations concerning the future prospects of listed securities.
- Continuing on the advisory side, investment banks *propose strategic advice and valuation services in mergers and acquisitions*, transactions dealing with the equity capital of corporations.

Available Products

All investment banks deliver their services to their clients through client-relationship managers.

In most banks, the client executive in charge of issuing institutions provides advice to companies on the full spectrum of the bank's products. These services are organized by industry sector.

On the investor side, client coverage is segmented by client classes. The private-client representative caters to individuals and works quite independently from the rest of the bank. The institutional salesperson develops business relationships with large institutional investors.

Nevertheless, investment banks are still managed to a considerable extent by product-line specialists because the client executive cannot master all the techniques. Corporate Finance is responsible for financial and strategic advice on a range of major transactions. Equity Capital Markets has responsibility for initial public offerings, privatizations, and secondary offerings.

Many divisions of an investment bank, and of trading in particular, are still specialized by product lines. For instance, the Equities division assists clients with their investing and trading strategies in the various equity and equity-linked markets. The

Fixed Income division deals in interest-rate securities. Others divisions specialize in currencies or in commodities.

Investment banks advertise their expertise through "league tables." Published by third parties like Thomson Financial, league tables rank the banks according to their success in broad categories of products. The lines of products in which investment banks deal are often classified as *advisory, equity capital market,* and *debt capital market.*

Financial Role

An investment bank can trade as a principal investor or as an agent. When trading as a principal investor (so-called proprietary trading), the bank is buying and selling for its own account. When the bank acts as an intermediary, this is an agency transaction. There is also a role in between, where the bank can be a counterparty. The investment bank stands willing to buy (or sell) the security (and thus creates a market). Even though they facilitate their clients' trades, investment banks risk their own capital in doing so.

The Investment Banks' Organizational Structures

An investment bank's structure is like a tango—one step forward and two steps backward—as it tries to find the best organization for cross-selling its wide range of services to its client base. "Structure follows strategy" was the motto of Goldman Sachs's strategy committee, which in 1998 was charged with surveying the terrain for the next five to ten years.[7] Here, we compare the structures of Goldman Sachs and Deutsche Bank in 2007.

Goldman Sachs

In 2007, Goldman Sachs was organized into three divisions: Investment Banking, Trading and Principal Investments, and Asset Management and Securities Services. Twenty years earlier, the firm had had four divisions: Investment Banking, Equities (stock trading), Fixed Income (bond trading), and Currency and Commodities Trading.[8]

The Investment Banking Division

This division developed and maintained long-term relationships with Goldman's clients as their lead investment bank. Organized by regional, industry, and product groups, the segment sought to combine client-focused investment bankers with execution and industry expertise. It was divided into two components: *Financial Advisory* (mergers and acquisitions, divestitures, corporate defense activities, restructurings, and spin-offs) and *Underwriting* (public offerings and private placements of equity and debt instruments).

In 2003, Goldman Sachs merged all its capital market activities to create its *financing group*. An important part of investment banking, the financing group delivers to clients a single and comprehensive source of expertise and advice across the capital structure. This is from the bank's Web site:

> *Our aim is to provide our clients with the best and most innovative financing and risk management solutions across the product spectrum (including equity, debt and derivatives). The group comprises all Goldman Sachs' capital markets departments and operates in close cooperation with our other divisions, primarily investment banking, FICC and Equities.*

The Trading and Principal Investments Division

This division included the Trading and Capital Markets area and Merchant Banking. In turn, Trading and Capital Markets contained the prominent Fixed Income, Currencies and Commodities division (FICC) and the Equities division.

FICC was active in all kind of financial assets:

- Credit products, including trading and investing in credit derivatives, high-yield securities, bank loans, municipal securities, emerging market debt and other distressed debt, and equity securities

- Mortgage-backed securities and loans and other asset-backed securities
- Interest-rate products, including interest-rate derivatives, global government securities, and money market instruments
- Currencies and currency derivatives
- Commodities, commodities derivatives, and power generation activities

In the equity business, Goldman Sachs had the largest institutional business in the world. The equities landscape changed rapidly and significantly in the early 2000s, and the main driver of success in the equity business was the ability to recognize these changes (as well as the changes in clients' needs). The bank offered securities, futures, and options clearing services. It was a specialist and a market maker in equity securities and options.

Merchant banking had become a forte of Goldman Sachs. The firm had increasingly moved from acting on behalf of clients to acting as a principal. By trading and directly investing for itself, Goldman Sachs put more of its capital at risk than its competitors did. An *Economist* article succinctly explained this: "Goldman applies capital not only to what has traditionally been perceived as proprietary trading —punts on the market—but to other businesses as well. Some of these, such as executing trades for clients in return for a commission, used to have no risk at all. With increasing frequency, investors no longer want a straight broker. They want someone to take on the risk of the transaction, and that someone must put up money and possibly suffer losses or make an outsized gain."[9] According to the then chairman of the bank, Henry Paulson, clients did not resent this role or see it as a conflict of interest.[10] At Goldman Sachs, clients are less clients in the traditional sense than partners.

The Asset Management and Securities Services Division

Asset Management offered mutual funds and an array of products as well as services for high-net-worth individuals. The Securities

Services division provided prime brokerage products and securities lending programs. The prime broker typically provides financing and back-office accounting services, as well as settlement services, to hedge funds. Goldman Sachs has become the premier provider of low-touch trading, an electronic trade execution service for institutional brokerages. According to Paulson, "A key area of growth has been low touch electronic trading. . . . We trade some 650 to 700 million shares per day through electronic trading systems. . . . More than 2,000 organizations use our low touch trading." These services enable investors to tap most markets directly and to develop automated buy and sell strategies.

Although it is not mentioned in the core group of activities, Global Investment Research provides in-depth analyses of markets, companies, industries, and currencies worldwide, and the Institutional Portal provides clients with online access to market intelligence and trading opportunities.

Deutsche Bank

Let us now take a minute to consider a European universal bank, just to give us an idea of how similar these banks are to American investment banks.

Deutsche Bank got into retail banking in 1959 by introducing small personal loans. Thirty years later, in 1989, the bank acquired the former arm of J.P. Morgan in London, the Morgan Grenfell Group. The bank was then able to strengthen its position in the international securities business. After expanding its presence in the important London capital market, Deutsche Bank acquired Bankers Trust in the United States in 1999. And in 2006, the bank completed the acquisition of the Russian investment bank United Financial Group (UFG).

In 2007, Deutsche Bank had three group divisions: Corporate and Investment Bank (CIB), Private Clients and Asset Management (PCAM), and Corporate Investments (CI). The CIB contained Global Markets (Deutsche Bank's capital markets business) and Global Banking.

Global Markets consisted of all sales, trading, and research in equity, debt, and other capital market products. Similar to Goldman Sachs's Financing group, Global Markets handled debt and equity origination jointly with Corporate Finance. Global Banking comprises Corporate Finance and Global Transaction Banking. Corporate Finance covers not only merger and acquisition (M&A) advisory services and debt and equity underwriting, like Goldman Sachs's Investment Banking division, but also Asset Finance and Leasing, Commercial Real Estate, and corporate lending businesses. Global Transaction Banking comprises Cash Management, Trade Finance, and Trust & Securities Services.

The PCAM division was Deutsche Bank's investment management business, together with its traditional banking activities for private individuals and businesses. PCAM comprised two corporate divisions: Asset and Wealth Management and Private & Business Clients. Asset Management provided institutional clients with a full range of services and retail clients with mutual fund products. Private Wealth Management served high-net-worth individuals and families worldwide with a fully integrated wealth management service. Private & Business Clients offered traditional retail-banking products, from current accounts to deposits and loans, along with investment management products and services.

The Revenue Mix

Investment banks receive their revenue from five sources: commissions, trading income, underwriting revenues, interest, and various kinds of fees.

- A *commission* is the revenue from many kinds of agency transactions (when the bank acts as an intermediary), stipulated as a percentage of the transaction value.
- *Trading income* is the realized and unrealized gains and losses when the bank "makes a market" (takes the other side of customer trades). This is a pretty complex notion, which will become clearer when we discuss it in Chapter 7.

- *Underwriting revenues* are the gross profits (or losses) from underwriting security issues.
- *Interest* can be margin interest (when customers borrow against the value of their securities to finance purchases) or interest from investment accounts (including repurchase agreements and reverse repurchase agreements).
- *Asset management fees* include fees from the sale of mutual funds and from the management of portfolios.
- *Other securities-related revenues* include advisory fees from mergers and acquisitions, but also dividends and interest from investment accounts (including repurchase agreements and reverse repurchase agreements).

Table 3–1 compares the sources of revenue for the U.S. investment banking and securities brokerage industry in 1999 and 2005 and shows how other securities-related revenues have increased during these six years.[11]

Other securities related revenues grew from 36.4 percent to 50.3 percent during the period. It is not so much advisory fees that have grown during the period, but rather the return from investment accounts.

According to the Boston Consulting Group, revenues from underwriting equity and debt issues and advising on M&A accounted for 21 percent of investment banks' revenues in 2005,

Table 3-1. Sources of Securities Industry Revenues (percent of total)

	1999	2005
Commissions	16.0	11.6
Trading income	19.9	7.7
Underwriting	8.7	7.7
Interest	7.3	4.9
Asset management	6.2	10.2
Other securities-related	36.4	50.3
Non-securities-related	5.5	7.6
Total	100.0	100.0

down from 26 percent in 2001. Advisory revenues fell from 10 percent to 6 percent of the total.[12]

The Main Clients

Table 3–2 shows the fees paid to American investment banks by their clients around the world for the whole range of investment banking services outside of trading. It is interesting to note that in 2001, more than half of the larger clients of investment banks were telecom companies. In 2005, more than half of the better clients for investment banks were private equity funds.

Table 3-2. Ranking based on corporate estimated spent on investment banking fees-mergers and acquisitions, equity capital markets, debt capital markets, loans

	2005	
Rank	Company name	Total fees ($m)
1	Blackstone Group	305
2	KKR	304
3	Telefonica	296
4	Warburg Pincus & Co	295
5	Carlyle Group	264
6	Goldman Sachs Merchant Banking	262
7	Apax Partners	245
8	Thomas H Lee	240
9	Apollo Management	217
10	EDF	201
11	Texas Pacific Group	197
12	Gazprom	194
13	CVC Capital Partners	189
14	Permira Advisers	182
15	Cinven Limited	177
16	Suez	175
17	Ripplewood Holdings	165
18	3i Group	161
19	CSFB Private Equity	160
20	First Reserve Corporation	159

Rank	Company name	2001 Total fees ($m)
1	Altria Group	**257**
2	France Telecom	**250**
3	Vodafone Group	**230**
4	Koninklijke KPN	**224**
5	BT Group	**223**
6	Nippon Telegraph & Telephone	**216**
7	Tyco International	**189**
8	KKR	**174**
9	Agere Systems	**168**
10	Time Warner	**166**
11	Orange	**162**
12	AT&T Wireless	**160**
13	Charter Communications Hldgs	**152**
14	Deutsche Telekom	**146**
15	Calpine Corp	**145**
16	Adelphia Communications Corp	**144**
17	Warburg Pincus & Co	**140**
18	JP Morgan Partners	**139**
19	Telecom Italia	**135**
20	Sprint Corp	**134**

Source: Thomson Financial / Freeman & Co

Note: the rankings exclude financial institutions and governments. Closed end funds' ECM activity is excluded.

How Do They Compare?

Investment banks are generally classified as bulge bracket; tier one; regional; and boutique, or specialized, firms.

- *Bulge bracket* firms provide the entire spectrum of invest-ment banking services for large-cap (more than $10 billion) and increasingly mid-cap firms ($2 to $10 billion). Small-cap and micro-cap firms (less than $2 billion) are covered by boutiques. In an equity issue prospectus, the underwriters are listed in brackets, with the more prestigious under-writers in the higher brackets underwriting more shares. The bulge bracket investment banks handle the majority of Wall

Street transactions. They include Morgan Stanley, Goldman Sachs, Merrill Lynch, Citigroup Global Capital Markets, and Credit Suisse.

- *Tier one*, or major bracket, firms are large full-line firms that do not have the same status as the bulge bracket firms. The better-known major bracket firms are Lehman Brothers, Wachovia Capital Markets, UBS (Warburg PaineWebber), and Bear Stearns.
- *Regional brokers* have branch networks in certain regions of the country. Raymond James Financial Inc. is an example. Regional banks have also become more active in the investment-banking business through acquisitions: the east coast bank PNC acquired a leader in mid-market M&A advisory, Harris Williams, in 2005 and, on the west coast, Wells Fargo & Co. purchased a boutique investment firm, Barrington Associates, in 2006.
- *Boutiques* tend to be small and focused on a class of service offerings. In Europe, there are Lazard and Rothschild, both of which specialize in mergers and acquisitions advice. Others include Houlihan Lokey Howard & Zukin, Hawkpoint, and Lexicon, which specialize in smaller transactions.

The latest strategic trend is for the largest investment banks to continue to expand at the expense of the mid-tier organizations. All together, there are less than ten of these investment banks in the whole world! While there may be some room for regional or specialty firms in niche markets, it will mainly be the large players that will gain market share in the near future. This is even more true with the rise of the universal bank model.

Under the Glass-Steagall act, American commercial banks, or money-center banks, were excluded from underwriting activities. With big corporations moving more and more of their borrowing to the capital markets over the past two or three decades, universal banks started underwriting stocks and bonds, advising on mergers and acquisitions, and trading in securities and commodities as soon as the regulations allowed them to do so. The large banks emerged as strong competitors in the brokerage and investment-banking industry by acquiring smaller investment banks and brokerages.

In 1985, all of the top ten investment banking and brokerage participants were stand-alone entities.[13]

In the mid–1990s, large commercial banks started returning to corporate investment banking as the restrictions imposed by the Glass-Steagall Act began to fall. These banks acquired investment-banking firms to gain market share.

The number of stand-alone houses shrank to eight in 1995 when Credit Suisse and J.P. Morgan entered the top ten list. After the repeal of the Glass-Steagall Act, American banks started to follow the European universal bank model, with a convergence of commercial banking and investment banking through mergers and acquisitions.

By 2005, large commercial banks, including Citigroup, JPMorgan Chase, Bank of America, and HSBC, had become major competitors in the global investment banking industry. Only five of the top ten investment banks were still stand-alone: Goldman Sachs, Morgan Stanley, Merrill Lynch, Lehman, and Lazard. Goldman Sachs ranked first among advisors in 2006, followed by Citigroup, Morgan Stanley, J.P. Morgan, and Merrill Lynch.[14] But Citigroup was the leader in global equity and equity-related underwritings. Citigroup had the biggest investment-banking revenues of any institution in 2005 except Goldman Sachs.[15]

Goldman Sachs was the most active trader on the NYSE in 2003, 2004, and 2005, with approximately 10 percent of the NYSE's trading volume, but it was rivaled in this role by UBS AG after 2003.

The five universal banks that were in the top ten in 2005 were:

- JPMorgan Chase after the merger with Banc One
- UBS Investment Bank, which had acquired Paine Webber, Warburg, and Dillon Read
- Citigroup after its acquisition of Salomon Smith Barney

- Deutsche Bank, which had bought Bankers Trust and Alex. Brown
- Credit Suisse, which had taken over DLJ

Of these five universal banks, three were European!

While there may be some room for regional or specialty firms in niche markets (like M&A) or for specific clients (like hedge funds), the boutique or specialized bank model is difficult to follow. Firms with a diverse range of services win business over specialists. But how do you acquire a broad range of services? The following illustration shows how a retail brokerage firm has become a full-service investment bank. The process took eighty years, but it is food for thought for competitors. The Merrill Lynch model illustrates a successful strategy in investment banking. Oftentimes, it will be applied through successive acquisitions.

Merrill Lynch: An Intelligent Design

The French philosopher Gilles Deleuze once said, "Rhizomes develop in terms of relays moving at different velocities and in many directions—similar to the way crabgrass branches out."[16] Throughout its history, Merrill Lynch has branched out from its retail brokerage franchise in much the same way as a rhizome, or crabgrass, does. Darwinian evolution is not everything in this case, but it helps.

Bringing Wall Street to Main Street

Charles E. Merrill invented the notion that securities could become a consumer product. Very early, he was intrigued by the use of mass merchandising for the sale of securities. While working in the fledgling bond department of the Wall Street firm George H. Burr & Co., Merrill wrote an article in the November 1911 edition of *Leslie's Weekly* addressed to "Mr. Average Investor": "Having thousands of customers scattered throughout the United States is infinitely preferable to being dependent upon the fluctuating power of a smaller and perhaps on the whole wealthier group of investors in any one section." The article also emphasized the broker's need to consider the customer's circumstances and objectives when suggesting investments.

In January 1914, Charles Merrill created his brokerage firm and was soon joined by his friend Edmund Lynch. Almost immediately, Charles E. Merrill & Co. won the contract to underwrite the $6 million offering of a chain store called J.G. McCrory Co. (Unfortunately, the New York Stock Exchange closed on July 31, 1914, because of the beginning of World War I, and didn't reopen until December 12. Nevertheless, Merrill did the IPO of the chain store in May 1915.) It is probably not a coincidence that Charles Merrill adopted chain stores' marketing to sell securities thereafter. By 1917, Americans were used to seeing movie stars like Charlie Chaplin drum up support for Liberty Bond sales. It was Charlie Merrill who created the first advertisements ever run for Liberty Bonds. After the war, Merrill Lynch specialized in underwriting chain stores, which were rapidly expanding across the country.

Brokerage and investment were intertwined at the time, and in 1926 Merrill Lynch purchased control of Safeway, then a southern California grocery chain. "The acquisition [represented] the firm's most significant investment outside the financial field to date," according to ML's Web site in 2007. Sensing the potential for financial instability, Charlie warned his clients of the risk of a crash as early as 1928. He advised them to "take advantage of present high prices and put your financial house in order." Of course, October 1929 proved him right. In February 1930, Merrill Lynch pledged to devote itself "to the continued development of its investment banking business" and transferred its retail brokerage business to the brokerage firm E. A. Pierce. The firm then focused on Safeway Stores, building it up to become the country's third-largest grocery store chain. In 1932, Merrill founded *Family Circle*, the first grocery store point-of-sale magazine.

In the late 1930s, Merrill started seriously putting into action his credo of using mass merchandising to sell securities to the average

American. During that period, E. A. Pierce had grown into America's largest brokerage house, but it was close to bankruptcy. In January 1940, Merrill Lynch reacquired its retail-brokerage business by merging with E. A. Pierce & Cassatt. Merrill proclaimed the bank's tenet: "Our business is people and their money. We must draw the new capital required for industrial might and growth not from among a few large investors but from the savings of thousands of people of moderate incomes. We must bring Wall Street to Main Street—and we must use the efficient, mass-merchandising methods of the chain store to do it."[17]

From Retail Brokerage to Equity Trading

When applying the mass-merchandising methods of the chain store to securities, how does an investment bank become not only "one of the world's leading financial management and advisory companies, with offices in thirty-five countries and private client assets of approximately $1.5 trillion," but also "a leading global underwriter of debt and equity securities and strategic advisor to corporations, governments, institutions, and individuals worldwide"?

As both the leading brokerage firm and the leading firm ensuring trading on the equity market, by 1941 Merrill Lynch had become the world's largest securities house, with offices in ninety-three cities and memberships in twenty-eight exchanges. In 1944, the firm handled about 10 percent of the NYSE's volume.[18]

After the war, Merrill Lynch bore a striking resemblance to Safeway: with branches all over the country, it had become a household name. It started to take its role of educating and advising the average investor very seriously. In 1948, the firm published "What Everyone Ought to Know about This Stock and Bond Business," an advertisement that explained the securities industry and defined such terms as *stocks* and *bonds* for the general public. Education and advising were the conditions for bringing Wall Street to Main Street. In so doing, Merrill invented equity research. The British Bankers Association had the occasion to write:

The whole reason for having research analysts has always been as a means of selling stocks in the primary market, and generating transactions, whether buy or sell, in the secondary market. The origin of the research analyst within securities' firms has been succinctly described as follows: "Charles Merrill [of Merrill Lynch] and his imitators soon adopted security analysis as a selling tool and established large research departments—quite unknown until the 1940s—to turn out stock recommendations and market letters."[19]

After having become the leading U.S. equity trading firm, the natural next step for Merrill Lynch was to apply the same strategy internationally—much later. In 1995, the bank acquired the largest brokerage firm in the United Kingdom, Smith Newcourt. Smith Newcourt was a hidden jewel for Merrill: it controlled nearly 25 percent of the equity transactions on the London Stock Exchange. With this acquisition, Merrill Lynch became the largest equity organization in the world, with unsurpassed research, trading, and sales capabilities. As it had done fifty years earlier in New York, Merrill could grow, from its rhizomes in London, in the direction of investment banking and the advisory field.

From Wire House to Financier

An initial public offering (IPO) is the first sale of a corporation's common shares to investors on a public stock exchange (see Chapter 10). IPOs generally involve a large group of banks, called an *underwriting syndicate*, to approach investors with offers to sell these shares. Syndicate formation begins with the selection of the book manager (or lead underwriter) by the issuing firm. With the largest market share on the NYSE, Merrill Lynch could start embracing the business of raising capital for corporations.

In 1956, Merrill Lynch was selected as one of seven managers to bring Ford Motor Company public. The record-setting $600 million offering gave the firm its first billion-dollar underwriting year. It was a public offering of a consumer stock, however, and Merrill Lynch was only one of the underwriters. Except for

Morgan Stanley, which was General Motors' primary banker, every major investment bank was included. This was a compelling reason for Ford to use the largest securities house to bring the shares of one of the better-known car manufacturers to the American public. The deal literally brought the cars of Main Street to Wall Street!

In 1964, Merrill Lynch became a dealer in fixed-income securities with the purchase of C. J. Devine. And it also became a real financier: the firm was selected to lead eleven managers in the $100 million public offering of Communications Satellite Corporation (COMSAT). Merrill Lynch went public in 1971, the second Big Board member to do so, but the first to have its shares listed on the NYSE.

Merrill Lynch, however, was still considered a "wire house" (a firm operating a private wire to its own branch offices). This was not a compliment. Before the early 1980s, a wire house was not seen as a real investment bank that was able to deliver powerful institutional investors to the corporate world in search of capital. CFOs were encouraged to think poorly of Merrill Lynch by top-notch investment banks like Goldman Sachs and Morgan Stanley. The common wisdom was that trading securities for retail investors could bring only small investors with limited amounts of new capital. In most cases, one or two investment banks take the lead role in setting up a new IPO. For serious people, one needed white-shoe bankers who were able to bring the large and influential institutional investors who alone were able to make a share offering successful. Merrill Lynch could be part of the bank syndicate, but the bank could not lead an equity offering.

Merrill Lynch tried to shake off its wire house image by making targeted purchases. In 1978, it acquired White, Weld & Co., Inc., an old-line international investment-banking house, to strengthen its investment-banking division. It also acquired Becker Paribas, another international investment bank, in 1984. But competitors still managed to keep Merrill Lynch from getting the top spot: lead managing an IPO. In 1987, under the leadership of Barry Friedberg (the head of investment banking, who had arrived with A.G. Becker), Merrill Lynch went on strike: it refused to participate in a syndicate only to bring its armies of brokers to sell to retail investors. Friedberg's argument was essentially to look at Merrill's market share in the equity market. Its dominance of trading meant that the firm had as strong a relationship with institutional investors as with private investors. Consequently, the big competitors like Goldman and Morgan could not expect to limit Merrill to retail investors. The gamble paid off. Since 1988, Merrill Lynch has topped the U.S. and global debt and equity underwriting chart.

In very much the same vein, in 1986 Merrill Lynch invented the zero coupon convertible bond. Liquid Yield Option Notes, or LYONs, are zero coupon bonds that are convertible (at the holder's option) into common stock. Because no other bank wanted to help Merrill underwrite the first LYONs, Merrill turned a weakness into a force and made a point of being sole manager for all the new issues. This strategic gamble paid off in 1990, when Merrill Lynch acted as sole underwriter for the Walt Disney Company's $2.25 billion LYONs. Today Merrill Lynch is a recognized world leader in the underwriting, trading, and distribution of convertible securities, and it manages one of the industry's largest daily inventories of issues. Merrill Lynch maintains an active secondary market not only in LYONs but in other convertible issues as well.

From Financier to Advisor

The goal of any investment bank worth its salt is not only to become a financier and structure a debt offering, but more specifically to help the company to raise capital on the equity capital market. The reason is probably that this kind of decision involving shareholders' funds has to be discussed and vetted by the board, and often by a shareholders' meeting. Once you are recognized as a financier on the capital structure side, it is relatively easy to act as an advisor in mergers and acquisitions and, from there, in takeover defenses.

To illustrate the point, Merrill Lynch France was selected as the bank advisor to the French government and put in charge of international placement for the privatization of the French steel company Usinor in 1996. In 2000, when Usinor merged with Arbed from Luxembourg and Aceralia from Spain to create Arcelor (then the largest steel company in the world), it was Merrill Lynch that advised Usinor. Finally, when Mittal Steel launched an €18.6 billion ($22.1 billion) hostile bid for Arcelor in 2006, the Luxembourg-based steelmaker was advised by five banks led by Merrill Lynch. Mittal was advised by Credit Suisse, Goldman Sachs, HSBC, Société Générale, and Citigroup.

Merrill Lynch engaged in additional acquisitions to complete the move from financier to advisor. For example, the bank purchased Petrie Parkman & Co., a firm specializing in advisory services for the oil and gas industry, in October 2006.

From Retail Brokerage to Asset Management

Until the mid–1970s, clients purchased securities from Merrill Lynch with the help of account executives (known today as *financial advisors*). Because the decision was the customer's, Merrill Lynch provided its private clients with education and advisory services. In 1976, Merrill Lynch created Merrill Lynch Asset Management (MLAM), a money management firm. MLAM extended the service of providing advice and began to allow its retail investors to have their funds professionally managed by buying shares in mutual funds or unit trusts. The Cash Management Account, introduced in 1977, combined a securities margin account with a money market account plus a checking account and a VISA debit card.

Twenty years later, Merrill Lynch acquired Mercury Asset Management, an international asset management group based in the United Kingdom. With combined assets of $450 billion now under its management, Merrill Lynch held a leading position in asset management in both the United Kingdom and the United States. This acquisition provided the company with an exceptional position from which to serve its clients and capitalize on the substantial amount of worldwide growth opportunities. Merrill Lynch, however, was not able to branch out from this acquisition, and its assets under management remained pretty much the same in the subsequent eight years while its competitors increased their assets by 50 percent. As a result, Merrill Lynch decided in 2006 to sell its asset management operation to BlackRock, a money manager serving wealthy investors and institutions, thus making BlackRock one of the world's biggest money managers, with about $1 trillion in assets and 4,500 employees in eighteen countries. In exchange, Merrill acquired a stake of just under 50 percent of BlackRock's capital in a transaction valued at roughly $9 billion (see Chapter 16).

Notes

1. The Standard Industrial Classification Codes that appear in a company's SEC filings indicate the company's type of business.
2. U.S. Supreme Court, *Board of Governors, FRS* v. *Dimension Financial*, decided January 22, 1986.
3. K. T. Liaw, *The Business of Investment Banking* (New York: Wiley, 1999).
4. Merrill Lynch 2004 Factbook.
5. Goldman Sachs 2003 annual report; see also www2.gold mansachs.com/.
6. "Intermediation supposes the existence of financial institutions like banks, mutual funds, insurance companies, etc., that collect excess financial resources from various economic agents to invest them in the securities issued by the economic agents with the financing needs" (vernimmen.com/html/glossary).
7. Lisa Endlich, *Goldman Sachs, The Culture of Success* (New York: Alfred A. Knopf, 1999), p. 250.
8. Ibid., p. 4.

9. "Goldman Sachs: Behind the Brass Plate," *Economist*, April 29, 2006.

10. Henry M. Paulson, Jr., Chairman and CEO, Presentation to the 2004 Merrill Lynch Financial Services Conference, November 16, 2004.

11. E. Robert Hansen and Justin Menza, *S&P Industry Survey: Investment Services*, May 2006.

12. Peter Thal Larsen, "Banks Face Big Test to Keep Clients," *Financial Times*, May 30, 2006.

13. Peter A. Horowitz, "Shifting from Defense to Offense: A Model for the 21st Century Capital Markets Firm," BearingPoint, 2005.

14. Standard & Poor's Industry Surveys—Investment Services, May 17, 2007.

15. "A Survey of International Banking: The Risk-Takers," *Economist*, May 20, 2006.

16. Gilles Deleuze and Felix Guattevin, *A Thousand Plateaus*, Vol. 2 of *Capitalism and Schizophrenia* (Minneapolis: University of Minnesota Press, December 1987).

17. Merrill quoted in Robert Sobel, *Dangerous Dreamers: The Financial Innovators from Charles Merrill to Michael Milken* (New York: Wiley, 1993), p. 30.

18. Staff of *Forbes* magazine and Daniel Gross, *Greatest Business Stories of All Time* (New York: Wiley, 1996).

19. British Bankers Association, Response to CP 171: "Conflicts of Interest: Investment Research and Issues of Securities," April 18, 2003.

4

Charting the Course

As we saw in Chapter 3, all investment banks do pretty much the same things. So how can they differentiate themselves from their competitors? Goldman Sachs's 2004 annual report had this to say: "As we often remind our people, Goldman Sachs cannot control the market environment in which we work. But we can control our relative performance." Likewise, sailors are fond of saying, "We can't direct the wind, but we can adjust the sails." Investment banks do not know which way the winds will be blowing, but they can develop a strategy to control their relative performance.

The Product/Client Matrix

The major rudder in investment banking is how to grow the franchise. Let's go back to the broad scope of investment-banking operations with their diverse range of customers. A simple product/client matrix goes a long way in explaining how a bank can grow its franchise. Traditionally, investment banking covered advisory services and underwriting. But today investment banks make a point of developing a much more complete portfolio of

Table 4-1. The Product/Client Matrix

	Capital Raising	Capital Markets	Advisory
Investors			
Financial			
institutions	Capital	Market maker	Sales
Individuals	Financing	Broker	Research
Issuers			
Corporations	Capital	Risk management	M&A
Government	Bond		
	underwriting	Government dealer	Privatization
Proprietary	Principal investor	Proprietary trading	Investment
			partnership

offerings designed to serve the full spectrum of financial needs. It is the three main service offerings of an investment bank that constitute the vertical columns of the franchise matrix:

- Role in primary markets
- Role in secondary markets
- Advisory services and M&A

In each of these three types of offerings, the bank caters to the needs of its clients: either investors (individuals and financial institutions) or issuers (corporations or governments). Each row refers to a type of client. And as the investment banks put more and more of their own capital at risk, an additional type of client has been added: the bank itself. Finally, each quadrant of the matrix corresponds to a service offered by the bank to a particular client. Table 4–1 helps in anticipating complex client needs to offer complete solutions.

Services

First I'll comment on each of the columns in turn. *Raising capital* has been one of the historical roles of investment banks. You will remember that the financier is one of two ancestors of investment banks. In its traditional role as financier, an investment bank will raise money either through the debt markets (these include new markets like the high-yield bond market) or through the equity markets (this includes new markets like the private equity markets). The successful investment bank has become an expert in raising capital in the form of both equity and debt. Global equity and equity-related underwritings[1] include domestic and international placements of equity offerings and equity-related transactions. This includes initial public offerings (IPOs), follow-on offerings, accelerated book buildings, block trades, and convertible bonds. Debt capital markets underwritings include all U.S. public, Euro public, and Rule 144a global debt transactions (including global bonds, euro/144a transactions, Yankee bonds, Eurobonds, foreign bonds, and preferred stock), as well as mortgage-backed securities (MBS), asset-backed securities (ABS), and tax munis. But the investment bank's role goes beyond that. It caters to the need of issuers by delivering to clients a comprehensive source of expertise and advice across the capital structure.

The second role of investment banks involves *capital markets*. The bank will distribute securities and also make a market in a given security (taking the other side of customer trades). An investment bank makes a market not only in securities, but also in derivatives, currencies, and other financial instruments to satisfy its clients' demand for these instruments. It also operates in public regulated markets or in OTC markets (see Chapter 7). When trading in capital markets, the bank assumes one of two roles: it is either trading in response to its clients' needs or trading as a principal investor. When responding to its clients' requests, the bank trades on behalf of its clients. When trading as a principal investor (so-called proprietary trading), the bank is buying and selling for its own account. The problem is that it isn't always easy to distinguish between the two. In markets with little liquidity,[2] the bank often has to commit its own capital to facilitate a client trade. Once the bank has invested its own capital, there is a proprietary aspect to the trading, even though it may have been driven by a client's request.

The third role is that of an *investment advisor.* Investment banks have sales relationships with institutional investors. In this role, they offer investment ideas and liquidity services to these investors, like block trading services for large transactions and prime brokerage (see Chapter 7). Also, we should not forget the role of investment banking research—whether macroeconomic, fixed income, or securities research.

Additionally, there is the role of investment banks as advisors to issuers—be they corporations, governments, or institutions. For corporations and institutions, investment banks play an advisory role in mergers and acquisitions. The bank may identify a target; it can also provide access to this target. It assesses the high-level strategic rationale of a proposed acquisition. It develops a deal structure and suggests a financing method. It develops the valuation of the target. In this case, the banker negotiates on behalf of the client to determine the price to be paid, the mode of payment, and other terms of the deal. For governments, investment banks can advise on privatizations or can simply underwrite an equity offering of previously state-owned enterprises. They can also underwrite government bonds and advise governments on financial matters.

Clients

In general, investment banks cater to a wide range of clients, both *investors* (institutions and individuals) and *issuers* (corporations and governments). Certain banks will focus on only a certain type of client. Finally, there is the *proprietary role,* when the bank puts its own capital at risk. In this case, the client is the bank itself. Arguably, Goldman Sachs is an investment bank that puts most of its capital at risk—in principal investments in trading and in creating private-equity partnerships. The following is an explanation of how it got involved in this role:

> *The Merchant Banking division invests in corporate and real estate assets worldwide through a series of investment funds managed by the*

Principal Investment Area (PIA), the Real Estate Principal Investment Area (REPIA) and the Urban Investment Group (UIG). Goldman Sachs began making principal investments in 1982, committing the firm's capital to long-term equity investment opportunities generated from the firm's investment banking and brokerage clients. In 1986, Goldman Sachs began to organize investment partnerships to allow outside investors to participate in private investments with the firm. This activity proved so successful and strategic that the firm formed the Merchant Banking division in 1998 to house the PIA and REPIA investment activities.[3]

Principal investing consists of buying equity (or deeply subordinated debt securities) in privately held companies and real estate assets and working with management and operating partners to enhance the value of the assets purchased over time. For the privately held company, this means raising capital. In capital markets, the bank puts its capital at risk when it is making a market. As we saw before, an investment bank puts its capital at risk in trading—not only when it is buying and selling for its own account, but also when it commits its own capital to facilitate a client trade. Finally, the bank—when making a principal investment—can create an investment partnership (as well as allow outside investors to invest in the partnership). Ultimately, principal investors seek to harvest investments in order to generate substantial returns. While investment bankers are financial advisors who charge fees for their services, principal investors take equity risk and make profits when assets appreciate in value or are sold at a gain.

In order to grow its franchise, the successful investment bank usually takes a premier position in one of the matrix's boxes and then moves in either direction (as in checkers). But Goldman Sachs often assumes all the roles for both the client and the transaction. Since the mid–1980s, cooperation with other departments has been included in formal performance evaluations used to determine compensation.[4] In the following illustration, the matrix will help us understand why Goldman Sachs in the 2000s was arguably the premier investment bank in the world.

Illustration: Why Is Goldman Sachs So Successful?

From 1998 to 2005, Goldman averaged a yearly return on equity of 24 percent, making it the biggest firm on Wall Street in terms of market value (excluding commercial banks). From 1984 to 2004, Goldman Sachs's net revenues grew on average at 16 percent, almost three times the growth in global GDP. At the Goldman Sachs presentation to the 2005 Merrill Lynch Financial Services Conference, Henry M. Paulson, Jr. (then Goldman Sachs's chairman and CEO) gave the following hint: "We focus very hard on generating attractive return on our business. But we also place a great premium on growing our franchise and see attractive opportunities ahead." To decode Paulson, what has driven Goldman Sachs's growth is anticipating clients' needs, but also taking advantage of the opportunities that arise from the financial markets' growth and the capital markets' changes.

Among the principal determinants of success in the investment services industry, one often finds trends in the market and the economy.[5] Certainly a recovering confidence did help, since the economy drives both investors' confidence and the CEOs' confidence: raising capital and doing mergers and acquisitions depend on the CEO's confidence, and the trading businesses and the capital-committing businesses depend on customers' activity (and hence on investors' confidence). But there are two main characteristics that better explain the bank's success over the long haul: the breadth of its operations on the one hand, and how it takes advantage of the changes in the capital markets on the other.

The Breadth of Goldman Sachs's Operations

Here's an example.

In 2005, Goldman Sachs advised the city of Chicago on the $1.83 billion private concession for the Chicago Skyway Toll Road (CSTR).[6] The Chicago Skyway is a 7.8-mile, 6-lane toll bridge that began operation in 1958. In the 2000s, when the city of Chicago undertook a substantial capital-improvement program to be completed by the end of 2004, it started looking at financing solutions. In the end, the city decided that the appropriate public policy decision was to sell a concession. Historically, in infrastructure financing, the first option is to raise taxes. If that fails, the second option is to issue tax-exempt bonds. Goldman Sachs developed a new option: a "public-private partnership," in which a public service is funded and operated through a partnership between the municipality and a private-sector company. Capital investment is made by the company on the strength of toll revenues. The municipality's contribution to the partnership is the sale of the concession. Public-private partnerships are a new source of capital for state and local governments. They can be structured to avoid any impact on taxpayers, and they provide a lot more capital (debt and equity) for a given project while shifting the operating risk to a private party. Equity investors look for future returns based on growth, and the sale of a concession provides an opportunity to capture the anticipated growth in future traffic flows and toll increases.

Goldman Sachs acted as an advisor to the municipality over three years. The bank used its worldwide network to contact over forty potential bidders and helped evaluate prospective buyers. Once the winner was selected—a consortium between Cintra of Spain and Macquarie from Australia—the Skyway Concession Company (the newly formed managing entity) raised $1.4 billion of long-term debt secured by expected toll revenues. The bank underwrote the debt as a lead manager. This included complex interest-rate swaps to tailor debt payments to toll cash flows. Goldman was counterparty to the interest-rate swaps with the company, providing its own capital to facilitate the transaction.

At this point, let's refer back to the franchise matrix. An investment bank aims to offer four types of services:

- Financing (raising capital)
- Markets (trading in capital markets)
- Advisory (investment and M&A)
- Proprietary (committing capital)

In the Chicago Skyway Toll Road project, Goldman Sachs provided all four types of services in the very same transaction. As Goldman Sachs senior executives like to say, the firm acts as a financier, an advisor, and a principal across the whole range of products. The firm has the stated objective of being the premier bank in each of these three roles, endeavoring to combine its whole range of expertise for the same client.

The Function of Financier

In order to deliver its expertise in capital raising to its clients, in 2003 Goldman Sachs merged all its capital market activities to create its financing group. As an important part of investment banking, the financing group delivers to clients a single and comprehensive source of expertise and advice across the capital structure. In the CSTR transaction, the financing group was able to provide a financial engineering solution to the winning consortium when Goldman underwrote the $1.4 billion of long-term debt secured by toll revenues.

In Capital Markets

In capital markets, the bank has built a complete and almost perfectly diversified offering across a whole range of financial assets. In the CSTR transaction, FICC provided the interest-rate swaps to tailor debt payment to cash flows.

Advisory

Advisory includes assignments with respect to mergers and acquisitions, divestitures, corporate defense activities, restructurings, and spin-offs. It includes helping to structure and execute an array of financial transactions. Of course, Goldman's initial role in the CSTR transaction was that of an advisor to the Municipality of Chicago for three years.

Acting as a Principal

"Almost all of the largest and most complex transactions began with the client asking Goldman Sachs to commit capital and to commit its risk management expertise." Complex transactions demand the spreading of risk and the sharing of expertise. In the Chicago Skyway deal, Goldman provided its capital to facilitate the toll bond financing. But that came only after Goldman selected the winning bidder for the transaction. Indeed, the risk of conflict of interest is not negligible.

Attracting New Clients and Taking Advantage of Market Opportunities

Goldman Sachs's strategy is to develop new products and services as financial markets change. For instance, twenty years after Goldman started its commodities business in 1980, trading commodities was the place to be. The Goldman Sachs Commodities Index went from 3,000 in January 2002 to more than 6,000 by the end of 2005. Another example of this success is the derivatives market. Credit derivatives allow a firm to spread the risk of complex transactions. As a new asset class, outstanding credit derivatives grew from $270 billion in 1997 to more than $5 trillion in 2005. Goldman Sachs is a world leader in derivatives. Paulson doesn't hesitate to state the obvious: "It is very easy to decide to be in the commodities (or derivatives) business in the midst of a bull market in commodities (or derivatives)." In other words, the key to successful investment banking is to identify potential growth areas well before they flower.

A good example of attracting a new range of clients is to be found in the private-equity business. Private pools of capital have developed very rapidly since the mid–1990s, and Goldman Sachs is now a leader with hedge funds[7] and private-equity firms. Hedge fund assets have trebled between 1997 and 2005. Hedge funds have become some of Goldman Sachs's best clients because of their heavy trading and financing needs. The bank became a leader in offering low-touch electronic trading for large-volume order flow from hedge funds. It is also one of the biggest providers of financing and deal-making services to private-equity firms. Private equity capital grew from $20 billion in 1995 to $315 billion in 2005. Finally, according to Paulson, "Restructuring and reform play to our combined strength as a financier, a principal investor, and an advisor." For example, he identified significant opportunities for the firm to benefit from corporate reform in Germany and Japan.

A Combination of Outstanding People and a Strong Culture

All investment banks stress the same competitive advantage: focused strategy and execution, global reach, focus on clients, the people and culture of the firm, and the firm's reputation. What holds true for Goldman Sachs also holds true for Merrill Lynch (and many other investment banks as well). The real strength of Goldman Sachs, therefore, is its ability to take advantage of unexpected opportunities and position itself accordingly. To do so, Goldman rides the product/client matrix for the same client. The bank acts as a leading financier, a market maker, an advisor, and a principal investor around the world, across the whole range of products, and often for the same transaction. As Lisa Endlich, a veteran of Goldman Sachs, explains: "Our clients are working with professionals who prefer to work in teams and are connected to many others through the firm."[8]

Merrill Lynch, by contrast, evolves across the matrix but does not focus on delivering the whole set of expertise to the same client. For Merrill, the challenge lies in creating seamless teams that are able to convert a structure that is still organized in product silos into a real client-focused organization.

Notes

1. Underwriting is buying a new issue of securities from the issuing corporation and reselling it to the public.
2. Liquidity is the ability of an investor to convert assets to cash quickly and without significant loss. The ease with which an asset can be turned into cash depends on the number of buyers and sellers. A liquid market enjoys continuous offers, bidding, and consummated transactions.
3. www2.goldmansachs.com/careers/inside_goldman_sachs/ business_snapshot/merchant_banking/index.html.

4. Lisa Endlich, *Goldman Sachs: The Culture of Success* (New York: Alfred A. Knopf, 1999), p. 22.

5. See, for instance, the Standard & Poor's yearly Industry Survey for investment banking.

6. "Public-Private Partnerships—The Skyway Sale and Its Implications for Municipal Finance," Presentation to the National Association of State Treasurers, September 21, 2005.

7. Hedge funds are difficult to define precisely, but they are not traditional investment funds. The term *hedge fund* comes from *hedging,* or taking both long and short positions to reduce risk. In practice, these firms tend to make riskier investments than conventional money managers.

8. Endlich, *Goldman Sachs*, p. 27.

5

The Global Reach

Merrill Lynch stretched its footprint in order to grow in size in the last years of the twentieth century. In a 2003 presentation to investors, Stan O'Neal, the then chairman and CEO of Merrill Lynch, explained how he had reviewed the international expansion of the firm:

> *The implications of that analysis were far-reaching for our business. For example, when we looked at Canada, South Africa and Australia we saw countries not very densely populated in terms of wealth . . . that required enormous costs related to real estate dispersed over large geographic areas. We saw brokerage cultures driven by transaction volumes. Given our view of the economic outlook . . . this was not a sustainable business model. So, we had to reconfigure our investment in those markets.*

Merrill Lynch had simply tried to open the door of an international market with the wrong key.

The Keys to an International Expansion

What are the drivers of a successful international strategy for an investment bank? In its 2007 report on the industry, Standard & Poor's identified four factors:

- Corporate clients' needs
- Restructuring and reforms
- International investment options for domestic clients
- Investment services for developing wealthy populations[1]

Access to business contacts, international capital, and financial products are needed for corporate clients. Goldman Sachs's first push on the road to international expansion came in the late 1970s when one of its clients, General Foods, approached the bank with an offer to acquire a French food company. Goldman Sachs had no office in France (or anywhere else in the world) at that time, and it had to turn down the business.[2] In addition, restructuring and reform, including privatization trends worldwide, have increased the supply of equity and the demand for capital, creating further opportunities for investment banks. Investment banks can develop a role in government advisory, pension advisory, restructuring advisory, and sale of cross-holdings. More and more, investors are looking to invest globally as a means of enhancing returns and reducing risk, putting pressure on asset managers to offer international investment options. Finally, increasingly wealthy populations of developing countries are looking for investment services from investment banks.

These are all good reasons for investment banks to expand their global footprint. But where should they go, and what kinds of services should they offer? What drives the choice of the markets to serve, in terms of both service offering and location?

Given the way investment banks have behaved in the past, it is likely that the drivers of global expansion will be capital markets' growth and liquidity. We believe that these are the two factors that will be especially important for an investment bank to consider in developing its global reach.

First (as Always) Growth

To reiterate, the key to successful expansion is to identify potential growth areas well before they flower—to recognize and anticipate patterns in a long-term evolution of the global capital market across geographies and asset classes. Over the twenty years from 1984 to 2004, the global financial stock market has grown much faster than world gross domestic product (GDP).[3] While in 1980 the global capital market was roughly the size of global GDP (109 percent of GDP), it was double the size of global GDP by 1993 (216 percent), and more than triple the size of global GDP by 2003 (326 percent). Between the years 1993 and 2003, the global financial stock grew on average at 8.4 percent, more than twice as fast as the growth in global GDP of 4.0 percent.

If one remembers that the core functions of an investment bank include acting as an intermediary between investors and/or issuers and matching sellers of securities with buyers of securities, it should come as no surprise that the revenues of investment banks have grown in accordance with global financial stocks, and therefore faster than global GDP. As we saw at Goldman Sachs, the revenue grew even faster than the global financial stock (GFS). The reason, of course, is that not all asset classes grow at the average rate. It's no surprise that a successful bank will have a keen interest in focusing on the fastest-growing products in the fastest-growing regions.

From 1984 to 2004, private debt securities contributed the most to the growth of the global financial stock. At the end of these twenty years, they were the largest asset class within the GFS, growing faster than equity securities or bank deposits. In contrast, government debt securities were the smallest asset class (17 percent of GFS) and had grown the most slowly since 1993. No wonder investment banks have been moving away from issuing debt for governments!

The ten years previous to 2003 showed very different growth stories. Some countries had experienced low growth in financial assets (5 percent or less): Japan, Argentina, and Mexico, for instance. Others had experienced high growth (10 percent or more): China, Korea, India, the United Kingdom, and Brazil. These fast-growing capital markets provided good opportunities for investment banks to enlarge their worldwide presence. China was the obvious story: huge and consistent growth. According to McKinsey, China's financial stock grew at 14.5 percent annually between 1993 and 2003. But Eastern Europe had been developing even faster, at 19.3 percent over the same period. Even in the euro zone, McKinsey found high growth rates (in the range of 15 to 21 percent) in Spain, Ireland, Greece, and Portugal. "Interestingly, we found that from 2000 to 2006, banking revenues in Greece grew more rapidly than those in China; India was outpaced by Australia, and Latin America by the United States."[4]

Countries vary significantly in the evolution, composition, and growth of their financial stock. For example, bank deposits made up 20 percent of the financial stock of the United States in 2003, but they represented 62 percent of China's financial stock at that time. For an investment bank, there was more business to be done in the United States or in Europe than in China, because China's financial markets were much smaller and geared toward bank credit during that period. However, though much smaller, China's and Eastern Europe's markets are growing rapidly and may contribute meaningfully to the global financial stock in the near future. This is why Goldman Sachs's Paulson could say in 2005: "As fast as this business is growing, we don't believe it can be a meaningful percentage of our revenues in the near term. But looking out five years, if things develop as we hoped, China may be an important contributor."

. . . And Then Liquidity

The bank should anticipate not only the growth of financial assets, but also the deepening of the capital market across geographies and asset classes. The depth of a country's market is measured by the ratio of its financial stock to the size of its underlying economy, as assessed by the country's GDP. There is a close link between the depth of a country's market and the country's per capita income: the higher the ratio, the higher the per capita income. Depth is a measure of the liquidity of a financial market. Liquidity is usually beneficial, giving households and businesses more choices for investing their savings and raising capital, and enabling more efficient allocation of capital and risk. In a liquid market, banks can trade in response to their clients' needs and can diversify across asset classes as a protection against the risk of global shocks.

A combination of low growth of financial markets and low depth is not very enticing. An investment bank cannot develop capital market activities in a market with little depth, because little depth means little liquidity. Unfortunately, this is the case for Argentina and Mexico; both are slow-growing markets with little depth. Fast-growing markets can also have low depth: the Brazilian and Indian markets are growing very fast, but with low depth (less than two times GDP). The best combination for an investment bank is a market that is growing briskly while exhibiting deepening liquidity. Such is the case for the United States, the United Kingdom, and the euro zone—but also China, South Korea, and Chile.

Recognizing the importance of depth plus speed, let's identify the factors encouraging market deepening:

- Growing savings rate
- Trend toward new financial assets like securitizations
- Move toward pension funds
- Development of IPOs and privatizations

If a low-depth capital market does not show positive trends in these factors, it may not be a good opportunity for a bank no matter what its growth rate may be.

A growing savings rate is a factor encouraging market deepening. Households invest a share of their savings in the financial markets, and other households, businesses, and governments can draw from these invested savings to fund attractive opportunities. So the higher the savings rate in an economy is, the wider and deeper that economy's financial market will be.

Securitization was a factor in deepening until the summer of 2007. The universe of securitized assets in the United States steadily increased. It included various residential and commercial mortgage-backed securities (MBS) issued by specialized institutions and various consumer and commercial asset-backed securities (ABS). As of June 2004, total mortgages in the United States reached $9.9 trillion (85 percent of GDP), of which $5.3 trillion were securitized. Investment banks acquired firms that specialized in subprime mortgages. In 2006, Morgan Stanley acquired Saxon Capital Inc., and Merrill Lynch the subprime and nonconforming mortgage businesses of National City Corp. In contrast, the mortgage market in many developing countries was underdeveloped (for example, mortgages were only 5 percent of GDP in Mexico), suggesting room for growth. The crisis of 2007 put a stop to these developments (see Chapter 17).

Another indicator of a deepening market is the demographic trends and their impact on retirement. In some countries, private pensions are still low relative to GDP. For example, Mexico, Argentina, and Brazil all have less than 15 percent of GDP in private pension-fund assets. By contrast, in the United States, pension funds reached 63 percent of GDP in June 2004. It's very likely that these other countries might buck their historical trend.

Finally, the development of initial public offerings (IPOs) and privatization depends on the rate of political reform (for privatization) and on the valuation of the equity market (for IPOs).

Many of these factors can be anticipated.

Where to Be and What to Do? The United States and Europe

The United States plays a unique role in the global capital markets, not only as the largest financial market (37 percent of GFS), but also as a global capital hub and conduit for capital. The relative importance of the United States in total private debt and equity securities has increased, reaching a 51 percent global share of private debt and 45 percent of equities in 2003. At the same time, the U.S. share of government debt and bank deposits has dropped to 25 percent each. The U.S. dollar maintains its unique position as the world's reserve currency despite its depreciation after 2003. Therefore, a successful investment bank must have a strong position in the United States, particularly in private debt and in equity (see, for example, UBS, Credit Suisse, and Deutsche Bank).

Europe is the second-largest region (31 percent of GFS) and is gaining strength through integration (although it still remains a collection of different markets). The euro zone constitutes two-thirds of Europe's financial stock; outside of the euro zone, the United Kingdom acts as Europe's financial hub, Switzerland acts as its global private bank, and, finally, Eastern Europe is the new hot spot for global financial growth. Europe's global share in each of the asset classes has increased modestly, reaching levels between 28 and 34 percent.

How can a successful investment bank grow its presence in Europe? First, an investment bank needs to be present in the United Kingdom. Second, a successful bank must be active in the three largest financial sectors in the euro zone—Germany, France, and Italy—which account for two-thirds of Europe's financial stock. Third, the bank must choose the asset classes in which it operates wisely. Even if the euro zone has experienced rapid deepening of its financial stock—from a low starting point of only 77 percent of GDP in 1980 to 314 percent of GDP in 2003—many of these markets are not particularly deep. For example, the markets in Germany (269 percent of GDP) or in France (324 percent of GDP) are not deeper than in China (323 percent).

Private debt has contributed the most to financial deepening in Europe (increasing from 14 percent of GDP in 1980 to 91 percent in 2003).

The two largest asset classes in the euro zone's financial stock are private debt securities and bank deposits, with a 30 and 29 percent share, respectively. Since bank deposits become bank loans, the addition of private debt securities and of bank deposits amount to the credit given to local economic agents. This is a field where investment banks may find it difficult to compete with local commercial banks. They will need to differentiate themselves by developing new asset classes like credit derivatives and securitization.

Equity securities play a smaller role in the euro zone than in the world as a whole. They account for only 19 percent of the financial stock, which is lower than their 28 percent of the global financial stock. Local banks do most of the equity trading, and a good way to penetrate this business is to buy a local trader, as Merrill Lynch did in 1995 when it acquired the largest brokerage firm in the United Kingdom, Smith Newcourt.

Government debt securities make up 21 percent of the financial stock in the euro zone, lower than in the United States (25 percent). Therefore, in a market like Germany, Goldman Sachs provides "government advisory." This is more germane than trading German government bonds! For instance, the firm helped the German government restructure its Paris Club debt to Russia. But the bank also advised the government on distressed asset investing, sale of cross-holdings, and restructuring. In the private sector, given the role of private debt, it will be no surprise that the bank has very successfully developed a premier role in high-yield markets and is doing principal investments. Finally, given the weight of pension and retirement costs in old Europe, the firm is also active in pension advisory.

The Netherlands has emerged as a preferred location for debt issuance. This shouldn't come as a surprise: it has been the case since the early 1700s, when Amsterdam became the hub for international debt. International debt securities still account for 74 percent of private debt securities in the Netherlands. Also, its financial stock grew at 14.1 percent between 1993 and 2003, which is much faster than the growth in Germany (9.1 percent), France (9.2 percent), or Italy (8.5 percent). Not only is the Netherlands the fourth-largest financial market in the euro zone, but it has also reached a financial depth of 569 percent of GDP, fueled by its hub role. Being active in capital markets in the Netherlands is a good move for an investment bank. (But you do not need to be physically based there; since trading in debt takes place electronically, the origin of the transaction taking place is in the country of the issuer.)

Finally, every investment bank managing money (and they all do) should have a presence in Switzerland, the global private bank of the Rhineland. McKinsey puts it succinctly:

> *The depth of the Swiss financial stock at 473 percent of GDP surpasses the US and the UK (397 and 385 percent, respectively), while in total the financial stock remains relatively small (about $1.5 trillion), accounting for 4 percent of total financial stock in Europe. However, measuring the size of a financial sector using financial stock issued in the country considerably understates the importance of the Swiss financial industry. If we took an alternative lens and looked at the amount of capital managed in the country, the value of Switzerland's financial stock could almost double as it would reflect the approximately $1.2 trillion private banking assets under Swiss management (of which a large share is not invested in financial stock issued in Switzerland).[5]*

Where to Be and What to Do? Asia

Asia is a region made up of markets that are both relatively isolated and very different, with Japan dominating two-thirds of the region's financial stock and China driving the region's financial stock growth. An investment bank will therefore position itself very differently throughout the region. It will expand in fast-growing markets like China while taking a different angle in Japan. Over the last fifteen years, Japan has been losing global share in all asset classes but government debt securities. However, the country has been involved in restructuring and reform. So how does an investment bank position itself in Japan?

Investment banks can develop a role in government advisory, pension advisory, restructuring advisory, and sale of cross-holdings. Take Goldman Sachs, for example. In Japan, it rode the trend of growing government debt securities. In 2005, the bank managed a very large debt offering for Japan's Housing Loan Corp. Goldman benefited from corporate reforms in Japan. With a certain amount of success, it has become the largest owner of Japanese golf courses.

More seriously, in 2002, Goldman invested $1.3 billion in Japan's Sumitomo Bank in a complicated deal that helped the firm extend loans to corporate clients. Again in 2005, Goldman Sachs Asset Management was one of only three firms (and the only non-Japanese firm) selected to provide money management services to Japan Post's $3 trillion savings system.[6] Unfortunately, a regulatory complaint led to the cancellation of this mandate.[7]

In the corporate sector, the firm provided pension fund advisory and asset management services, and underwrote high-yield debt and mezzanine finance[8]—and it made principal investments.

China is a completely different story. It accounts for more than 4 percent of the world's financial assets, with $5.1 trillion. Also, the country has amassed a sizable share of global bank deposits (9 percent). It is experiencing financial deepening across all asset classes. China's financial depth is a whopping 323 percent, more than that of the euro zone (314 percent). However, nearly two-thirds of China's financial stock is held in bank deposits, compared with 30 percent of Europe's total.

Most companies in China are state-owned enterprises, and the government held up to three-quarters of all outstanding shares in 2005. China has not developed much of a market for corporate debt securities, which constitute only 5 percent of China's total financial stock. But China's corporate debt stock has grown by 18 percent annually from 1995 to 2005. China's national savings rate is a huge 40 percent. In addition, foreign direct investment in China equaled 3.7 percent of GDP in 2003. As a result, China's economy has been able to finance investment and accumulate physical capital (which includes infrastructure, machinery, and buildings). In 2002, the country's investment in physical capital was 40 percent, which may explain why China has invested more in heavy industry and manufacturing than India, for instance, which has had success in the less capital-intensive business-service-outsourcing sector.

China needs to continue encouraging foreign direct investment through private equity and mergers and acquisitions, IPOs, and privatization. This is a good battleground for an investment bank.

Illustration: How China Became a Battleground for the World's Largest Investment Banks

Here's a bird's-eye view of the Chinese capital markets as of 2003:

- A very high share of bank deposits (62 percent) that was more than twice the world average share of 30 percent
- Nonperforming loans on the balance sheet of Chinese banks above the international standards[9]
- A small percentage of debt (both of government debt and of private debt)
- Equity securities accounting for a relatively high share of total financial stock (27 percent) in a very thin market with little trading

Now, let's take a look at the consequences for investment banks.

The Four Drivers in China

As of 2003, we could expect international investment banks to invest in bank deposits and help banks to restructure private debt, avoid government debt, and find a way into equity financing without becoming stuck in the local market for equities. What was the situation in 2006?

Although foreign ownership of Chinese banks was limited to 25 percent until 2007, almost all investment banks had invested in the equity of the larger national banks by deposit. For example, Merrill Lynch was part of a group led by Royal Bank of Scotland that made an investment of $3.1 billion for 10 percent of Bank of China (BoC) in 2005. In spite of putting its money where its mouth was, Merrill Lynch missed out on an advisory mandate on BoC's IPO, which took place in 2006. Instead, it was Goldman Sachs that led the $10 billion IPO. But the same thing happened to Goldman the same year. The bank had led a group of investors, which also included Germany's Allianz and American Express, in the purchase of a 10 percent stake in ICBC (Industrial and Commercial Bank of China, the country's largest lender) for $3.8 billion. Goldman's $2.6 billion investment for a 7 percent stake in ICBC did not help it to win the mandate for ICBC's IPO. It was Merrill Lynch, along with four other banks, that led the $12 billion initial public offering in the fall of 2006. As is usual in privatizations, the government managed to spread the deals around. The management of the IPO was shared by five firms: Merrill Lynch, Credit Suisse, Deutsche Bank, China International Capital Corp. (China's only domestic investment bank), and an ICBC subsidiary based in Hong Kong.

Other big banks have chosen a slightly different route, investing in smaller banks. In 2002, Citigroup acquired a near 5 percent stake in China's eighth-biggest bank, Shanghai Pudong Development Bank, which it increased to 20 percent in 2006. At the time, Citigroup was leading a consortium to acquire 85 percent of Guangdong Development Bank, another medium-sized bank. In 2004, HSBC had taken a 20 percent participation in Bank of Communications (BoCom), then China's fifth-biggest bank (but with only one-eighth the number of branches that ICBC had). In addition, HSBC started building up a branch network in the fifty largest and fastest-growing cities in China.

The results of these transactions are summarized in Table 5–1.

In the future, we should also see investment banks involved in the restructuring of nonperforming loans. In 2005, Goldman Sachs and Morgan Stanley had each purchased a substantial

Table 5-1. Stakes in Chinese Banks as of October 2006

Purchaser	Target	Date	%
Bank of America	China Construction Bank	June 2005	8.50%
Goldman Sachs	ICBC	January 2006	5.80%
HSBC	Bank of Communications	August 2004	19.90%
Temasek	China Construction Bank	July 2005	6.00%
Temasek	Bank of China	August 2005	4.70%
Royal Bank of Scotland	Bank of China	August 2005	4.30%
Allianz	ICBC	January 2006	2.30%
UBS	Bank of China	August 2005	2.00%
Merrill Lynch	Bank of China	September 2005	1.30%
American Express	ICBC	August 2005	0.70%
Morgan Stanley	Nan Tung Bank	October 2006	100.00%
Citigroup	Shanghai Pudong Development Bank	January 2003	19.90%

number of bad loans from China's financial institutions. In line with its expertise in debt products, Lehman Brothers chose to focus on corporate balance sheet restructurings. As part of their investment in commercial banks, the foreign investors helped to improve the credit management.

As expected, foreign investment banks had not been very active in government debt by 2006. As for the private debt, Chinese regulations did not allow securitization at tat time.

We expected investment banks to be active in Chinese firms' equity since equity securities accounted for more than a quarter of the country's total financial stock. However, the Chinese market for equities lacked liquidity, and many companies were thinly traded. As a consequence, its local brokerages were in serious crisis. Between 2003 and 2006, the Chinese regulator eliminated about 20 percent of the country's securities firms because of irregularities such as misappropriation of clients' funds, illegal acquisitions, and mismanagement. Needless to say, trading shares on China's exchanges wasn't exactly an exciting proposition.

Nevertheless, many foreign investment banks bought into Chinese brokerages with the aim of being able to act as middle-men in the sale of local shares—again, foreign investment was limited. Chinese regulations did not allow a foreign firm to own more than 33 percent of a securities firm. In 2004, Goldman Sachs was the first foreign investment bank to gain effective control of a securities firm. First, Goldman agreed to fork out $68 million in 2001 to help the brokerage Hainan Securities, with which it had no connection. Then the firm financed a group of nationals led by China's best-known banker, Fang Feng-lei, to launch Gaohua Securities, a new brokerage allowed to distribute locally listed stocks to domestic investors. Finally, it created Goldman Sachs Gaohua, an investment-banking joint venture in which Gaohua holds 67 percent and Goldman owns 33 percent. Following this trend, in 2005, Merrill Lynch announced that it would buy a 33 percent stake in a venture with Huan Securities. In 2006, UBS purchased a 20 percent stake in Beijing Securities, one of China's ailing brokerage firms.

And the Winner Is . . .

In 2005, the top investment bank in China was Morgan Stanley. The year before, it was Goldman Sachs. Both had a common strategy, which was to create a local investment bank in partner-ship with a local player. In 1995, Morgan Stanley set up the first investment bank in the country with China Construction Bank Corp., a joint venture called China International Capital Corporation (CICC). Morgan took a 34 percent stake in CICC and effective control. Initially Fang Feng-lei was CICC's senior banker. But after CICC lost the IPO of the telecommunications giant China Mobile to Goldman in 1997, the relationship between CCB and the American bank turned sour. Fang Feng-lei left for Goldman Sachs, and in 2000 Morgan Stanley pulled out of the management, becoming only a passive investor in CICC.

Nevertheless, Morgan Stanley was chosen as lead underwriter for China Construction Bank's Hong Kong listing in 2005. Because of the weakness of the domestic equity markets in China in the early 2000s, many Chinese companies looked for a foreign listing. Initially, the strategy of American investment banks was to bring Chinese companies to the NYSE or the Nasdaq—the first foreign IPO was in 1992, when Brilliance Auto floated shares on the New York Stock Exchange—but in the late 1990s, Chinese firms chose Hong Kong instead. In 2005, mainland firms accounted for a third of all companies listed on the Hong Kong exchange and half its market value.

For an investment bank, leading an international IPO was the door to cross-border mergers and acquisitions. And Chinese firms became important actors in M&A. Completed M&A deals involving Chinese firms reached a record $28.5 billion in 2005, up sharply from $1.9 billion in 1995. Historically, it was Goldman Sachs that helped China's largest companies raise capital, acting as a financier and an advisor. Goldman led the 1997 foreign IPO for the state-owned telecommunications giant China Mobile, the first megadeal in China. A year later, it managed China Mobile's secondary offering.[10] In 1999, the bank advised China Mobile on an acquisition. Then Goldman Sachs led an offering of additional China Mobile shares in 2000, and it advised on another acquisition in 2002. The bank led PetroChina's $2.9 billion listing in 2000. Then it helped PetroChina in a 2002 acquisition, and it led the 2004 follow-on offering.

In some cases, an investment bank may have to put some of its capital in order to get an IPO mandate. Together with HSBC and Morgan Stanley, Goldman Sachs invested in the Chinese insurer Ping An. Goldman made its initial investment in 1994, and the three banks were picked as advisors on Ping An's $1.8 billion Hong Kong listing in 2004. Ten years to become a coadvisor may seem a long time for a Wall Street firm, but . . .

Notes

1. Matthew B. Albrecht and Justin Menza, "S&P Industry Survey: Investment Services," May 2007.

2. Lisa Endlich, *Goldman Sachs: The Culture of Success* (New York: Alfred A. Knopf, 1999), p. 75.

3. The data I use in this chapter are from the seminal work of Diana Farrell and the McKinsey Global Institute, "$118 Trillion and Counting: Taking Stock of the World's Capital Markets," February 2005.

4. Miklos Dietz, Robert Reibestein, and Cornelius Walter, "What's in Store for Global Banking," *The McKinsey Quarterly*, January 2008.

5. Farrell and McKinsey Global Institute, "$118 Trillion and Counting."

6. Japan Post is a public corporation offering postal services, banking services, and life insurance.

7. "Goldman Sachs: Behind the Brass Plate," *Economist*, April 29, 2006.

8. I discuss *mezzanine finance* in Chapter 12.

9. A 2006 study by the accounting firm Ernst & Young estimated bad loans at China's four largest state-owned banks at $358 billion—more than twice what officials acknowledged and nearly half of China's foreign currency reserves. Ernst & Young had to go back over its estimate, however.

10. An offering of shares after a company's initial public offering; also called a follow-on offering.

6

The Strategy of Relationship Management

Goldman Sachs is credited with having invented a new function. "Modeling itself on a manufacturing, rather than a service, industry, Goldman Sachs would build a sales department that would do nothing but sell. Taking a radically different approach from that of its competitors, the member of Investment Banking Services (IBS) would fan out and cultivate business, then turn over its execution to specialists."[1] Other banks quickly adopted Goldman's model.

In today's investment banks, these people have different names, but they all have the same goal. The purpose of "relationship managers" (RMs)—or "client executives" or "senior bankers" or simply "bankers"—is to build and manage client relationships. RMs spend most of their time paying visits to CEOs and CFOs, finding new clients, and servicing existing clients. They are not focused on one specific product, but provide advice on the full range of the bank's products. That means offering the right solution at the right time, and not being skewed toward any particular product offering. In other words, it's about putting the clients' needs first.

Senior bankers and RMs must have an excellent understanding of their clients' financial and business strategies and day-to-day management concerns, making them the preferred partners of their bank's clients. This understanding also enables them to effectively coordinate the activities of product specialists, with a focus not only on promoting revenue generation across all product lines, but also on building trust.

Trust Me, I Am a Banker

Paul Myners, chairman of Marks and Spencer, said very judiciously, "The selection of an investment bank is, at its heart, about people. And here, personal relationships are hugely important because, in the end, the decision should come down to trust, based on prior experience or recommendation. Do you trust the banker? People tend to trust individuals, not organizations."[2] Contrary to this positive view, a career guide to investment banking gives a rather cynical definition of the job of relationship managers: "The MD [managing directors]'s most important task includes schmoozing in the industry, finding potential deals, and pitching them with confidence and poise. Public speaking skills, industry awareness, demonstrated experience and an ability to sell combine to create the best bankers. Importantly, however, MDs must still be able to grasp the numbers side of the business and be able to explain them to clients."[3] Frankly, this latter view is wrong. The relationship manager may be the most important asset of an investment bank—even if his only asset is his reputation and the trust of his clients, it is quintessential to the firm's success.

Three Keys to Successful Relationship Management

KPMG, a consulting firm, conducted a survey of wholesale banking relationship management in 1998 to identify leading RM strategies and how investment banks were differentiating themselves in that respect. Wholesale bank senior executives and the information technology managers at fifteen dominant North American wholesale financial services firms were interviewed extensively.[4] Based on the survey results, KPMG identified three elements that together form the core of relationship management:

1. *Customer segmentation.* Leading firms have a deep understanding of customer needs. These firms understand their strengths and seek to match those strengths with their most potentially profitable customers. These customers command the lion's share of the firm's marketing efforts and resources.

2. *Organizational structure.* Leading firms organize their resources to deliver the right solution to the right customer at the right time. Market leaders successfully overcome turf issues and facilitate continual communication among product specialists and relationship managers to better serve the customer.

3. *Information structure and IT systems.* In this global economy, where one corporation can be buying dozens of discrete services from an institution, no single relationship manager can stay on top of monitoring and executing against customer needs.[5] In the middle market, relationship managers face the challenge of managing an increasing number of customers. Institutions must rely on comprehensive and integrated information systems to provide a more holistic view of customers, and also to link that knowledge to the relationship manager.

Types of Relationship Managers

There are four types of RMs:

- Super banker
- Coordinator of product specialists
- Tandem RM (a generalist and an M&A banker)
- Functional RM (product specialists work as RMs for middle-market clients)

The "super banker" is the cornerstone of the bank's relationship with its corporate clients. His or her job is to know both the
client's business and its leadership well enough to bring in specialists to meet any of the company's financial needs. This model
prevails for the bulge bracket firms (see Chapter 3).

For middle-market banks, which offer specialized services, the
RM pulls together the total marketing effort, but product experts
market directly to customers.

The tandem system to be found essentially in commercial
banks has two separate relationship managers, one for commercial bank and one for investment bank activities, who oversee
product specialists.

In the functional model, different specialists are responsible for
the sale of their own products, and there is no central customer
contact point. Banks have found that this is not an ideal way to
develop customer relationships. Some banks believe that spe-
cialization of customer coverage in a same industry is an advantage vis-à-vis the client, the RM becoming an expert in the sector. Others think that the RM should not cover customers in the
same sector in order to preserve confidentiality between competitors. In general however, banks select key areas of focus for
their client coverage. At Goldman Sachs in 2008, for example,
Investment Banking's key areas of focus included:

- *Industries.* Financial institutions, technology, media and
  telecommunications, health care, real estate, industrial, consumer and retail, natural resources, public sector, and infrastructure
- *Products.* Equity, leveraged finance, debt, financial advisory, and mergers and acquisitions
- *Regions.* Americas, Europe, Asia, Japan, Middle East, and
  Africa

The Model: Goldman Sachs

A consultant, Steven I. Davis, sought to gain perspective on key
management issues by conducting off-the-record interviews in

2002 with key players in European investment banking. The thirty interviews covered all global players, most European second-tier players, and many specialists.[6] To the question, "Who is the most respected/feared competitor?" the answer was mixed: Goldman Sachs got nineteen votes, Citigroup got thirteen, and Morgan Stanley, ten. (No one else had more than three votes.) But when asked the question, "Who has the most successful culture and operational model?" the nearly unanimous answer was, "Goldman Sachs." So, what is Goldman's secret? Here's a brief rundown:

- *"One bank"* with total communication and collaboration across businesses and genuine teamwork. "An idea hatched on a Friday afternoon by a group of traders sitting around a bag of microwave popcorn might lead to an early morning meeting on Saturday; the lawyers and accountants would check all the angles on Sunday, and by Monday morning the salesman would be ready to put a new idea before the client."[7]
- *One compensation/bonus pool* after remunerating stockholders to keep the spirit of partnership in place.
- *A highly selective client focus with exceptional service quality.* "All this seems to make Goldman people work just a little bit harder. Clients get called before anyone else on the Street has thought to make a call."[8]
- *A single investment banker capable of selling the full range of products.* The "RM as super banker" at Goldman Sachs targets client CEOs for mergers and acquisitions (M&A) and equity products that generate other transactions.

So, How Does the Banker Target Clients for M&A Mandates?

It helps to look at what matters to M&A clients. According to the consultant Greenwich Associates, the factors determining M&A mandates are, in order of importance,[9]

- Credibility with the company's CEO and board of directors
- Capability of M&A specialists

- Creative and innovative ideas
- Understanding of the company's M&A strategy

In short, a relationship manager needs to be credible to a company's CEO in order to be able to sell that CEO M&A advice. One could thus conclude that a good way to be credible is to be working with Goldman Sachs. Is this 100 percent true? Do clients buy the firm, or do they buy the banker? Well, both; but not simultaneously. The clients want expertise first. And they buy expertise through the reputation of the firm. But once they have chosen the bank, they also want to work with an RM that they trust. If they don't trust the banker, well, they no longer trust the bank—and they may then choose to take their business elsewhere. Therefore bankers must sell their character, interpersonal skills, and judgment, not just their degrees and content knowledge.

How Do You Develop Trust as a Banker?

First, *focus on the client.* Continually have the client's best interests in mind—well beyond the mere bounds of the existing project. At root, a good banker really cares about the client, not just the problem. He views issues from the client's perspective. He thinks strategically. By understanding a particular client's problems, he devises a new solution to deal with that situation. The good banker takes a long-term perspective. He is not a transaction-oriented cog but a relationship-driven person.

Second, *engender trust.* From day one, when a banker starts talking to a client, he or she should try to strengthen the relationship by developing trust. There are three components to trust. In Chinese, the word *trust* is written (in Pinyin) as *xin ren.* The first part of the ideogram means "credit" or "credibility." (I can trust what he says about . . .) The second appears in words like *task* and *appointment* and suggests reliability (I can trust him to do . . .) I would add to these two components of trust a third one: integrity.

First, a client generally seeks an advisor who is experienced and knowledgeable. One gains credibility through content expertise and accuracy. A good RM is intellectually honest and expertly examines various sides of an issue, making sure that everything has been covered. He spends an enormous amount of time trying to figure out where he might be wrong. "If it feels right, don't worry so much about the prevailing wisdom." He remains level-headed, honest, and in control.

Reliability stems from aligning promises with actions, words with deeds. Reliability is the repeated experience of expectations fulfilled. The real measure of a good RM's talent is his sustainability throughout difficult periods.

Integrity derives from the Latin *integrare*, "to make whole." A person of integrity is a person whose conduct and principles operate in happy harmony. There are two ways to become whole: either make your conduct and your principles whole or do the reverse. David Luban at the Georgetown University Law Center puts it this way:

> *The high road, if you choose to take it, requires you to conform your conduct to your principles. That occasionally demands agonizing sacrificial choices: to resign from your job, for example, when continuing to do what your client asks requires you to cheat and shred and cover up. . . . The low road is so much simpler—that, of course, is what makes it the low road. If your conduct conflicts with your principles, modify your principles. This is the path of least resistance, so much so that apparently we follow it unconsciously all the time.*[10]

It is important that you take a stand, forge your own path, and be unafraid to share opinions. Take the high road.

Beware. Ego is the cardinal sin of relationship management. There is no greater source of distrust than advisors who appear to be more interested in themselves than in trying to be of service to the client. Charles H. Green, an advisor on trust-based relationships, says: "Frequently professionals have only the best motives, and are unselfish—but they are also self-conscious and self-absorbed. They worry about their credentials, about how they are being perceived, about how smart they seem, and about whether they'll get the job. To that extent, they are not focused on the client in front of them—and to that extent they won't be trusted."[11] In other words, "Good firms worry about competition. Great firms worry about their clients."[12]

In their book *The Trusted Advisor*,[13] David Maister, Charles Green, and Robert Galford suggest that there are four primary components of trustworthiness, that they arrange in an equation: T=(C+R+I)/S where:

$$T = \text{trustworthiness}$$
$$C = \text{credibility}$$
$$R = \text{reliability}$$
$$I = \text{intimacy}$$
$$S = \text{self-orientation}$$

For them, winning trust requires that you do well on all four dimensions (in the client's eyes), unless you are so superb at one or two dimensions that you can overcome some relative weaknesses in the others. They use the two same components of trust as in Chinese (credibility and reliability) but they add intimacy. Intimacy is about "emotional closeness" concerning the issues at hand. "It is driven by emotional honesty, a willingness to expand the bounds of acceptable topics, while maintaining mutual respect and by respecting boundaries. Greater intimacy means that fewer subjects are barred from discussion."[14]

The correct level of intimacy is closely linked with cultural background and depends of the country of origin.

Illustration: How Merrill Lynch–France Displaced Goldman Sachs to Advise the Largest M&A in the World

In the early 1990s, the French company Société Nationale Elf Aquitaine (Elf) was one of the world's top ten oil companies, the fourth-largest producer of natural gas in Europe, and the continent's fifth-largest refiner and marketer. The company had a strong presence in Africa also. Through Elf Atochem, it was the world's thirteenth-largest chemical maker, while through its 15 percent equity interest in Sanofi, a midsize drug company, it was the eighteenth-largest pharmaceutical firm in the world. Elf was France's largest industrial corporation. The French government was the main shareholder (with 64 percent), although the stock Elf Aquitaine was quoted on the stock exchange. Its ADRs (American Depositary Receipts)[15] were quoted on the NYSE. Goldman Sachs was then its preferred foreign investment bank; however, Merrill Lynch's oil analyst, Sue Graham, was the darling of Elf's people.

How Did Merrill Get Its Foot in the Door?

Merrill Lynch had to convince the finance people at Elf that Merrill was worth talking to on financial issues. This is the rule of engagement. You need to earn the right to engage in a mutual exploration of ideas. Merrill began with an analysis of the client's problems, then looked at how the bank's expertise could be helpful, and, finally, determined how the banker could create enough trust to displace Goldman Sachs.

First, the bank tried to clarify the many issues involved in the client's problems. What were Elf's needs? The company was facing very high capital expenditures and could not raise equity capital because the French government did not want its equity ownership to be diluted. Elf had used debt issues extensively in the past to finance its investment. The firm enjoyed an AA credit rating, but that rating was somewhat at risk. In order to improve its rating, Merrill Lynch recommended that the company increase the average maturity of the debt (the time at which the debt is due), since rating agencies pay a lot of attention not only to the size of the debt, but also to when it is due.

So Merrill Lynch offered a solution to the maturity problem. American investors were used to investing in corporate bonds, and a ten-year bond was not a problem. What could be a problem in this case was that many small financial institutions could not invest in a firm that was not listed in the United States. But Elf had listed its ADRs on the NYSE four months before, with Goldman Sachs as the lead underwriter.

How to Help the Client?

The banker first tries to understand how to combine the bank's product capability with the customer's needs, and then identifies the strengths it has that can be put to use to develop a solution. In the case of Merrill Lynch, it had an intimate knowledge of the debt markets in the United States and a huge network of retail investors looking for financial assets that offered a decent return for little risk. In addition, Merrill Lynch had a good angle: it could help with the trading of the bonds in the secondary market.

Once issued, debt securities are traded in the secondary market. However, most Yankee bonds, because they come from non-U.S. firms, are not easily traded in the marketplace. Investors often find that they must hold on to their bonds rather than sell them. This leads to low liquidity (the ability to trade bonds at stable prices) and higher transaction costs. There is a market in the bonds only in the first few days after issuance, as part of the "allocation process." After this period, liquidity is typically low, reflecting the small number of buyers and sellers and low trading volume. The lack of liquidity is evidenced by a sizable difference between bid and ask prices (generally called the bid-ask spread). The two-way pricing is provided by the lead underwriters of the issue and very few other brokers, if any. Merrill could commit to provide liquidity because of its strong customer base of private investors.

In addition, Elf had used Goldman Sachs for its NYSE listing of ADRs, and it did not want to give the impression that all finance transactions would be given to Goldman. As a result, Merrill Lynch won the lead management of a plain-vanilla U.S. debt issue, a Yankee, in July 1991. The co-lead managers were Goldman Sachs and J.P. Morgan. The $300 million ten-year debt issue was the French firm's first in the United States.

A Preferred Solution

A year later, Merrill convinced Elf to issue auction-market securities.

Auction-market securities are preference shares issued by a company that have a variable dividend that is set at a market rate every seven days through an auction between investors. The dividend is reset at a rate that is fixed until the next auction seven days later, when a new yield that reflects market conditions is determined. The security is a form of equity security that has priority over common stock for the payment of dividends. It is a money market instrument (since the interest rate is for seven days) with a longer legal term (since it is a preferred share).

Created in 1984, these securities had previously been referred to as auction-market preferred stock (AMPS), as well as variable-rate preferred (VRP), money market preferred (MMP), and periodic-auction-rate (PAR) securities. Here again, Merrill had an angle: more than 91 percent of the auction-market securities in which Merrill Lynch participated were rated AAA or AA, the two highest credit ratings. Merrill Lynch's private clients were heavy investors in these securities. With Elf's rating and the priority over common stock afforded by these securities, the issue of auction-market securities received an AA+ rating. Merrill convinced the company to give it the lead management of the issue. This was a tremendous success in the eyes of Merrill's private investors' base.

In 1993, Merrill came up with a new idea and convinced Elf to issue preferred shares in the United States. Preferred shares are taxed like equity and paid like bonds. For an issuer, preferred shares rank in between debt and equity for rating purposes. They are what we call "mezzanine financing." The firm first issued $350 million of preferred shares in April 1993 and did a second issue later that year; for both, Merrill Lynch was the sole manager. In a few years, Merrill had displaced Goldman Sachs in the financing of Elf. While the group's debts increased from $7 billion to $10 billion between 1992 and 1995, Merrill Lynch raised a third of the increase!

Raising the Ante

During the spring of 1993, France elected a new government that planned to privatize state-owned enterprises, among which was the largest of them all, Elf. At that time, the only listing procedure in France for new equity was a special kind of

Dutch auction (see Chapter 10); the French did not use the book-building method that was prominent in the United States at the time. Book building is a process that allows large stock offerings to be marketed.

Merrill Lynch started working with lawyers to convince the government of the merits of the book-building procedure. The work paid off, and all privatizations in France began to follow along.

The new government announced the complete privatization of Elf in the summer of 1993, which opened a competition between investment banks to lead the sale of the French government's shares in the company. The French administration held its contest in October, but Merrill Lynch did not make the group of winners, which included, of course, Goldman Sachs. Since Merrill Lynch had gained Elf's trust in the issuance of debt, it was able to convince Elf to retain it as the company advisor in the privatization. In addition, Merrill Lynch won the lead management of the equity offering in the United States, the goal being to create more liquidity for the ADRs trading on the NYSE. In January 1994, the sale of a 64 percent stake in ELF for FF385 per share generated FF14.9 billion ($3 billion), and was one of the biggest privatizations in the world. Merrill had successfully taken over from Goldman as Elf's financier.

The Cherry on Top—Texas Gulf

In 1994, Merrill had the opportunity to displace Goldman Sachs completely in the most coveted role of M&A advisor. Elf wanted to sell its U.S. chemical subsidiary, Texas Gulf. The company held a "beauty contest" (a pitch in which investment banks compete against all the other investment banks for business) to select its advisors. It chose three: Merrill, Goldman, and Morgan Stanley. The advisors, in turn, proposed a "dual-track procedure," which is an attempt to sell the company to another firm or to financial investors while preparing to have the shares listed and offered on the stock exchange as a backup. The IPO is a guarantee in case the auction sale does not work. Unfortunately for Merrill Lynch (and Morgan Stanley), Goldman Sachs, as the sole advisor to

Elf, was the lone executor of the trade sale of Texas Gulf. Merrill had lost its role as the company's preferred bank. It continued to provide a few services in the following years—for one thing, the bank was able to help structure a project finance solution on an oil field in Qatar—but nothing of substance happened between 1994 and 1999.

A Total Success

In 1998, the group Albert Frère, the main shareholder of a medium-size Belgian oil company called Petrofina, wanted to merge that company with a bigger oil company. Albert Frère called on Elf, but Elf turned it down. So the group tried Total, a French oil company half the size of Elf. In December 1998, Total, whose advisors were Credit Suisse First Boston and the French bank Paribas, announced a friendly offer for Petrofina. The market reacted negatively to the announcement. But Merrill knew the U.S. oil investors very well, and its European oil analyst was still Sue Graham, who had the total trust of European oil investors. Merrill recognized the value of the merger and proposed to Total and to Petrofina that it explain their strategy to the investors.

The merger between Total and Petrofina would create the biggest industrial group in France. There were large economies of scale[16] that could be achieved in oil and gas. Hadn't Exxon recently merged with Mobil? Hadn't British Petroleum acquired Amoco and then Arco? Total hired Merrill to be the guide. Merrill Lynch organized various investors' meetings for Total in America and in Europe. It worked; not only did the stock price recover, but the merger turned out to be a major success.

The transaction was completed on July 2, 1999. That very same day, Merrill Lynch received a call from Total Fina (its new name after the merger with Petrofina). It was not to celebrate the completion of the merger, but rather to explain that Total Fina was about to launch a hostile bid for Elf Aquitaine and to check if Merrill Lynch had a conflict. The answer came back a bit later: no, Merrill did not have any conflict in advising Total. The following

Monday, the board of Total Fina announced its offer for 100 percent of the capital of Elf through an equity swap. Total Fina's advisors were Paribas, CSFB, and Merrill Lynch. Elf responded by launching its own offer for Total Fina, a procedure that is known in the industry as the "Pac-Man defense."[17] In a Pac-Man defense, the key is to organize a proxy fight and to lobby the institutional investors to convince them to vote for one side rather than the other. Elf was advised by no less than Lazard, Goldman Sachs, Banexi, Morgan Stanley, and, in the end, Crédit Agricole-Indosuez. The presence of large commercial banks indicated that Elf was trying to raise cash through debt in order to buttress its defense. But the strategy did not work. Elf could not muster the majority of votes it needed to increase its capital. Total Fina absorbed Elf to become Total Fina Elf (now Total), thus becoming the fourth-largest oil and gas producer in the world.

This merger was one of the largest in 1999, but it was also the key to the largest merger worldwide in 2004. After its acquisition of Elf, Total Fina Elf had become a shareholder in Sanofi, with 15 percent of the capital, the same percentage as the other main shareholder, the beauty czar L'Oréal. Sanofi was the second-largest pharmaceutical company in France, behind the Franco-German Aventis.

In 2002, Merrill Lynch was retained by Sanofi to be its strategic advisor for a couple of years. In April 2004, Sanofi launched a $50 billion hostile bid for Aventis with two advisors, Merrill Lynch and the French bank BNP Paribas. This merger was completed in the summer of 2004. It was the largest M&A transaction in the world that year.

Notes

1. Lisa Endlich, *Goldman Sachs: The Culture of Success* (New York: Alfred A. Knopf, 1999), p. 61.
2. "Guide to Investment Banks: Pick the Bankers Rather than the Bank," *Financial Times*, June 27, 2006.

3. *Vault Career Guide to Investment Banking*, 2003. The author refers to the RM as an MD because relationship managers are often managing directors. However, MD is the title and RM the function.

4. Kevin Neylan, "The Urgent Need to Rethink Relationship Management in Wholesale Banking," 2002 (this is research by KPMG available on the Internet as of January 2008).

5. According to KPMG, Citigroup experiments with double coverage because no one individual can sell all products.

6. His presentation was at the UBS Warburg 2002 Global Financial Services Conference.

7. Endlich, *Goldman Sachs*, p. 22.

8. B. McLean, "Goldman Sachs: Inside the Money Machine," *Fortune*, September 6, 2004.

9. Steven I. Davis's presentation to the UBS Warburg 2002 Global Financial Services Conference.

10. Donald Luban, "Integrity: Its Causes and Cures," Georgetown University Law Center, 2003.

11. trustedadvisor.com/articles/13/.

12. Henry Paulson, cited by Endlich in *Goldman Sachs*, p. 250.

13. David Maister, Charles Gree, and Robert Galford, *The Trusted Advisor*, new edition (New York: Free Press, 2002).

14. Ibid., p. 77.

15. Depositary Receipt (or ADR) represents ownership in the shares of a foreign company trading on U.S. financial markets. They carry prices in U.S. dollars, pay dividends in U.S. dollars, and can be traded like the shares of U.S.-based companies.

16. Economies of scale are the reduction in unit cost resulting from higher overall physical volume produced (Glossary Vernimmen).

17. In the video game "Pac-Man," ghosts roam the maze, trying to catch Pac-Man. Fortunately, "energizers" can provide Pac-Man with the temporary ability to eat the ghosts; hence an attempt to turn the tables on a corporate raider is called the Pac-Man defense against a hostile takeover.

7

Trading and Capital Markets Activities

Trading was the main source of profit for Goldman Sachs in the early 2000s. But in the mid–1990s, trading broke one of the oldest investment banks in the world, Barings Brothers. The globalization of markets, increased transaction volume and volatility, and the introduction of complex products and trading strategies have led capital markets and trading activities to take on an increasingly important (and risk-prone) role at financial institutions over the last decade. The Federal Reserve Board's "Trading and Capital-Markets Activities" manual states, "The risk dimensions of these products and strategies should be fully understood, monitored, and controlled by bank management. Accordingly, adequate risk-management systems and controls at financial institutions are essential to prevent losses and protect capital."

There are basically three different dimensions to the analysis of trading models for capital markets:

- Over-the-counter (OTC) markets as opposed to organized exchanges
- Quote-driven markets as opposed to order-driven markets
- Floor-based exchanges as opposed to electronic markets

OTC Markets vs. Organized Exchanges

Organized exchanges (formed as a result of the 1934 Securities Exchange Act, which required every national security exchange to register with the SEC) are market centers that systematically bring buyers and sellers together to carry out transactions in standardized products. In contrast, OTC markets do not have a central location where trading takes place. Instead, securities transactions are privately negotiated, via a telephone and computer network, by a decentralized group of dealers who "make a market" by buying and selling for their own account. OTC-traded securities are not standardized, but rather are tailored to meet specific client needs, unlike securities traded on an exchange. In 1971, the National Association of Securities Dealers Automated Quotation system, or Nasdaq—an electronic quotation network without a physical trading floor—was introduced as an enhancement of the traditional telephone-based over-the-counter market. Thirty years later, the Nasdaq Stock Market applied to the SEC to operate as a national securities exchange, which the SEC approved in 2006. Nasdaq is now an organized exchange, reporting trades that had always been considered OTC market trades. The SEC moderated its longstanding position that exchanges must have a central limit order book with priority over dealer trades on the exchange.

Exchanges are characterized by the type of financial instruments listed for trading on the market. There are two broad types of products: cash and derivative instruments.

The price of cash instruments is directly determined by the market; they include securities (stocks, bonds, T-bills, and commercial paper), currencies (spot foreign exchange), loans, and certificates of deposit. Exchanges typically list cash equities (stocks and to some extent bonds), exchange-traded funds, indexes, commodities, and sometimes currencies.

The price of a derivative is based on the value of an underlying asset, such as commodities, equities and bonds, interest rates, exchange rates, and indexes (a stock market index, index of inflation, or index of weather conditions, for example).

In 2007, there were six U.S. equity-options exchanges competing in many of the same products: the four traditional floor-based options exchanges (AMEX, the Chicago Board Options Exchange, NYSE Arca, Inc., and the Philadelphia Stock Exchange) and two fully electronic exchanges (the International Securities Exchange and the Boston Options Exchange). The electronic trading systems emerged in the 1990s for highly liquid markets like the U.S. Treasuries market. These systems operate as quasi exchanges, defined by centralization of orders, more open market information, and more standardized rules. Trading on the telephone, also called voice brokering, remains more prominent in other fixed-income securities markets, such as corporate and municipal bonds.

Trading in fixed-income securities is conducted almost exclusively on the OTC markets, whether through direct bilateral trading between counterparties, intermediation services provided by interdealer brokers, or proprietary trading platforms operated by banks. Derivatives are transacted mainly on OTC markets. The Bank for International Settlements has estimated that OTC-traded derivatives had a notional outstanding value of approximately $284 trillion in 2005, representing 83 percent of the total notional value of all derivatives contracts traded worldwide over the same period.[1]

OTC-traded derivatives may be divided into four broad categories: futures/forwards, options, swaps, and credit derivatives.[2] These categories can be segmented further based on the underlying assets: forward-rate agreement, repurchase agreement, foreign exchange (FX) forward; equity swaps, interest-rate swaps, currency swaps, credit default swaps; bond options, stock options, warrants, FX options, interest-rate caps, and floors.

Transactions on OTC markets are conducted by different groups of traders, called "desks" in an investment bank. Within a desk, the traders work with salespersons in very integrated teams. The following desks can be found in an investment bank:

- Equity-based products and activities: cash equities, equity options, warrants, and swaps

- Interest-rate products: fixed-income securities, governments, agencies, money markets and repos; swaps, futures, forward-rate agreements (FRAs), options, caps, and floors
- Currency-related activities: customer-driven and discretionary foreign-exchange trading, cross-currency transactions, and currency derivatives (for example, currency options, forwards, futures, and swaps)
- Credit-based products: investment-grade, junk bonds, and credit derivatives
- Mortgages: liquid products, asset-backed products, and structured products
- Commodity-based products and activities: commodity futures, options, and forwards typified by underlying assets—for example, oil products, natural gas products, power assets, metals

Quote-Driven Markets vs. Order-Driven Markets

Quote-Driven Markets

In a quote-driven system (aka a price-driven market), prices are determined according to quotations made by market makers, or dealers. Investment banks are the main actors in a quote-driven system. The trader in an investment bank makes a market in the assets he trades; his clients are other banks and institutions. A market maker maintains a firm bid and ask price in a given security by standing ready, willing, and able to buy or sell at publicly quoted prices. When making a market, the trader acts as a principal who takes the other side of customer trades.

Traders make public to their clients the price at which they will buy and that at which they will sell, and if these prices are met, they will immediately buy for or sell from their own accounts. The purchase price (the "bid") is always lower than the sale price (the "ask"), thus allowing a profit margin on the turnover (in principle, at least, as we'll see in a moment). The difference between the bid and ask prices for a given security is the "trader's spread." Clients can execute an order electronically against the posted prices. The bid price at any given time is the price at which clients can sell a trader a security, while the ask price is the price at which they can buy the same security from him or her.

It's a rather risky undertaking. Traders are market makers who provide liquidity for the financial asset they trade: they stand ready to immediately buy the securities on offer or sell the securities on demand. Traders need to keep inventories to satisfy the investors who are looking to buy. The problem with carrying inventory is that the price of a financial asset can move dramatically. A trader will lose a lot of money if the price of an asset held in inventory falls. This is so because the value of the inventory is marked to market, that is to say, it is priced on the basis of the previous day's close. If the asset is not quoted, the price should nevertheless reflect the trading value of the asset. On the flip side, carrying inventory leads to making money when prices are on the rise.

What compensates the market maker for taking this risk? The bid-ask spread.

Because of this price risk, traders attempt to ensure that the bid-ask spread is big enough to absorb the shock of a fall in price. However, if the spread is too big, they may find it difficult to execute trades. Generally speaking, the more liquidity a stock or bond has, the narrower the spread tends to be.

The level of inventories of the financial asset being traded is an important indicator for a trader. He or she will adjust the quotes in order to restore inventories to some desired level.

Let us suppose that the equilibrium price (P^* in Figure 7–1) for a share at a given moment is $63. This is the "clearing price," the price at which all buy orders will equal all sell orders. The cumulative demand curve is decreasing; it shows the number of buy orders for different prices. The cumulative supply curve is increasing; there are more sell orders as the price increases. (Of course, nobody knows that the clearing price is $63, but it is the trader's job to make the best estimate of what the clearing price is.)

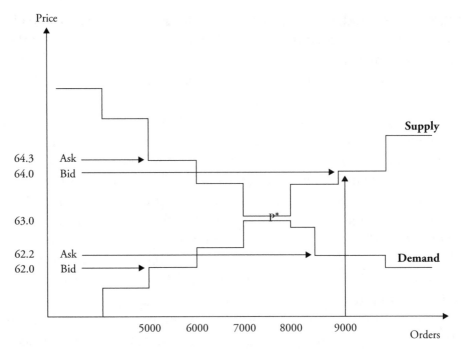

Figure 7-1. Price discovery in a quote-driven market

Let us suppose that one trader quotes a price of 64–64.3. This is a bid to buy at 64 and an offer to sell at 64.3, along with the sizes (the number of shares) that the two quotes are good for. Since his quotes are above the market-clearing price of 63, our trader will tend to receive more sell orders than buy orders: why would a customer want to pay 64.3 for what can be bought at 63? The trader will receive 9,000 sell orders per hour (the intersection of his bid price with the supply curve), and he will receive only 5,000 buy orders per hour (the intersection of his ask price with the demand curve); our trader will thus buy 4,000 shares per hour. A trader who has bought a stock that he cannot sell is "carrying a position" or "carrying inventory." When a trader carries inventory, he is "long the stock." Positions must be financed, and this costs money. Additionally, in case of a big price drop, our trader would lose money on his position (and would lose big if his inventory is large). So, when the trader sees his inventory rise by 4,000 thousand shares, he will move his quotes down toward 63, the clearing price.

The same holds true in reverse for a trader with a lower quote. Suppose that another trader posts a bid-ask spread that is below 63, say 62/62.2. She will receive many buy orders at 62.2, but she won't be able to buy many shares at 62 if the equilibrium price is 63. Why would you sell at 62 if you can do it at 63? Our trader will receive 8,500 buy orders per hour (the intersection of her ask price with the demand curve), but she will receive only 5,000 sell orders per hour (the intersection of her bid price with the supply curve). Since a trader provides liquidity to the market, she usually owns shares that she is ready to sell when asked. Her inventory of shares will go down by 3,500 thousand, leading her to move her quotes up toward 63.

If a client wants a particular security that the trader does not have in stock, she sells it to the investor without owning it. Where does she get the security? She borrows it from someone else. This is called "short selling" or "shorting" the shares. The problems with shorting stock are the opposite of those that a trader faces when she is long the stock. In a short position, a trader worries that the stock will increase in price. She has locked in her selling price up front, but she has not locked in her purchase price. If the price of the stock moves up, then the purchase price moves up as well. The trader must then buy the shares to pay back the short at a higher price. Bear hunters can face a similar dilemma: the selling price is locked in up front, but they have not locked in the purchase price, the "kill." The skin has been sold before the bear has been killed; if the price on skins goes down, the trader who is short makes money. But if the price goes up, she loses.

Order-Driven Markets

Order-driven markets are auction markets in which prices are determined by the publication of orders to buy or sell shares. The largest agency auction-trading market in the world is the

New York Stock Exchange (NYSE). The NYSE operates an auction market in which orders are electronically transmitted for execution. Specialists on the trading floor are charged with maintaining fair, orderly, and continuous trading markets in specific stocks by bringing buyers and sellers together and, when circumstances warrant, adding liquidity by buying and selling stock for their own account. Floor brokers act as agents on the trading floor to facilitate large or complicated orders.

Today the purest order-driven markets are electronic structures in which new orders are either "matched up" with standing orders that were previously submitted to the market or are themselves placed in an electronic book—a central limit order book (CLOB)—until an offsetting order is submitted. These markets are structured as two-sided auctions in which there is no market maker; instead, a broker acts as an agent for a customer's orders.

Take, for example, Euronext, a subsidiary of NYSE Euronext and the largest central-order-book cash market in Europe. Securities are traded on the Euronext trading platform either continuously for securities that are liquid enough or that have a liquidity provider that is willing to accept certain obligations or, when they are less liquid, by auction. On the trading platform, orders for a given security are automatically stored by direction (i.e., sale or purchase) and price limit, with those at the same limit ranked by the sequence in which they enter the central limit order book. Most orders are limit orders, with an associated limit price above which a buyer, or below which a seller, will not trade.

The CLOB functions like an electronic, continuously matching auction, in which orders are executed according to price-time priority.

First, the price: a limit buy order is filled before all others with lower limits, and a limit sale order is filled before all others with higher limits. A limit order entered during the trading session is executed either fully or partially, as market conditions permit. Failing this, it gets logged in the order book in descending buy-price order or ascending sell-price order (the "price-priority principle") and joins the queue of orders having the same price (the "time-priority principle").

Second, the time of entry: orders of the same kind and at the same limit are filled in the same order as they were entered into the order book. The "book," therefore, is a collection of unexecuted limit orders. An incoming order is said to "walk through the book": the buy order moves to successively higher prices, while the sell order moves to increasingly lower prices. At the opening, on the basis of all orders recorded on the book, the central computer automatically calculates the opening price at which the largest number of bids and asks can be matched. Once the opening auction is completed, trading takes place continuously until the preclosing phase. The arrival of a new order immediately triggers one or several transactions if the central order book contains an order or several orders of the contrary kind at a compatible price. If there are no such orders, the incoming order is recorded, remaining on the order book at the specified limit.

Let us suppose that the order book looks like Table 7–1.

If a buy order for 5,000 shares at a limit price of 5.70 is entered into the central order book at 15:21, the system compares it with the sell orders that are already in the order book and are compatible with a buying price of 5.70. The algorithm will immediately execute the following sales at the following prices: 1,000 shares at 5.60, 1,500 shares at 5.65, and 2,000 shares at 5.70—that is, a total of 4,500 shares out of the bid for 5,000.

Table 7-1. The CLOB at 15:20

BUY ORDERS		SELL ORDERS		LAST TRADES		
SHARES	PRICE	PRICE	SHARES	TIME	SHARES	PRICE
4,500	5.55	5.60	1000	15:20	2500	5.60
1000	5.50	5.65	1500	15:20	1500	5.55
3000	5.45	5.70	2000	15:19	3000	5.45
1000	5.40	5.75	3000	15:18	1000	5.50
2500	5.35	5.80	2500	15:18	3000	5.45

Table 7-2. The CLOB at 15:21

Buy Orders		Sell Orders		Last Trades		
Shares	Price	Price	Shares	Time	Shares	Price
500	5.70	5.75	3,000	15.21	2,000	5.70
4,500	5.55	5.80	2,500	15:21	1,500	5.65
1,000	5.50			15:21	1,000	5.60
3,000	5.45			15:20	2,500	5.60
1,000	5.40			15:20	1,500	5.55

In this example, 500 shares remain on demand at 5.70 each, so
that the book looks like Table 7–2.

From Quote-Driven to Order-Driven Markets

There seems to be a hierarchy of trading structures: the more
mature the exchange, the more likely it is to be an order-driven
market. To paraphrase Darwin, it may be said that capital markets
are striving to seize their place in the economy of nature, and that
order-driven exchanges are the normal evolution of trading mechanisms. In 2002, a survey of the market structure of exchanges
around the world showed that the proportion of order-driven markets was much higher in developed countries (52 percent) than in
emerging and frontier countries (at most 24 percent). Equity
exchanges were more often order-driven (42 percent) than derivative exchanges (only 20 percent of the latter were order-driven).

These simple statistics suggest that the degree of economic
development as well as the type of asset traded may affect the
choice of trading mechanism used by financial exchanges. The
results are consistent with a hierarchy from systems in which
market makers provide liquidity, such as open outcry, to systems
where the market participants provide liquidity, such as a limit
order book. Less developed countries are more likely to choose
the former trading mechanism, whereas highly developed countries are more likely to choose the latter trading mechanism.[3]

Floor-Based Exchanges vs. Electronic Markets

An exchange is a regulated market that lists registered instruments such as stocks, bonds, and derivatives. It used to be a physical forum where brokers met face-to-face on the floor of the exchange. For more than two hundred years, trading at the NYSE has used this "open outcry" auction system, where "specialists" representing sellers cry offers and specialists representing buyers shout counteroffers. In floor-based exchanges, trading is conducted in a single physical location, with floor brokers executing customer orders in a continuous market. These exchanges have integrated, to varying degrees, electronic trading into their floor-based models.

Electronic trading allows order flow to migrate more freely across competing market venues. In addition, electronic agency systems match trades without dealer intervention. Practically all the electronic, screen-based systems involve a CLOB (in many cases it is the sole or dominant method of trading on the system).[4]

The major European markets have used electronic, order-driven systems since the early 1980s. The Paris Bourse developed a cash-market trading system in the late 1980s, and this system had been adopted by more than fifteen exchanges on four continents in 2006. That same year, much of the volume in the U.K. market was traded on the London Stock Exchange's SETS system. In Germany, Deutsche Börse operated the Xetra system for cash trading (there was still some floor-based trading in Frankfurt, but it was limited) and the electronic Eurex platform for derivatives trading. The electronic trading platform for derivatives developed by LIFFE, LIFFE CONNECT, was adopted by the Chicago Board of Trade, Kansas City Board of Trade, Minneapolis Grain Exchange, Winnipeg Commodity Exchange, and Tokyo Financial Exchange.

In the United States, major markets were slower to adopt the new technology. Until the creation of the International Securities Exchange (ISE) in 1997 as an all-electronic options exchange, all U.S. securities exchanges used the floor-based exchange model.

By September 2002, the ISE had a larger market share than its main competitor, the Chicago Board Options Exchange (CBOE). When the New York Mercantile Exchange (Nymex) launched the WTI (West Texas Intermediate) crude oil futures contract in 1983, it succeeded in determining the price of oil—which is not set by the Organization of Petroleum Exporting Countries but on the trading floor of Nymex. However, it took twenty-three years for Nymex to realize that an electronic platform would be more efficient than open outcry.

In June 2006, Nymex launched (partial) electronic trading of its WTI contract on the Chicago Mercantile Exchange's Globex system. On this platform, electronic trades accounted for 15 percent of the volume of all trades in 2000; in 2005 it was 70 percent.[5] The order-handling rules adopted by the SEC in 1996 led to the rapid emergence of electronic trading systems that competed with traditional U.S. market centers.[6] Ten years later, much of the volume in Nasdaq-listed securities was handled by electronic trading systems. In NYSE-listed securities, a significant portion of trading still occurred on a trading floor (as of 2008), but electronic trading on the NYSE's electronic system, crossing systems, and electronic communication networks (ECNs) was growing.

Illustration: LTCM, a Near-Fatal Trading Strategy

LTCM was a hedge fund that applied a market-neutral strategy that in theory entailed little risk. LTCM endeavored to profit from price differences between closely correlated assets. For example, it held long positions in high-risk, high-yield bonds such as the debts of emerging countries, and short positions in bonds of higher quality and lower yield (such as U.S. Treasury bonds). In principle, the prices for these positions would evolve in a parallel manner, and, as a result, LTCM investments were supposed to escape interest-rate movements and seemed to be subject to only minimal risk.

LTCM had invested more than 25 times its capital of $4.1 billion in various assets, including government bonds, Russian bonds, mortgage-backed securities, and select U.S. equities. In order to amplify the low returns on theoretically low-risk arbitrage operations, the leverage was extremely high. Moreover, LTCM was quite active on the derivatives markets, with over $1.25 trillion of notional value. There were more than fifty LTCM counterparties on the over-the-counter markets, where the world's leading financial institutions were to be found. LTCM was also widely present on the organized markets; and it accounted for a sizable percentage of the positions opened on a dozen futures markets. Each organized market and each counterparty was evidently aware of the status of its contracts with LTCM, but no contracting party was cognizant of the consolidated status of LTCM's commitments to all the others. The large-scale financial establishments that worked with LTCM on the over-the-counter markets had guarantees providing them with the necessary security—or, at least, so they thought.

The Difficulties (and Perils) of Forecasting the Future

The models employed by LTCM could not foresee what was at the time unforeseeable: the sudden appearance of divergences between the prices of financial instruments (prices that had historically moved in a parallel manner). The avalanche swallowed up chalets that had long seemed invulnerable. Prices no longer followed traditional logic—and neither, so to speak, did the snow! At the end of the summer of 1998, the fall of the ruble and the near cessation of payments by Russia panicked investors, most notably those who had invested in Russian government short-term bonds (GKOs). The contagion then spread to the other emerging countries, and shortly after to the stock markets of the developed countries.

So what happens at LTCM? The flight toward quality and security reduced to next to nothing the value of the high-risk bonds in which LTCM was long and, at the same time, led to a rise in the prices of the low-risk bonds in which LTCM had short positions. Well, you can just imagine the pandemonium that ensued as investors rushed to sell their securities in whatever way possible. The leverage of 25 to 1 correspondingly amplified the losses, and LTCM found itself obliged to sell off its high-risk long positions at a time when no one knew where the market would bottom out.

These sell-offs correspondingly amplified the price fall of the high-risk bonds, rendered the price variances between high-risk and low-risk bonds even more pronounced, and made LTCM's potential losses and margin calls even greater. By mid-August the losses had grown staggering, and LTCM had to seek out equity capital. It did so, but to no avail. By the end of August, following a loss of $1.18 billion over the month, LTCM was left with capital of just $2.3 billion and assets of $125 billion, for a leverage of 50 to 1. By mid-September, its capital had melted down to $600 million and its assets still amounted to $100 billion: leverage had skyrocketed to 150 to 1!

Systemic Risk

If LTCM had been left to its own devices, thus unable to fulfill its commitments, it would have gone into liquidation. All its counterparties would have had to liquidate the financial instruments given as security. All the coverage instruments would have had to be unraveled, which would have entailed serious losses for the counterparties (some of which would have also gone bankrupt). If LTCM had had to liquidate its positions, and if the financial establishments acting as counterparties had likewise had to liquidate at scrap value, the cumulative worth of the public and private debts put up for sale would have suffered an abrupt downturn. High-quality collateral would have been deprived of its value; the prices of the debts of numerous countries might have fallen dangerously, and their interest rates would have shot up. From the beginning of August to October, the spread on high-yield bonds jumped from 350 to 750 basis points (a basis point is one one-hundredth of a percentage point, or 0.01 percent), a doubling in two months! In a last-ditch effort to avoid a financial panic that would wreak havoc on financial markets throughout the world, the New York Federal Reserve "invited" a group of financial establishments to look into ways of avoiding the liquidation of LTCM.

On September 23, 1998, following four days and four nights of strenuous negotiations, sixteen global investment banks invested $3.6 billion in exchange for 90 percent of LTCM's assets. It must be emphasized that at no point were public funds allocated; private establishments provided the funds necessary for the firm's survival. It also bears mentioning that on the occasion of the bailout, the hedge fund's shareholders relinquished over 90 percent of their investments. The fund was salvaged, yet LTCM investors failed (to put it euphemistically) to get back their outlay.

Last but not least, the creditors turned shareholders took on the fund management. In four days, the New York Federal Reserve worked out a solution analogous to an out-of-court restructuring alternative, which could have taken months. And by November 1999, the new leaders of LTCM were almost ready to complete repayment of 90 percent of the $3.6 billion owed to their creditors-shareholders. By March 2000, the incident was closed—well done, but only after coming dangerously close to the edge.

Notes

1. NYSE Euronext, "Registration Statement Form S–4," September 21, 2006.
2. Futures/forwards are contracts to buy or sell an asset at a specified future date. An option gives its holder the right (but not the obligation) to buy or sell an asset at a specified future date. Swaps are contracts to exchange cash flows. Credit derivatives are contract whose value derives from the creditworthiness of a third party.
3. Matthew J. Clayton, Bjorn N. Jorgensen, and Kenneth A. Kavajecz, "On the Presence and Market-Structure of Exchanges

around the World," *Journal of Financial Markets*, February 2006, pp. 27–48.

4. Stephen Wells's report to the FIBV annual meeting, Brisbane, "Price Discovery and the Competitiveness of Trading Systems," October 3, 2000.

5. "Nymex Relents and Allows Electronic Trade," *Financial Times*, June 12, 2006.

6. Under the order-handling rules adopted by the SEC in 1996, a market maker that receives a limit order at the same price or better than its own published quote, for more than a *de minimis* size, must generally execute the order, incorporate the limit order price into its published quote, or pass the order on to an ECN for public display and execution access.

8

The Strategies in Trading

If you've ever been in an investment bank's trading room, you've seen the mess: the noise, the TV on mute, the piles of financial reports and newspapers, half-finished cups of coffee, and wall-to-wall computer screens flashing numbers. How could there be strategies at work amid such chaos? Investment banks must develop strategies in order to become and, perhaps more importantly, remain experts in the fast, price-driven OTC markets. In addition, being exchange members, investment banks cannot be completely indifferent to the evolution of organized exchanges.

The Competitive Strategy of Exchanges

To understand the game, one has to look at exchanges around the world. Since the end of the 1980s, regulated financial exchanges have come to play a major new role in international finance. At the beginning of this century, there were about 250 financial exchanges competing in nearly two hundred countries around the world. The competitive intensity of the industry can be analyzed with the help of Michael E. Porter's "five forces" model:[1]

1. The threat of new entrants
2. The power of suppliers
3. The power of buyers
4. The availability of substitutes
5. The competitive rivalry

Here are some examples of the intensity of each force in the industry in 2006.

The Threat of New Entrants

Because there are practically no barriers to entry into the industry, noncash exchanges have found it easy to become stock exchanges, which has led to an increase in competition between the two types of exchanges. On July 27, 2006, the Chicago Board Options Exchange announced that it was entering the cash equities market through the formation of the CBOE Stock Exchange LLC.

Also, with the development of new technologies, in the last ten years it has become easy to launch electronic trading systems. On April 19, 2006, the International Securities Exchange announced that it was entering the cash equities market through the launch of the ISE Stock Exchange.

The Power of Suppliers

The freedom of companies to choose where they want to list their securities places pressure on an exchange. Issuing companies may in fact list their securities on multiple exchanges; a company's main listing is referred to as its "primary listing," while subsequent listings on other exchanges are referred to as "secondary listings." The vast majority of issuing companies obtain only a primary listing, invariably on a domestic exchange.

When there are multiple equity exchanges in one country, competition can be intense. In 2006, the principal competitors for trading listed equity securities in the United States included NYSE Euronext, Nasdaq, the American Stock Exchange, and regional exchanges in major cities like Chicago, Boston, and Philadelphia.

Cross-border capital movements and the demand for international listings have led to increased competition for listings and trading among domestic and international exchanges. U.S. stock exchanges face competition for international listings from a number of foreign stock exchanges, including NYSE Euronext, London Stock Exchange plc, Deutsche Börse Group, and exchanges in Tokyo, Hong Kong, Toronto, Singapore, and Australia.

The Power of Buyers

Investors also can place pressure on an exchange. Greater geographic diversification of investments, investment opportunities in the fast-growing markets of China and India, and expanded cross-border commercial activities are leading to increasing levels of cross-border trading and capital movements. Financial institutions, investment firms, and other financial intermediaries are increasingly trading across national boundaries, in numerous markets and asset classes, outside traditional exchanges, and even directly among themselves.

The Availability of Substitutes

Major customers and brokers are likely to either internalize order flow or transact orders through bilateral agreements. In July 2006, eight large European-based investment banks, from ABN Amro to UBS, announced their intention to launch an alternative for their trade and transaction reporting called Boat. Boat was initiated to help reduce market participants' costs by providing the pre- and posttrade reporting facilities required of investment firms, enabling them to meet regulatory requirements. But it could also provide an alternative to trading on the London Stock Exchange, Deutsche Börse, or Euronext.

The Competitive Rivalry

Last but not least, there is the competition among existing exchanges. In January 2006, the SEC approved Nasdaq's application to operate as a national securities exchange, which meant that Nasdaq would function according to its own trading, listing, membership, and other rules—with its own members and its own regulations.

The Consolidation of Exchanges

The need to respond to this intense competition among exchanges and the desire to provide cross-border services to clients has led to a series of consolidations across products and geographies to diversify revenues and gain the operating efficiencies necessary to compete for customers and intermediaries.

Until recently, the structure of the industry prevented the exchanges from consolidating. In 1996, most of the world's securities exchanges were not-for-profit private clubs, whose member-owners were stockbrokers and investment banks. Ten years later, nearly all of the world's stock markets have transformed themselves into for-profit, publicly traded companies, with shareholders made up of asset managers and hedge funds. A 2005 survey of the World Federation of Exchanges indicated that, of the thirty-eight respondents, twenty-six were private limited companies, demutualized exchanges, or publicly listed companies.

Why the big shift? Many of the exchanges had to become for-profit companies in order to get a listing and be able to merge. In Europe, exchange trading had historically been highly fragmented: each country operated its own exchange, which was linked to its own central securities depositary (CSD). The transactions taking place on the national exchange were settled by the national CSD. International users were therefore obliged to interface with multiple national systems. Naturally, the need to coordinate these systems and obtain a listing appeared very early in Europe.

Europe

Public listings give exchanges the resources they need to further expand their businesses—either by offering more services or by acquiring rivals. In order to broaden their revenue sources, many exchanges have been combining equity and derivatives markets and moving to a multiproduct business model. OM, an equity-options exchange created in Sweden in 1985, became the world's first publicly listed exchange in 1987. After its merger with the Stockholm Stock Exchange in 1998, OM took a new name, OMX. In 2003, OMX merged with HEX, the Helsinki Stock Exchange (which included the Tallinn and Riga exchanges). Then it acquired the Vilnius Stock Exchange in 2004. Then OMX merged with the Copenhagen Stock Exchange in 2005 and with the Iceland Stock Exchange in 2006. With exchanges in Copenhagen, Stockholm, Helsinki, Iceland, Riga, Tallinn, and Vilnius, OMX offered access to approximately 80 percent of the Nordic and Baltic securities markets.

The three largest markets in Europe—Euronext, the Frankfurt Stock Exchange, and the London Stock Exchange (LSE)—conducted their initial public offerings in 2001. The Madrid Stock Exchange (Bolsa de Madrid) was listed in 2006.

Before their listing, the exchanges of Paris, Brussels, and Amsterdam combined in 2000 to create Euronext N.V., the first cross-border European exchange. In 2002, Euronext acquired LIFFE (the London International Financial Futures and Options Exchange) and merged with BVLP (Bolsa de Valores de Lisboa e Porto), a Portuguese exchange.

The United States

Until 2007, the major stock and derivatives markets in the United States remained largely separate, even though their customers were increasingly trading in multiple asset classes. In 2005, for example, the NYSE still specialized in stocks and bonds; the Chicago Mercantile Exchange in currency futures; the CBOT in futures on stocks, bonds, and commodities; the Chicago Board

Options Exchange in equity and index options; and the Philadelphia Options Exchange in foreign options.

Investment banks started buying equity in the electronic trading systems that competed with traditional U.S. market centers. In 2004, Goldman Sachs had a 28 percent stake in Archipelago ECN, the first ECN[2] to link traders to pools of liquidity throughout the U.S. securities markets. The bank had also made investments in a number of other electronic platforms: an electronic options market maker, a firm specializing in online underwriting, and a computerized order-matching system.

Nasdaq, the Stock Market Inc., and the Chicago Mercantile Exchange Holdings Inc. (CME) conducted their IPO in 2002 and the Chicago Board of Trade Holdings Inc. (CBOT) in 2005. The NYSE was listed through its reverse merger with the listed Archipelago ECN.

In April 2004, a merger was announced between the NYSE and Archipelago; its completion in March 2006 created the New York Stock Exchange Group. As a result, the NYSE Group operated two securities exchanges: the NYSE and NYSE Arca (formerly known as the Pacific Exchange). In early 2006, NYSE Group and Euronext started discussions that led to a merger between the two companies in March 2007. NYSE Euronext brought together six cash equities exchanges in five countries and six derivatives exchanges. In 2007, it was a world leader in listings, trading in cash equities, equity and interest-rate derivatives, bonds, and market data distribution.

On April 2005, Nasdaq announced that it had entered into a definitive agreement to acquire two other ECNs, Island ECN and Instinet ECN, which became subsidiaries a year later. Nasdaq launched a £2.4 billion takeover approach to the LSE in March 2006, and started accumulating a stake that reached 25 percent by mid-2006.

The Philadelphia Stock Exchange, the oldest stock exchange in the nation (founded in 1790), sold itself to five investment banks and a hedge fund in 2005. It closed its equity trading floor in 2006, bolstered its core business of trading options (as part of the deal, the six investors funneled their options business to the exchange), and relaunched its futures market, the Philadelphia Board of Trade. On November 7, 2007, the Nasdaq Stock Market announced that it had entered into a definitive agreement to acquire the Philadelphia Stock Exchange.

The Chicago Mercantile Exchange and CBOT had signed a merger agreement in October 2006. Six months later, the Intercontinental Exchange had submitted an unsolicited proposal for CBOT. In July 2007, Chicago Mercantile Exchange Holdings and CBOT Holdings, having revised the terms of their definitive merger agreement, finalized their merger to create one of the world's most liquid marketplaces.

The Strategies of Investment Banks in OTC Markets

In order to increase their competitiveness, investment banks have developed electronic trade-processing systems in OTC markets. For instance, Goldman Sachs has become the premier provider of "low-touch trading," an electronic trade-execution service for active traders such as hedge funds. "Two thousand organizations use our low-touch trading," said Goldman's chairman and CEO, Henry Paulson, at the 2005 Merrill Lynch conference. These services enable investors to tap most markets directly and to develop automated buy and sell strategies.

Morgan Stanley, Goldman Sachs, and Bear Stearns are also leaders in "prime brokerage," providing institutional investors with everything from electronic trade-execution services to margin loans. In 2006 they had two-thirds of the market in hedge fund prime broking, where plenty of newer arrivals in the segment were trying to make their mark[3]—Citigroup, Lehman Brothers, and Merrill Lynch, for example. Credit Suisse, Deutsche Bank, and UBS also seem to be gaining market share. Prime brokerage is a high-barrier-to-entry business and has been a good strategy for the investment banks from 2000 until 2007. The 2007 United States subprime crisis put a stop to these developments.

In OTC markets, an investment bank often has to commit its own capital to facilitate a client trade. So, even when the bank is buying and selling for its clients, there may be a proprietary aspect to the trading. "The factors of success in Fixed Income Currencies and Commodities (FICC) are trading in response to our clients' needs and diversification by asset classes as a protection against risk of global shocks," said Paulson. Lloyd Blankfein, president and COO of Goldman Sachs, had this to say: "Our trading revenues are nowhere near as unstable as they would be at a hedge fund. . . . Our traders come in every day and clients call them up with ideas."[4]

Nevertheless, the value of the capital earmarked for trading by investment banks is regularly increasing.

In addition to providing liquidity for the bank's clients, traders also may take their own trading positions on behalf of the firm. This is called "proprietary trading," or "prop trading," in our jargon. Prop trading uses the firm's capital in order to make capital gains called "trading income." (It sometimes ends up as losses.) Trading income is the sum of the realized and unrealized gains and losses on securities held for sale or investment. Trading on behalf of clients and trading on behalf of the firm are normally performed by the same trader. It is therefore difficult to distinguish between the two functions. Some investment banks have a strategy to commit capital if the client asks for it.

The Value of the VaR

"No firm has immersed itself as deeply in the risky world of proprietary trading with the same consistent level of profitability as Goldman Sachs. . . . The firm revived its proprietary trading business in 1995, and over the following three years many of the firm's businesses developed a proprietary element."[5]

The "value at risk" (VaR) measures the potential loss in value of trading positions as a result of adverse market movements over a defined time period with a specified confidence level. To take an example, let us suppose that the VaR was $1 million at a one-day, 99 percent confidence level. A VaR of $1 million with this confidence level means that there is only one chance in 100, under normal market conditions, that a loss greater than $1 million will occur. The value at risk at Goldman Sachs,[6] which purports to measure the amount the firm could lose in one very bad day of trading, has almost tripled between late 2000 and late 2004 to $69 million, according to Bethany McLean in *Fortune* magazine.[7] The problem is that in 2006, two years later, the *Economist* noted that "over the past two years, Goldman's 'value at risk,' or the amount it can lose in a really bad (but not really, really, really bad) day has risen strongly."[8]

Table 8–1 comes from Goldman's third-quarter results for 2006 (variations calculated by the author).

The "diversification effect" in Table 8–1 equals the difference between total VaR and the sum of the VaRs for the four risk categories. This negative effect arises because the four market-risk categories are not perfectly correlated. The two risk categories that rose the most in one year's time are "interest rates" and "equity prices" (by about 50 percent). The diversification effect also rose substantially, meaning that the bank knows how to manage the risks.

From 2002 to 2005, negative trading days at investment banks happened less than 50 percent of the time, fortunately for the

Table 8-1. Goldman's Third-Quarter Results

Risk Categories	Three Months Ended		Variations
	August 2006	August 2005	
Interest rates	55	38	145%
Equity prices	61	40	153%
Currency rates	21	19	111%
Commodity prices	31	25	124%
Diversification effect	–76	–46	–165%
Total	92	76	121%

banks and their shareholders.[9] But they happen more often at Goldman Sachs than at Lehman Brothers, for example (in fact, about five times more often). The gains (and the losses) are also bigger at Goldman Sachs. But the same holds true at Lehman Brothers. Conclusion: investment banks take huge bets in their trading operations, and this pays off.

Arbitrage Trading

The key driver of trading is not so much the direction of prices as the need to have discernible price trends and some volatility to drive a client's activity. Prices are difficult to predict, and they can react rapidly to shocks in the financial system. Today, investment banks use more complex computer models to identify how volatility drives clients' activity and find new "arbitrage" opportunities in equities, interest rates, derivatives, and foreign currencies. Arbitrage is the simultaneous purchase of one security deemed to be mispriced and the sale of another in order to profit from price distortions. For instance, index arbitrage is the simultaneous purchase (sale) of stock index futures and the sale (purchase) of some or all of the component stocks that make up the particular stock index, to profit from sufficiently large intermarket spreads between the futures contract and the index itself.

Another example of arbitrage opportunities arises as a result of the public announcement of a hostile bid by one company for another. Risk arbitrageurs bet their analytical and trading skills against the market. Robert Rubin at Goldman Sachs (who later became secretary of the treasury), one of the best in the field throughout the 1980s, said this: "You had to stick to your discipline and try to reduce everything in your mind to pluses and minuses and do probabilities. If a deal goes through, what do you win? If it doesn't go through, what do you lose? It was a high-risk business, but I'll tell you, it did teach you to think of life in terms of probabilities instead of absolutes."[10] Unlike speculators, arbitrageurs do not bet on where the market is heading, but reason in terms of relative value: they buy one product and sell another, thereby "mutualizing" their risks on numerous operations.

An Over-the-Counter Revolution

Two types of markets have undergone a revolution in the last few years: the credit derivatives market and the commodities market. The credit derivatives market barely existed before the mid-1990s. It developed as part of the effort to find new ways of managing risks: fixed-income traders were trying to find ways to hedge against interest rates and price volatility; banks wanted to transfer and disperse their credit exposures using new credit instruments such as credit-default swaps and collateralized debt obligations. And investors were looking to take on credit risks in exchange for higher investment yields. "The market for credit derivatives is mostly dominated by credit-default swaps (CDS)," said Wharton finance professor Krishna Ramaswamy. He describes a CDS as "an 'insurance' contract in which the buyer of protection pays a periodic and ongoing premium in exchange for a payment from the protection seller when a well-defined event is triggered."

This is from a recent reference book on the subject: "In these newly transparent credit markets, credit risk is not simply the risk of potential default. It is the risk that credit premiums will change, affecting the relative market value of the underlying corporate bonds, loans, and other derivative instruments. In effect, the 'credit risk' of traditional banking is evolving into the 'market risk of credit risk' for certain liquid credits."[11] Interest rates and prices are not as influential in fixed-income trading thanks to the use of credit derivatives.

Oil: The Long End and Short End of the Stick

Investment banks have long been active in oil products and natural gas power because of the volatility in the oil and natural gas industries and the operators' need to hedge their risk. There are derivatives exchanges such as futures to hedge the simplest risks. The principle of protection against price fluctuations consists of taking positions on the futures market opposite to those that one has on the physical market. As I mentioned before, all actors who fear a rise in the prices of the goods they buy and use in their production are said to be "short," meaning that they will want to buy futures contracts and take a long position on the futures market.

Let's take, for an example, a refinery. What does the refiner fear? The price of crude oil may rise, and that increase cannot necessarily be passed along to the price of refined products. The refiner notes that while the spot price is 60, the three-month future (the price in three months) is 61. And while production at 61 is profitable, this would no longer be the case at 70. Wishing to shield himself from such risk, the refiner buys futures contracts and is thereby enabled, as of today, to set the purchase price of the crude oil he will use in the near future. He will buy three-month contracts corresponding to a price of 61 per barrel. He thereby guarantees for himself a cost of 61 in three months, and he covers the risk of a cost increase. If by the payment date the spot price has gone up to 70, the contracts he had bought at 61 will be worth 70, and he will sell them at that price, thereby making a gain of 9 on each contract. His costs will come down to 61, which is the purchase of the crude oil at 70 minus the gain on the futures market of 9.

That having been said, such coverage has a cost. It entails a loss of opportunity. Suppose that three months later, crude oil is quoted at 55. In that case, the refiner will bear a refining cost higher than the market price; he will buy his oil at 55, but he will also sell his contracts at 55 and will consequently lose 6 on each contract, thereby raising his total cost to 61.

In terms of the goods they produce, manufacturers are said to be "long" because they run the risk of a price decline over time. The refiner does not fear a crude oil price rise alone; he may also, at other moments, anticipate lower prices for refined products (gasoline, fuel, kerosene) that he has in stock or will produce at some time in the future. To hedge against this decrease, the refiner must sell petroleum-product futures (contracts for fuel or gasoline). By doing so, he may thereby set, as of now, the selling prices for products that perhaps have yet to be refined, and the risk is covered through a short position on the futures market.

Let's return to the case of the refiner who lives in fear of a rise in the price of crude oil. Wishing to hedge against this risk, he buys futures contracts. Who will sell them to him? Quite probably his fellow professionals, such as manufacturers or industrialists who own a stock of crude oil and want to protect themselves through the sale of contracts. Herein lies the beauty of a futures market: it brings together traders who have differing anticipations of the upcoming price evolution and who act accordingly. These are speculators who foresee the future and act before it transpires. Buying and selling futures enables one and all to predetermine prices so that they are not affected by the risks of rises and falls.

The supply of and demand for contracts for purposes of coverage will in all likelihood not be equal. It is statistically impossible that at a given moment, there will be exactly the same number of professionals wishing to protect themselves from an oil price hike and professionals wishing to shield themselves from the opposite. This explains the intervention of "speculators" who underwrite the residual risk (that which the professionals cannot take care of). The primary interest of such speculators is to make a short-term profit over a period of a few months. They have no interest in the production or processing of a commodity. It is difficult to establish the exact percentage of transactions engaged in by actors who are covering their commercial operations and by operators who intervene in speculation. Yet these much-maligned speculators in fact play a positive role, which is basically that of an insurer providing coverage for the commercial operations of a market actor.

Futures markets consequently allow for redistribution of the risks that the professionals do not wish to incur. The operators who agree to underwrite these risks are in a better position to do so: they have less apprehension of risk or a different perception of the future. Speculators buy the risk that industrialists wish to be rid of. Investment banks are very active in intermediating this market or in acting as principals.

But futures markets do not exist for every asset. When futures are not available, an investment bank may be the counterparty of a "forward contract." Forward contracts are arranged between two principals, with complete flexibility as to exactly what property is being transferred and when the transfer will occur. They are agreements that are directly entered into between a buyer and a seller, calling for delivery of a specified amount of a specified asset at a specified future date. The buyer and the seller are direct contractual counterparties to each other. Buying or selling forward involves agreeing immediately on price and article; delivery and reception are slated for later. The contracting parties agree today on a time or term price. On the due date, the buyer is obliged to take the delivery and settle as stipulated. The seller is compelled to deliver the goods. Parties to forward contracts may require some form of collateral security in the form of compensating balances or a performance letter of credit.

In July 2005, Goldman Sachs Capital Partners acquired an oil refiner and fertilizer maker. The bank Goldman Sachs provided the "crack-spread"[12] hedges to mitigate the risk of refining. Because refiners are on both sides of the market at once, their exposure is greater than that of companies that simply sell crude oil at the wellhead, or that sell products to the wholesale and retail markets. These hedges were structured as forward contracts to lock in the differential between refinery input and output prices, and to protect against changes in that value. In the late 1990s, Goldman Sachs was not only a major player in natural gas but even a shipper of natural gas into California. The firm has pulled out of this business, but it has remained a leader in the trading of oil and power assets.

Commercial banks have also become very active in energy trading, leveraging both their credit ratings and their customer relations. For example, Bank of America says that it can trade wholesale energy contracts on behalf of customers in the airline, oil, and utility sectors. The activity of the banks in the derivatives markets is increasingly self-sustained. When banks propose a new coverage instrument, they take on the risk at their own expense and evidently endeavor to cover it with other derivative instruments. This creates a new activity: the banks try to diversify the risks of being long or short by selling various commodity products to their institutional and industrial clients.

The Role of Investment Banks in the Evolution of Financial Markets

Liquidity (the ability to buy or sell a security immediately without materially affecting the market price) is a key word in understanding the role of investment banks in the evolution of financial markets. The life of a financial instrument from birth to maturity illustrates this role. Typically, a product invented by a bank will be imitated, generalized, and finally negotiated on an organized market. Investment banks encourage the evolution of organized markets toward electronic order-driven markets.

Initially, an investment bank creates a product in response to the needs of two clients: an issuer and an investor. Other clients, issuers, and investors become interested in the new instrument. The bank will then start making a market in the product to provide liquidity for its investor clients.

Unfortunately, there is no copyright in investment banking! Other banks will start issuing the product for their issuing and investing clients, thus making an OTC market in these issues. When there is enough liquidity, the need for market makers diminishes, and the product can be traded in an order-driven organized market. Investment banks free up capital in the latter.

One function of exchanges is to provide a point at which orders can congregate to maximize liquidity. Liquidity is a key to attracting and retaining customers. The greater the number of users trading a security on a given exchange, (1) the more companies will be attracted to issue securities on that exchange, and (2) the more traders will use that exchange. This virtuous cycle creates the highest possible levels of liquidity.

Take as an illustration the development of financial products based on the need to control pollution. Sulfur Financial Instruments (SFIs) are based on emission allowances used for compliance with the Acid Rain Program established by the Clean Air Act of 1990. In this program, the Environmental Protection Agency (EPA) set an overall limit on the amount of emissions permitted from all power plants combined and then allocated a certain number of emission allowances to each power plant. If a particular plant cannot meet its quota, it can buy additional allowances from plants that have not used up their allotments.

SFIs were traded over the counter until the Chicago Climate Exchange (CCX), the world's first exchange for the reduction and trading of greenhouse gas emissions, announced the creation of a cash market for SFIs by the end of 2004 and later an exchange for standardized and cleared futures contracts. In April 2007, CCX started offering standardized and cleared options contracts on SFI. CCX applied the same market-based strategies for carbon emissions trading under Europe's Emission Trading Scheme of 2005 when the European Climate Exchange (ECX) started trading European Union Allowances. ECX offered standardized and cleared futures contracts, and it attracted over 80 percent of the exchange-traded volume in the market by 2006. These contracts were then traded on the electronic order-driven platform of the Intercontinental Exchange. The seventh annual World Bank carbon market intelligence study, released in April 2007, showed that the global carbon market tripled in 2006—from US$10 billion in 2005 to US$30 billion. During this time, the market was dominated by the sale and resale of European Union Allowances at a value of nearly US$25 billion.

Notes

1. Michael E. Porter, *Competitive Strategy: Techniques for Analyzing Industries and Competitors* (New York: Free Press, 1980).
2. ECNs, or electronic communication networks, are electronic trading systems that automatically match buy and sell orders at specified prices; they are registered with the SEC as broker-dealers.
3. *Financial Times*, August 15, 2006.
4. Quoted in Bethany McLean, "Goldman Sachs: Inside the Money Machine," *Fortune*, September 6, 2004.
5. Lisa Endlich, *Goldman Sachs: The Culture of Success* (New York: Alfred A. Knopf, 1999), pp. 224–225.
6. VaR at Goldman Sachs is the potential loss in value of the firm's trading positions as a result of adverse market movements over a one-day horizon with a 95 percent confidence level. Paul Glasserman at Columbia Business School (1999) quotes an executive at the bank: "At Goldman Sachs, we commonly focus on an amount of capital that we should expect to lose no more than once per year in a given day. We think of this not as a 'worst case,' but rather as a regularly occurring event with which we should be comfortable."
7. McLean, "Inside the Money Machine."
8. "Behind the Brass Plate," *Economist*, April 27, 2006.
9. Ibid., Table 2.
10. Cited in Endlich, *Goldman Sachs*, p. 109.
11. M. Crouhy, D. Galai, and R. Mark, *The Essentials of Risk Management* (New York: McGraw-Hill, 2006).
12. The term derives from the refining process, which "cracks" crude oil into its constituent products.

9

Equity Research

As we saw before, Merrill Lynch is credited by no less than the British Bankers Association with having created equity research after World War II.[1] Ironically, Merrill had to pay a $100 million fine in 2002 as part of a settlement: New York Attorney General Eliot Spitzer had accused the firm's Internet research analysts of publishing, on a regular basis, ratings for Internet stocks that were misleading. What went wrong?

The Research in Question at Merrill Lynch

Merrill Lynch was built on selling and trading equities to individual investors. Research was a way to educate clients. When research became more sophisticated, it was aimed at the Merrill Lynch brokers who were advising the firm's clients. In the 1990s, equity research was mainly geared toward the large institutional investors: "The whole reason for having research analysts has always been as a means of selling stocks in the primary market, and generating transactions, whether buy or sell, in the secondary market."[2]

The business model was simple: hire high-priced analysts, get rankings up, and (in theory) watch the investment-banking revenue pour in. "That strategy at Merrill Lynch produced high rankings, but it also produced Henry Blodget . . . who later became a symbol of research marred by investment banking conflicts."[3] The research analyst was at the center of a perfect storm that almost destroyed Merrill Lynch[4] and, ultimately, equity research at investment banks.

In June 2001, Spitzer initiated an investigation into the causes of the failure of Merrill Lynch's research. His conclusion was that the research analysts were acting as quasi-investment bankers for the companies at issue, often initiating, continuing, and/or manipulating research coverage for the purpose of attracting and keeping investment-banking clients. The general terms of an agreement for a "global settlement"—which included Spitzer, ten of the top U.S. investment banks, the SEC, the NYSE, the NASD, the North American Securities Administrators Association, and state regulators—were announced in December 2002. And on April 28, 2003, regulators announced that enforcement actions against the major investment banks had been completed, thereby finalizing the so-called Global Analyst Research Settlement. The settlement mainly focused on insulating research from investment banking. And, starting in July 2004, the banks had to finance independent research during the next five years.

What Exactly Do Research Analysts Do?

"Sell-side" equity research analysts (stock analysts working for investment-banking and brokerage firms) typically follow, analyze, and advise investors on roughly a dozen public companies operating within a given industry. In addition to producing original research, analysts typically spend between one and two weeks each month visiting the offices of their buy-side clients to pitch their latest investment ideas. Most large institutional investment managers employ portfolio managers who invest their clients' capital in diversified baskets of assets, such as open-end mutual funds. Given the wide scope of their mandate, fund managers are supported by their firms' internal research analysts, who follow companies within broadly classified sectors. These buy-side analysts turn to sell-side analysts for their in-depth knowledge of the various industries within the sectors they cover, as buy-side research analysts are typically responsible for as many as five times the number of companies that their more specialized sell-side counterparts follow.

Sell-side equity-research analysts produce written reports that include buy/sell recommendations, target prices, and earnings forecasts. An analyst's first report on a company, an "initiation of coverage" report, contains the most detail, including an analysis of industry drivers, competitive positioning, and risks, in addition to a robust financial analysis and specific trading recommendations. The most provocative initiation reports highlight interesting investment themes and provide investors with compelling, original investment ideas. Also included in these reports are the stock's target price or price objective and its investment rating. Once an analyst assumes coverage of a company, he or she will issue short comments and follow-up reports whenever significant incremental information about the company, industry, or macroenvironment surfaces. Additionally, analysts issue either comments or reports when they adjust their investment ratings and price objectives.

To develop their recommendations and investment themes, analyst teams evaluate the companies they follow from a number of perspectives. At the highest level, they consider the macroeconomic environment and its relative effect on their industries. Take advertising as an example: consumer cyclical stocks, such as advertising agency holding companies, are heavily affected by the overall economic climate. Analysts who cover these companies must develop views on the macroeconomy, although, in practice, many of them rely on their firms' market strategists for these opinions.

Digging deeper, analysts consider the dynamics of the specific industries they cover. Again using advertising as an example, an analyst in the early 2000s could very well observe that advertising agencies had faced rapid consolidation over the previous decade. She would mull over the direction of advertising spending in a world in which media channels are converging and disruptive technologies, such as the digital video recorder, are changing the way marketers deliver their branding messages to customers. At the micro level, analysts try to determine which individual firms within their coverage universe are best positioned to benefit from changes in the macro and industry environments, and which firms are at risk. Analysts then derive the financial implications for the companies they cover from this comprehensive strategic analysis.

Analysts model and project the financial statements of the companies they cover to determine the fair value of those companies' equity securities. Taking as a given the idea that a stock's share price reflects the company's discounted stream of future free cash flow available to equity holders, securities analysts typically value company shares using cash-flow-based relative-valuation multiples—such as price-to-earnings-per-share and enterprise-value-to-EBITDA (earnings before interest, taxes, depreciation, and amortization)—and foot the results of their analyses with discounted-cash-flow-based methods to arrive at an intermediate-term price objective, or "target price."

Analysts also compare the valuations of the companies they follow to those of other companies in their respective industries or to their own historical trading ranges. The basis of comparison is generally a barometer of cash flow, such as the forward-year price-earnings ratio or enterprise-value-to-EBITDA multiple.

Analysts Produce Buy/Sell Recommendations

Typically sell-side firms define the intermediate-term time horizon of their price objectives as roughly twelve months. These firms assign specific investment recommendations such as "Buy,"

"Hold," or "Sell" to stocks they follow based on the implied upside—the difference between the current stock price and an analyst's twelve-month price objective—of a stock. For example, Merrill Lynch ratings would obey the following explicit methodology in 2002:

Merrill Lynch Investment Ratings Key

OPINION KEY: Opinions include a Volatility Risk Rating, Intermediate-Term and Long-Term Investment Ratings, and an Income Rating.

VOLATILITY RISK RATINGS, indicators of potential price fluctuation, are: A–Low, B–Average, C–Above Average, D–High.

INTERMEDIATE-TERM INVESTMENT RATINGS, indicators of expected total return (price appreciation plus yield) within the 12-month period from the date of the initial rating, are: 1–Strong Buy (minimum 20%–more for High Risk securities); 2–Buy (minimum 10%); 3–Neutral (0–10%); 4–Reduce/Sell (negative return); 6–No Rating.

LONG-TERM INVESTMENT RATINGS, indicators of fundamental company factors demonstrating potential total return for the 3-year period from the date of the initial rating, are: 1–Strong Buy (aggregate minimum 40%); 2–Buy (aggregate minimum 20%); 3–Neutral (aggregate 0–20%); 4–Reduce/Sell (negative return); 6–No Rating.

INCOME RATINGS, indicators of potential cash dividends, are: 7–same/higher (dividend considered to be secure); 8–same/lower (dividend not considered to be secure); and 9–pays no cash dividend.

Source: Merrill Lynch & Co. equity research in 2002.

The Enron Fiasco

How detailed is the method of financial analysis used by analysts? There is some concern that analysts in the United States did not always do their homework and were more interested in strategic analysis than in financial models. For instance, it is now obvious that most analysts did not anticipate Enron's problems in large part because they did not read the fine print in Enron's financial statements. When they did not understand something, they would give Jeff or Andy[5] a call instead of looking into the accounts.

At the beginning of 2000, Enron was the largest energy broker in the entire world. At one point, the company was worth more than AT&T: the stock hit an all-time high of $90.56 in August 2000 and closed the year at $80. By the end of 2001, however, Enron had devolved into the largest bankruptcy case in the entire history of the United States. The questions started in March 2001, when Bethany McLean, a reporter for *Fortune* magazine, wrote an article provocatively titled "Is Enron Overpriced?" The caption read: "It's in a bunch of complex businesses. Its financial statements are nearly impenetrable. So why is Enron trading at such a huge multiple?" During the summer of 2001, several analysts finally buckled down and focused on several major concerns regarding Enron. Nevertheless, in October 2001, sixteen of the seventeen analysts covering Enron still called it a strong buy or a buy.

On October 9, 2001, Goldman Sachs published a report on Enron with the title "Still the Best of the Best." The stock price was then $33.5 and Goldman had a target price of $48. Nine days later, on Thursday, October 18, Enron's stock dropped to $29, and it sank to $20 the following Monday, a quarter of its value nine months earlier. In the report, the Goldman Sachs analysts had commented on each of the concerns surrounding Enron. They reiterated their conviction that Enron was going to experience high and sustained growth prospects.

> *What was their take on Enron?* "We view Enron as one of the best companies in the economy, let alone among the companies in our energy convergence space."
>
> *Their recommendation?* "We expect Enron shares to recover dramatically in the coming months. We view the current period as an extremely rare opportunity to purchase the shares of a company that remains extremely well positioned to grow at a substantial rate and earn strong returns in the still-very-young and evolving energy convergence space.

We strongly reiterate our Recommended List rating on Enron stock." The main reason for the recommendation was that the authors of the report had spoken recently with most of top management. "Our confidence level is high," they wrote.

Goldman Sachs classified Enron as a "gas-and-power producer." The balance sheet showed that Enron had in fact become a natural gas and electricity derivatives trading company. What appeared as "assets from price risk management activities" in the balance sheet were $2.2 billion in 1999 and stood at $12 billion in 2000. Liabilities from price risk management activities were $1.8 billion in 1999 and $10.5 billion in 2000. Total assets from price risk management activities—that is to say, "power derivatives"—reached $21 billion in 2000, representing 32 percent of the total assets. So, how come the return on capital for Enron was less than a third of the profitability of other financial institutions, including Goldman Sachs itself?

Goldman's report was aimed at "addressing the major concerns about Enron." So the authors asked the obvious question: "Have earnings been invented writing up assets using fair value accounting?" They answered this question in the negative: "Any net gains in our view have been a modest portion of earnings over the years and a negative in 2001." However, Enron's revenues included "other revenues," which should have been posted as nonoperating income. These revenues represented $7.2 billion in 2000, compared with less than $2 billion in operating income. In addition, Enron's investment-banking activities produced a substantial part of its operating income.

The next question in the Goldman report was the following: "Are customers and competitors concerned about credit exposure?" We know today that Enron invented deals involving off-balance-sheet partnerships and special-purpose entities to hide debt. There were many clues concerning these off-balance-sheet treatments in note 9 of the 2000 annual report. For those few who read it, the report showed that the company was responsible for a total of nearly $16 billion of debt through its unconsolidated affiliates. With more than $8.5 billion of long debt on the balance sheet, Enron had in reality $24.5 billion in debt and $11 billion in shareholders' equity at the end of 2000. No wonder that Enron's bankruptcy examiner would later discover more than $26 billion of debt: it was right there in the 2000 balance sheet!

Another concern regarding Enron was that cash flow from operations had lagged earnings. Goldman's explanation was that "in the past, financial discipline did not appear to be a top priority as the company spent whatever it took to rapidly build its industry-leading capabilities. It now appears that financial discipline is dramatically improved." And indeed, "cash from operating activities" (excluding working capital) grew from $1.873 billion in 1998 to $2.228 billion in 1999 and to $3.010 in 2000;[6] and the income before interest, minority interests, and income taxes (IBIT) grew in the same way, from $1.582 billion in 1998 to $1.995 billion in 1999 and to $2.482 billion in 2000.

Why the fuss? This IBIT looked like the classical EBIT (earnings before interests and taxes). But it was quite different, because it included many types of financial nonoperating income: gains on sales of nonmerchant assets, gains on the issuance of stock (by TNPC, Inc), and interest income. The traditional EBIT had undergone a very mountainous trip between 1998 and 2000, while the IBIT showed an impressively growing steadfast tendency. This is, of course, why Enron published these numbers: it was better to focus on the IBIT than on the more classical and less glamorous EBIT. On the first page of the annual report for 2000, the financial highlights focused on numbers showing "an impressive revenue growth" and "a regularly growing source of cash from operating activities." But Enron's so-called figure for cash from operating activities excluded changes in working capital requirements, a fact that was spelled out in the 2000 published financial reports:

	2000	**1999**	**1998**
Cash from operating activities (excluding working capital)	$3.010	$2.228	$1.873

Elsewhere this very same item of cash from operating activities was also called "Funds Flow from Operations."[7] In reality, this funds flow from operations had nothing to do either with cash or with operations. It was not a cash figure, since it excluded the working capital requirements. It was not linked with operations, since it included many nonfinancial sources of income, such as interest and related charges; net dividends on company-obligated preferred securities of subsidiaries; minority interest; income tax expense; net income before cumulative effect of accounting changes; cumulative effect of accounting changes, net of tax; and proceeds from sales.

Enron's consolidated statement of cash flows gave a lot of indexes (as usual), for who dared to read it? It seemed that the firm was able to generate a huge pile of cash from its activities. But a large proportion of this cash had nothing to do with its activities and was more linked to merchant assets and investments. In addition, a large part of the net cash provided by operating activities was a result of the changes in working capital requirements, not of earnings. An analysis of Enron's accounts could have showed that it was heading for trouble. Enron did cook the books, but it also gave the recipe for the cooking—many analysts just didn't read it.

Two Puzzles in Research

The first puzzle is well known: if markets are efficient, then research cannot be efficient. That is, if markets are efficient, all information about the value of shares, currencies, or bonds is already reflected in the price, and research is useless. In an efficient market, traders cannot profit from trading on publicly available information (and that includes research reports) in a way that allows them to "beat the market." But if there is no research, how can markets be efficient?

This puzzle is best illustrated by the joke about the economist who is walking along the street when his wife points out a ten-dollar bill on the pavement.[8] "Don't be silly," he replies. "If there was one, someone would have already picked it up." There is no point bending down to pick up a ten-dollar bill because someone would have done so already. The sidewalk is efficient. But if nobody bends down to pick up the money, it will still be there.

For our purpose, the equivalent of the ten-dollar bill would be information that makes it possible to gain ten dollars. If there is public information that makes it possible to gain ten bucks on a stock, people will buy this stock until there is nothing more to gain. Thus, there is no information that makes it possible to gain ten dollars in an efficient market, because any such information will have already been used (and therefore will have lost any value). To return to the joke of the economist: if there was information making it possible to gain ten dollars, somebody would have already collected it!

Experience would suggest that markets are inefficient because of delayed response ("underreaction") and overreaction to new information. However, significant deviations from intrinsic value are rare, and markets usually revert to share prices commensurate with economic fundamentals within about three years.[9] Therefore equity research may be useful in identifying significant deviations from intrinsic value.

The second puzzle is, if research can be useful for identifying significant deviations from intrinsic value, why is it that institutional investors do not care about analysts' financial models, earnings estimates, or stock selection? Each year, these investors vote for their favorite analysts in *Institutional Investor* magazine's annual "All-America Research Team" poll.[10] Since at least the October 1999 issue of *Institutional Investor,* "industry knowledge" has been rated as the single most important attribute of an equity analyst. In the October 2005 survey, poll voters ranked "integrity/professionalism" second behind "industry knowledge," much higher than "stock selection" and "earnings estimates," which are in only eleventh and twelfth place.[11]

Why aren't institutional investors interested in accurate earnings forecasts, timely buy and sell recommendations, and insightful written reports? One reason is that recommendations are public information, and public information has no value to institutional investors. As Professor Jay Ritter said at the *Journal of Banking and Finance* thirtieth anniversary conference in Beijing in 2006, "Value can be measured as the ability to generate positive abnormal returns. While the private value of public information is zero, the private value of private information can be considerable." Information has value to the degree that it is not already incorporated into the price, which comes later. Published recommendations and written reports are disseminated simultaneously to scores, if not hundreds, of investors, and unless there is a lagged market reaction, any price impact should occur immediately. And Jay R. Ritter adds "an analyst provides value to a money manager by answering questions and supplying information in individual telephone calls before the information is fully reflected in market prices."[12]

While academic research focuses on public, measurable information like price objectives or earnings estimates, institutional investors don't care much about this information. They are more interested in useful telephone calls with information that is not (yet) reflected in the price. This information does not need to be inside information, and it'd better not be. It's the nature and job of investors to be interested in information that allows them to gain, lawfully, positive abnormal returns.

James S. Chanos was one of the first investors to see information that was not reflected in the stock price in Enron's 1999 financials. Chanos was struck by Enron's return on capital, which was a paltry 7 percent before taxes. In his witness testimony to the Committee on Energy and Commerce on February 6, 2002, Chanos testified,

This is important for two reasons; first, we viewed Enron as a trading company that was akin to an "energy hedge fund." For this type of firm a 7 percent return on capital seemed abysmally low, particularly given its market dominance and accounting methods. Second, it was our view that Enron's cost of capital was likely in excess of 7 percent and probably closer to 9 percent, which meant, from an economic cost

*point-of-view, that Enron wasn't really earning any money at all, despite
reporting "profits" to its shareholders. This mismatch of Enron's cost of
capital and its return on investment became the cornerstone for our
bearish view on Enron and we began shorting Enron common stock in
November of 2000.*

The other reason why institutional investors are not interested
in buy and sell recommendations is that analysts do not really
forecast stock prices. Their recommendations are not really based
on their expectation of total shareholder return (contrary to what
the banks' ratings indicate). Take the case of Merrill Lynch, for
instance. As noted previously, analysts at Merrill Lynch give a rating reflecting the expected total return (price appreciation plus
yield) within the twelve-month period from the date of the initial
rating. The price appreciation depends on the stock price in
twelve months time. But is their price objective a forecast of the
stock price in twelve months? No. They provide an intrinsic value
for the stock, but they do not forecast future stock prices. After
all, what makes a stock move? The answer is *expectations*. But
then the next stock price will be based on new expectations. The
analyst cannot forecast what the expectations are going to be one
year hence. Nobody can.

If you look at the way analysts establish their twelve-month
price objective, you will see that their price objective is the future
price (provided the market does not change). Take, for example,
this recommendation from an analyst: "Our price objective is
$100–$105/share (12–17 percent upside), based on a 25 percent
premium to the S&P 500 consensus twelve-month estimates." What
are these S&P 500 consensus twelve-month estimates? Financial
analysts make earnings forecasts; S&P calculates a consensus as
an average of these earnings forecasts, what it calls "bottom-up
estimates of operating earnings by economic sector." The S&P
500 Consensus Price/Earnings (or P/E) is the average of current
prices/estimated earnings for the 500 companies. Our analyst's
price objective is therefore equal to her estimate of the earnings
per share for the company she covers, multiplied by 125 percent,

times the average of current price/estimated earnings for the S&P 500. Please note the words "current price" in that phrase. The analyst does not forecast how the average P/E for S&P 500 companies might change. The information that will make this P/E change would be very valuable, but it is not reflected in her price target.

Another analyst values the company's shares using discounted-cash-flow (DCF)–based methods to arrive at his target price. He uses a discount rate that reflects the current expected market return. Information that will make the expected market return change would be also very valuable, but it is not incorporated into his price objective.

Thus, the price objective is not really a prevision; it is the analyst's view of the stock's intrinsic value. It is not a forecast of a market price, contrary to what Merrill Lynch (and other investment banks) makes it look like.

A third reason could be that the analyst's forecasts are systematically biased. The common wisdom about sell-side analysts is that their recommendations tend to be overly optimistic as a result of pressure from their investment-banking colleagues. However, research by Fleuriet and Yan[13] shows that it is not the optimistic analyst but the good analyst (one with superior stock-picking ability) who increases the chance of winning equity mandates for investment banks. We found that the performance of analysts' recommendation can explain their investment banks' chances of winning future mandates. There is a positive relationship between the performance of an analyst's recent buy and strong buy recommendations and his bank's chance of winning future underwriting mandates. The effect is significant for both raw stock performance and industry-adjusted stock performance. In contrast, the relationship between an analyst's optimism and his bank's chance of winning future mandates is weakly negative. We conjecture that stock picking earns analysts credibility among investors, and that this reputation plays an integral role in investment banks' underwriting process. The key finding of our research identifies a countervailing force to the well-documented incentives for analysts to be optimistically biased. The current organization structure of investment banks (i.e., the affiliation between equity research and investment banking) has been blamed for analysts' optimism because of the conflict of interest problem. The feedback effect identified in our research suggests that the affiliation also provides analysts with incentive to be good rather than optimistic.

The Business Model of Research

In the traditional model (that is, before the Global Analyst Research Settlement), equity analysts had three types of clients: issuers, individual investors, and institutional investors. There were allegations of unlawful interactions between underwriters' research and investment-banking divisions during the bubble of the late 1990s. According to Eliot Spitzer, at the time the attorney general of New York, research analysts were acting as quasi-investment bankers for the purpose of attracting and keeping issuing clients.

> *What do issuing companies want?* They expect analysts to deliver a positive earnings forecast and also to bring along enthusiastic investors when they issue equity. The problem is that you may not be able to have both (for example, see the case of Jack Grubman at Citigroup, which I discuss later in this chapter). If you make positive forecasts but are wrong, you simply cannot deliver the investors. But then, if you make negative forecasts, the CEOs shut you down and complain to your manager. Issuers should understand that analysts need to be good in order to provide access to capital for businesses worldwide.
>
> *What do individual investors want?* To the best of our knowledge, there is no public survey of what individual investors want. However, one thing's for sure: they do not want to lose money. After a while, analysts lose the trust of investors by making wrong recommendations. Individual investors want analysts with good stock-picking abilities.

What do institutional investors want? More and more, they have their own stables of buy-side analysts. In addition they may have better access to management (depending on their buying power) than sell-side analysts. Therefore, institutional investors are not so much interested in the investment ratings provided by analysts as in their industry insights. They are looking for expertise factors like industry knowledge, useful calls, management access, and special services, as well as personal factors like integrity, accessibility, and skills. Some institutional investors just want investment ideas. But more and more often they want extra bang for their buck. For example, hedge funds want "sell ideas" (or "short ideas") as well as buy recommendations. In 2004, Goldman Sachs created a group of analysts with fifty stocks to follow—only to find investment ideas, whether short or long. There is no longer a prevailing pressure (either internal or external) to be overly optimistic.

Finally, research as a business may not be judged by the immediate revenue it provides to the bank, but by its long-term effect. Sell-side research analysts do not earn revenue directly from sales of their services to clients. Institutional investors typically compensate investment banks for the research they produce by directing trades through their brokerage divisions at a slight premium, a practice known as "soft dollaring." Recent years have seen major changes: the commissions per share paid by institutional investors in the United States collapsed in the period from 2000 to 2006, from an average of about 4.5 cents per share to about 1.5 cents per share.[14] It seems that the slight premium paid for research may be disappearing. In 2005, Fidelity Investments, an asset manager, agreed with both Lehman Brothers and Deutsche Bank to pay for stock research, while also getting a reduced commission rate. This is called unbundling. Fidelity reportedly was paying $7 million to Lehman Brothers annually for research, while Lehman was charging commissions of $0.020 to $0.025 a share.[15]

In Europe, the U.K.'s Financial Services Authority (FSA) has encouraged unbundling, and the French authority, the AMF (Autorité des Marchés Financiers), followed suit in 2005. In the wake of the Global Analyst Research Settlement, many investment banks considered eliminating their research departments altogether.[16] Goldman Sachs was mentioned among them, but the firm refuted this: "As a premier institutional sales house, our research is critical to our franchise." The other big investment banks made similar comments. As Andy Kessler, a former equity analyst, said in an excellent book written about his experience:

> Analysts and salesmen and traders and bankers all make a living providing access to capital to business worldwide. For that task, the Street, as a group, gets to keep half of the revenues they generate. But it's an information business. When you work on the Street, all you have is your reputation. Longevity comes from maintaining that reputation with all your constituents, including companies, institutional investors, and Joe Six-Stock retail investors. Taint it, and someone else will fill your shoes.[17]

I think it's safe to say that the traditional model of equity research is here to stay. Research is critical to the franchise of investment banks, whether on the buy side or on the sell side. The banks simply need to keep in mind, in formulating their strategy for equity research, that neither side should take preeminence. So this begs the obvious question: is there anything new?

Illustration: How Citigroup's Research Model Went Wrong

One of the most notorious cases of an alleged conflict of interest on Wall Street involves the star telecom analyst Jack Grubman at Salomon Smith Barney (SSB). In the 1990s, Grubman built a strong reputation among investors for his ability to pick stocks.[18] In 1999, Salomon's retail force ranked Grubman fourth among all equity research analysts.[19] During 1999 and 2000, Salomon was awarded thirty-five mandates in the telecommunication sector, which Grubman covered. In early 2000, however, Grubman issued a number of buy and strong buy recommendations on

AT&T, Global Crossing, WorldCom, and Qwest, all of which performed poorly.

In 2000 and 2001, as the performance of Grubman's recommendations suffered, his internal rank among Salomon Smith Barney retail brokers dropped to last.[20] SSB was not selected as manager or comanager in any of the fourteen telecommunication stock offerings in 2002. Grubman's optimism not only cost investors money but also cost his bank opportunities for winning future mandates.

As Charles Gasparino pointed out in *Blood on the Street*:

> *In December 2000, the* New York Times *began a series of stories on conflicted research of the superstar analysts, targeting Grubman as "one of the many analysts who got it so wrong," in a long, detailed account of the Chinese Wall straddling that made Grubman one of Wall Street's highest-paid analysts. . . . [The NYT] presented evidence of Grubman's hyped research and inflated ratings on companies that returned the favor by kicking back investment-banking fees to Salomon.[21]*

These articles were the beginning of a chain of events that ultimately led to Grubman's resignation in August 2002, after accusations leveled by Eliot Spitzer that he had issued biased research to clients to win investment-banking business for SSB. A year later, the SEC brought an action against Grubman covering the very period of his success, 1999 to 2001.

The SEC alleged, among other things, that "Grubman was the linchpin for SSB's investment banking efforts in the telecom sector. He was the preeminent telecom analyst in the industry, and telecom was of critical importance to SSB. His approval and favorable view were important for SSB to obtain investment banking business from telecom companies in his sector."[22]

Not Commendable Recommendations

In the late fall of 1999, AT&T decided to list a tracking stock for its wireless unit—the largest equity offering in the United States. Grubman, who had always been negative on AT&T, issued a "strong buy" rating on the company. In February 2000, AT&T

named SSB as one of the lead underwriters and joint book runners for the IPO. On October 9, Jack Grubman dropped AT&T from a "buy" to an "outperform," a lesser rating in Wall Street's lexicon, after news reports claimed that he had issued the better recommendation to win Salomon an underwriting role in the IPO for AT&T Wireless Group. According to Heather Timmons, "Some observers say Grubman's buy rating so angered Wall Street that Salomon has been kept out of other upcoming telecom deals."[23]

As early as 2000, Salomon Smith Barney's retail sales force had started rating Grubman the worst of the investment bank's more than 100 analysts. So, how could SSB win investment-banking business with Grubman as a research analyst after 1999, i.e., after he had lost the trust of its retail sales force? In fact, an analyst who issues a positive call to curry favor with clients can ultimately lose favor in his own firm. This is precisely what happened to Grubman.

It is true that Grubman's importance to the business was reflected in high scores and evaluations from investment bankers, who ranked him first among all analysts in 2000. But their esteem quickly dropped in 2001, when they ranked him twenty-third. Likewise, SSB's institutional sales force rated Grubman sixteenth out of 113 analysts in 2000 and forty-sixth out of 115 in 2001. The opinions of retail brokers were even worse. For 1999, the retail sales force ranked Grubman fourth out of 159 analysts evaluated. In 2000, the brokers at Salomon Smith Barney ranked him dead last among all analysts (the same was true for 2001).

Moreover, Grubman received a litany of scathing written evaluations from the retail sales force during this time:

- "Poster child for conspicuous conflicts of interest."
- "I hope Smith Barney enjoyed the investment banking fees he generated, because they come at the expense of retail clients."
- "Let him be a banker, not a research analyst."
- "His opinions are completely tainted by 'investment banking' relationships (padding his business)."

- "Investment banker or research analyst? He should be fired."
- "Grubman has made a fortune for himself personally and for the investment banking division. However, his investment recommendations have impoverished the portfolio of my clients and I have had to spend endless hours with my clients discussing the losses Grubman has caused them."

Additionally, many criticized his support of companies that were SSB investment-banking clients:

- "Grubman's analysis and recommendations to buy (1 Ranking) WCOM [WorldCom], GX [Global Crossing], Q [Qwest] is/was careless."
- "His ridiculously bullish calls on WCOM and GX cost our clients a lot of money."
- "How can an analyst be so wrong and still keep his job? RTHM [Rhythm NetConnections], WCOM, etc., etc."
- "Downgrading a stock at $1/sh is useless to us."
- "How many bombs do we tolerate before we totally lose credibility with clients?"

A Matter of Trust

After a while, analysts lose the trust of investors by making wrong recommendations. After 1999, Grubman had lost the trust of Salomon's sales force. It got to the point where two former Salomon Smith Barney stockbrokers sued Jack Grubman, claiming that his "buy" ratings and bullish reports on WorldCom stock had misled their clients. (The suits were later dismissed.)

Investment banks want their investment research to be well respected and their individual investor clients to be successful over time. Analysts lose their reputation when they make too many wrong calls. When this happens, they prove useless in securing new mandates for investment banking. As Andy Kessler put it, "I had figured out long ago you work on Wall Street to get paid. But my clients were institutions for which I felt an obligation to make smart and right stock calls. All you have on Wall Street is your reputation. If you lose that, you are toast."[24]

Notes

1. British Bankers Association, Response to CP 171, "Conflicts of Interest: Investment Research and Issues of Securities," April 18, 2003.
2. Ibid.
3. Landon Thomas, Jr., "The War between the Street and Floor," *New York Times*, November 23, 2003.
4. In 2003, Blodget was charged with civil securities fraud by the U.S. Securities and Exchange Commission. He paid multimillion-dollar fines in his settlements with the prosecutors and was barred from the securities industry for life.
5. Jeffrey Skilling, who focused Enron on new markets for energy products, was promoted to president and chief operating officer in 1997. He resigned in August 2001. Andrew Fastow, who developed creative accounting and structured finance, was promoted to senior vice president of finance in 1997. In 1999, he received an award for excellence as a CFO.
6. Enron's 2000 Annual Report, p. 7.
7. See "Selected Financial and Credit Information," in Enron's 2000 Annual Report, p. 52.
8. This joke and its implications for the efficient market theory was beautifully recounted in a short article by John Kay, "A Fortune Built on Defying the Pull of Theory," *Financial Times*, March 24, 2004.
9. Marc Goedhart, Timothy Koller, and David Wessels, "Do Fundamentals—or Emotions—Drive the Stock Market?" *McKinsey Quarterly*, 2005 Special Edition: *Value and Performance*.
10. *Institutional Investor* (*I.I.*) is a highly recognized monthly trade publication targeted at buy-side investors—finance professionals who manage portfolios of securities on behalf of their clients.
11. See Exhibit 4 from *Institutional Investor*'s 2005 rankings.

12. Daniel J. Bradley, Bradford D. Jordan, and Jay R. Ritter, "Analyst Behavior Following IPOs: The 'Bubble Period' Evidence," July 2005, at SSRN: ssrn.com/abstract=758388.

13. Michel Fleuriet and Jinghua Yan, "Deal Making and Stock Picking: Better to Be Optimistic than Good?" 2006, unpublished.

14. Jay Ritter at the *Journal of Banking and Finance* Thirtieth Anniversary conference in Beijing, 2006.

15. Matthew B. Albrecht and Justin Menza, "S&P Industry Survey: Investment Services," May 2007.

16. Thomas, "War between the Street and Floor."

17. Andy Kessler, *Wall Street Meat* (New York: Harper Business, 2003), p. 231.

18. Ibid., p. 213.

19. *Securities and Exchange Commission* v. *Jack Benjamin Grubman*, April 28, 2003; www.sec.gov/litigation/complaints/comp18111b.htm.

20. Ibid.

21. Charles Gasparino, *Blood on the Street* (New York: Free Press, 2005), p. 185

22. *Securities and Exchange Commission* v. *Jack Benjamin Grubman*.

23. "Investment Banks: Let Analysts Do Their Jobs," *BusinessWeek*, October 30, 2000.

24. Kessler, *Wall Street Meat*, p. 155.

10

The Business of Equity Offerings

Raising equity capital is the traditional role of investment banks. It is, in fact, their core business, which they do either for companies that are already listed on a stock exchange or for a company's initial offering. An offering of a stock that is already listed is called a "seasoned equity offering" (SEO), as opposed to an "initial public offering" (IPO). An IPO is needed for a company to sell stock to the general public for the first time and get a listing (a necessary precondition to the trading of securities on an exchange). The stock is sold either by existing shareholders, in what is called a "secondary offering," or by the company itself as a "primary offering."

The IPO Conundrum

If you look at the experience of the different financial markets in the world, you will find three substantially different mechanisms for completing an IPO: auctions, fixed-price offerings, and book building. In an auction, the shares are offered for sale, on a predetermined schedule, to several competing potential buyers. Under a fixed-price offering, a certain number of shares are offered to retail investors at a preset price, which is generally identical to the price offered to institutional investors. Book building is the process whereby the bank marketing the IPO gets to know the price investors intend to offer and the volume of the security they are interested in.

In 2004, two academics examined the IPO methods used in forty-seven countries and found that book building, which was rare outside North America in the early 1990s, had become common around the world.[1] According to recent estimates, about 80 percent of foreign IPOs now use the book-building method. The IPO conundrum is as follows: why is it that, while companies in most countries are giving up auction methods to use a book-building technique, in the United States companies like Google are doing just the opposite?

IPO auctions have been tried in many countries—Italy, the Netherlands, Portugal, Sweden, Switzerland, and the United Kingdom in the 1980s and Argentina, Malaysia, Singapore, Taiwan, and Turkey in the 1990s. But they were abandoned years before book building became popular. "IPO auctions were most robust in France, being used alongside both fixed-price public offers and a restricted form of book-building for many years. Even in France, however, IPO auctions were abandoned once standard book-building/public offer simultaneous hybrids were allowed."[2] We saw how Merrill Lynch teamed up with a French law firm to convince the French government to use book building for privatizations in the country. Before that, the French had used auctions and fixed-price methods to sell their IPOs. Today, though, nearly all IPOs in France rely on book building.

In order to answer the conundrum, it is necessary to be familiar with the three IPO mechanisms. By way of example, we'll look at the experience of France in auction and fixed-price IPOs and the experience of the United States in book building. France is interesting because many mechanisms have been used in this country. According to Jay Ritter, "More than any other country in the world, the French IPO market has been characterized by multiple mechanisms being used to sell IPOs without government interference."[3]

Auction Mechanisms

IPO auctions are similar to what happens at Sotheby's or eBay: the winner bids above the equilibrium price. The difference is that, in the auctions at Sotheby's or on eBay, the winning bidder is the one who offers the highest price, and the price is whatever that person's final bid is. This is not necessarily the case for IPOs. There are two types of IPO auctions used in the world: single-price and discriminatory auctions. In a single-price auction, also called a "uniform-price auction," all winning bidders pay the lowest price regardless of the prices they bid. This mechanism is often used for IPOs. In a discriminatory auction, also called a "Dutch auction"[4] or "pay what you bid," winning bidders pay the amount they bid. This is the mechanism used in many countries for selling government bonds. In an auction, neither the issuer nor the underwriters can choose either the stock's price or its investors. Both the price and the winning investors result from the mechanism itself: the auction process is very perfunctory.

In France, the traditional IPO mechanism was, until the 1990s, a single-price auction managed by the Paris Bourse, *l'offre à prix minimal* (OPM). For this type of offering, the company and the issuing bank indicated the number of shares offered to the market and the minimum price, or "floor price." When placing an order, the investor had to indicate the number of shares wanted and the price range for acquiring them. The Paris Bourse centralized all the orders and ranked them by price. The exchange could then eliminate extreme orders to establish a price range within which most of the demand fell. The gap in price between the two ends of the range had to be at least 5 percent. All orders with prices within this range were executed at a price corresponding to the low end of the range, but not necessarily for 100 percent of the amount desired. The orders could be executed in part if there was more demand than the number of shares offered. The ratio between the number of shares allocated and the number of shares demanded might also significantly differ—the higher the price of the bid, the higher the pro rata allocation percentage.[5] There was therefore an incentive to bid high in this system.

Fixed-Price Offerings

In a fixed-price offering, the firm indicates the number of shares it is putting on the market and the proposed price, without any consideration for the demand. Any interested investor indicates to his bank the number of shares he wishes to purchase at that price. In the OPF, buy orders were transmitted by the underwriters to the Paris Bourse and centralized. If the number of shares demanded exceeded the number of shares offered, the exchange, together with the firm and the underwriters, decided on a pro rata allocation percentage. Given the lack of consideration of the demand in this process, it should come as no surprise that this mechanism tended to result in a high level of underpricing, which in turn generated inflated orders because of the pro rata allocation system. This mechanism is almost never used now.

The French still employ a fixed-price offering, but within a book building. The process starts with a book building for institutional investors. The price is set, but trading does not start immediately; after that, there is a fixed-price offering for retail investors that typically lasts for five days. The private investors can buy the offered stock at the price of the book building (or at a discount to this price). True, the underwriters are at risk during the five days of the fixed-price offering. But this mixed system could be a good strategy for investment banks to consider, as it allows small investors to participate in an IPO. This process is used not only in France but also in China.

Book Building in Detail

An underwritten issue means that the underwriter guarantees the proceeds. It is called a "bought deal," or a "firm commitment" transaction, because the issuer sells its securities outright to the underwriter, who then resells the securities to dealers and/or the general public. Alternatively, the company can decide to sell its shares directly to the public without the help of underwriters, what we call a "direct public offering" (DPO). In some cases, banks agree only to do their best to sell shares to the public; this is called a "best-efforts underwriting" or "standby agreement." Best-efforts underwritings are more common for IPOs than for secondary offerings, and more common still for very small IPOs.

The book-building process reduces the underwriters' risks in a bought deal by allowing them to test the demand through the advance gathering of indications of interest. There is a premarketing phase, a "road show," during which underwriters gather indications of interest from would-be investors—how many shares they would be interested in purchasing, and at what price. The final price and allocation of IPO shares will depend on the responses received during the premarketing phase. In a book-building offer, the underwriter has some influence on the offering price and on the allocation. Because allocations are dependent on the information reported, investors have a built-in incentive to provide an accurate report.

Because the IPO process in the United States is highly regulated, the calendar revolves around registration with the SEC.[6] From a regulatory standpoint, auctions, fixed-price offerings, and book building are alike. Two dates matter most in U.S. regulation: the filing date and the effective date. As a result, there are three important periods: the prefiling period, the waiting period, and the posteffective period.

The Prefiling Period

In the United States it is unlawful for anybody to sell an issuer's securities, through a prospectus or otherwise, unless the issuer has filed a registration statement with the SEC.[7] Selling securities on the basis of information that is not included in the prospectus is also strictly forbidden. The day the company turns in the registration statement to the SEC is known as the *filing date*. Contained in this registration statement are a description of the issuing company; biographical material on its officers and directors; the number of shares each insider (officers, directors, and shareholders owning more than 10 percent of the securities) owns; complete financial statements, including existing debt and equity securities and how they are capitalized; where the proceeds of the offering are going (the "use of funds"); and any present or impending legal proceedings involving the company, including strikes, lawsuits, antitrust actions, and copyright/patent infringement suits.

During the prefiling period, the firm prepares the IPO and chooses an investment bank to lead the transaction. The "lead manager" is responsible for preparing and executing the deal, and serves as book runner with a prominent role in pricing and allocation of IPO shares. It also helps choose the other members of the syndicate—the group of underwriters selling the shares to the public.[8] The lead manager's name almost always appears to the left of the other banks' names on the cover of the prospectus.

The duties of the lead manager during the prefiling period include the following: preparing the prospectus, overseeing legal due diligence and completion of the SEC registration, and selecting the other underwriters. A typical list of tasks for the lead manager during the prefiling gives you an idea of what is involved: holding the organizational meeting, starting business and financial due diligence, starting legal due diligence, drafting the registration statement, drafting the letter of comfort, and drafting the underwriting agreement.[9]

Five departments, no less, of the lead manager are involved:

- The banker, or relationship manager, gets the mandate. Then *corporate finance*—called IBK (investment banking) in certain banks—participates in the due diligence process and helps to develop marketing material, writes the MD&A (the extremely important "management's discussion and analysis of financial condition and results of operations"), and organizes the road show. All along, corporate finance works on the valuation of the company.

- The *equity capital markets group* (ECM) is in charge of the relationship with the other underwriters, the "syndicate members." ECM gives its opinion on the timing and controls the distribution of the stock. Usually, ECM identifies a target investors list, controls the book building, participates in the pricing, and provides aftermarket support.
- *Equity sales* take care of the relationships with potential investors.
- *Equity traders* are needed for market support.
- *Sell-side analysts* used to be as involved as the bacon in eggs and bacon. But since the Global Analyst Research Settlement, their role has been more indirect, like the rooster's. Now analysts attend due diligence sessions and participate in customer calls, as well as providing valuation opinions, reviewing the prospectus, and providing feedback on due diligence disclosure. Though they cannot be involved in the marketing (no analyst is allowed to attend the road show), they are still very important for the commitment committee (as was Jessica Reif Cohen, whom I discuss in the next chapter).

The Waiting Period

The waiting period, also known as the "cooling-off" or "quiet" period, takes place between the filing of a registration statement with the SEC and its being declared effective by the SEC. A lot actually happens during this so-called waiting period. After filing the registration statement, the underwriter performs a due diligence investigation; receives SEC comments and files amendments accordingly; and prepares the road show, including the presentation, the retail information memorandum, and the preliminary prospectus.

The Securities Act of 1933 requires an issuer of securities to disclose all material information to potential investors or be held liable for its absence. This applies to the firm's management, the underwriters, and the underwriters' counsels. The due diligence process has many benefits for the lead underwriter: to wit, it enables the underwriter to do the following:

- Understand the business, strategies, and operations of the company
- Assure investors that the company is a good investment opportunity
- Address the risk factors for the underwriting committee of the bank
- Understand the strategic story, which will help in drafting the MD&A

During this quiet period, issuers are prohibited from talking about their stock. It typically lasts 90 days from the filing date. In addition, following an IPO, NYSE and NASD rules impose a quiet period of forty calendar days on underwriting managers and comanagers (as opposed to ten calendar days following a secondary offering) and a quiet period of twenty-five calendar days on other members of the underwriting syndicate or selling group.

After the registration statement is filed, but before it becomes effective, actual sales are still prohibited. The issue is "in registration," which means that the SEC will investigate and make sure that full disclosure has been made in the registration statement. Amendments can be made to the registration statement if the SEC deems that changes are necessary. The registration statement will be the source of the "offering circular," or prospectus. The offering circular, required by the Securities Act of 1933, is the extremely important document that offers securities for sale. It includes all the information that the investor should need to help him make up his mind about investing in the security. In the prospectus are a description of the company, a description of the securities to be issued, who the selling shareholders are (if applicable), the company's historical financial statements, its current activities, the MD&A explaining the company's strategy and the nature of its competition, who the management is, and the use of funds from the issue (if new securities are issued). The public offering price and the effective date are not contained in the preliminary prospectus, because the information is not yet known.

The preliminary prospectus is also known as a "red herring" because of the red warnings across the top and down the side explaining that "this is not a solicitation for sale." No written information about the offering can be published other than the red herring. No analyst can publish a research report on the company during this period, and no journalist can write stories about the IPO that include the issuing firm's or its banks' involvement. Only the red herring can be a source of information. In Europe, however, where there is no quiet period, analysts can publish research and the value of the company can be discussed.

The preliminary prospectus is the basis of the premarketing that takes place during the quiet period. The underwriters elicit offers, but none of these offers may be accepted (i.e., sales concluded) until the registration statement is effective. With the preliminary prospectus in hand, the company and its bankers then embark on the road show—the traveling presentation by company managers addressed to would-be investors. (The bank also organizes a series of meetings with the most important of the potential investors, called "one-on-ones.") The first objective of the road show is to promote the issuer. A road show is especially important for IPOs because it is usually the first opportunity for the public to examine the company and its management. The second objective of the road show is to build the order book. The road show starts with a price range, or "price talk"—the one indicated to the SEC in the filing.

The price range is the preliminary indication of the price at which the stock is to be offered. To choose this price range, the lead bank usually selects a subset of comparable listed companies and calculates various ratios for these companies. Companies are matched based on how close their ratios are to the ratios of the target company. A price multiple is found for each company in the subset, and a median multiple for the subset is calculated. Applying this median multiple to the targeted company gives a price. Suppose, for example, that the price talk is $18 to $20. Investors provide their indications of interest (IOI). These IOI are not commitments to buy (remember that it is forbidden to sell shares before the registration statement is effective) but indications of how many shares an investor would demand at a given price (or at the price range). The book runner uses these IOI to build the order book.

The order book organizes the IOI in order of descending price (i.e., it establishes a demand curve). The third objective of the road show, then, is to prepare the placement of the shares. During the road show, the underwriters canvass institutional investors, using the banks' target investor focus list. These target investors can be longstanding clients of the bank, but there has to be enough potential interest in investing in the company; if there isn't, the banks risk losing both the investor and the issuer.

If demand in the indicated price range is too strong or too weak, the underwriter may want to revise the range and file the revised range with the SEC. Suppose that the demand is good and a revised price range of $20 to $22 is filed. At the pricing meeting, the price can be set 20 percent above or below the price range without the need to do another filing; in our case, it can be between $26 and $16 without a further pricing amendment. Under current SEC rules, issuers must amend their registration statement when the offering in the aggregate changes by more than 20 percent.

The Posteffective Period

Once the company receives SEC clearance and the shares become available for sale, many things happen in a short amount of time:

- The offering price is set.
- Shares are allocated to investors.
- The decision to sell, or not to sell, more shares than offered is made.
- The underwriting agreement is signed.

- A press release with the terms of the offering is issued.
- The final prospectus is printed.
- The transaction closes.

The effective date, or "offering date," is the date on which the SEC opines that full disclosure is included in the prospectus. (If the SEC does not approve the prospectus, a "letter of deficiency" is issued and the effective date is postponed.) The prospectus then becomes effective. On that date, the offering price is set, and the company files it with the SEC in a last amendment. The red herring is blacked out—the offering price and the date of subscription are added, and all the warnings are removed. The red herring then becomes the final prospectus. When the underwriting agreement is signed, the underwriters become the owners of the issue. At this point, the stock can be offered to the general public and the underwriting risk starts.

The offering price is the price at which the public buys the shares from the underwriters. The price that the IPO company (and/or its shareholders) receives is the public price minus the underwriting fee. The offering price is a business decision of the issuer based on the lead underwriter's pricing recommendation. The latter knows the book, which gives it a good picture of the demand for the offering at different price levels, as demonstrated by the indications of interest that the underwriters gathered during the marketing period. At this point, it is the job of the lead underwriter to explain to the issuer the context and significance of indications of interest from various investors, and to share its perspective on this demand.

Setting the offering price is a difficult balancing act. If the offering price is too high, the banks can be stuck with the issue. But if the price is too low, there is likely to be "money left on the table." An offering price is too low if it is below the first quoted price. The money left on the table is the first-day capital gain multiplied by the number of shares offered. As you can imagine, finding whether the price is too high or too low is a matter of a few hours of trading—at most one trading day. Remember that the underwriters buy the company's shares, then turn around and sell them to investors. Their gain is the underwriting fee. Therefore, they may lose the capital on the shares they cannot sell. Like all financial institutions, investment banks have to "mark to market" the shares they keep in inventories. If they cannot sell all the shares, the market price will stay below the offering price. The market will know that at some point the banks will have to unload the shares, therefore putting additional pressure on the price.

The book runner has discretion over who receives allocations of IPO shares. Only the lead bank's manager has real knowledge of the book that compiles all indications of interest. The book runner often gives priority to larger customers and institutions. However, the lead underwriter should disclose and explain to the issuer the final allocation of its IPO shares. After all, the chosen investors will become shareholders of the IPO company.

The strategy of investment banks in allocating stock has frequently been denounced, as it is understood as giving favors to a coterie of friends and customers. "Spinning," or allocating IPO shares to an executive in a company in exchange for the company's future investment-banking business, is unlawful. So are "quid pro quo arrangements," where investment banks allocate hot IPOs to their favored customers in return for commission business. The SEC brought a groundbreaking IPO case against Credit Suisse First Boston (CSFB) that was finally settled for $100 million in sanctions. In the late 1990s, CSFB had allocated hot IPO shares to chosen customers, charging between 33 and 65 percent of these customers' trading profits in those IPO shares—not a good strategy, obviously.

"Issuer-directed securities" are amounts of stock that the issuer reserves for its employees and friends. The practice is legal. Obviously, when doing an IPO, it is good business for a company to reserve stock for its customers and others who can help the firm in the future. Since the NASD is interested, however, in bona-fide public offerings, it insists that the amount of issuer-directed securities bear a "reasonable relationship" (interpreted by one commentator as 10 percent) to the total amount offered and that the favored purchasers be "directly related to the conduct of the issuer's business."

"Flipping" is the opposite of what underwriters look for. The flipper buys shares at the offering price and resells them as soon as trading begins. Flipping is most profitable in a hot IPO market, when the price often rises dramatically above the offering price on the first day. The agreement among underwriters may provide for a penalty for selling IPO shares to an investor that flips the shares. In the United States, the discouragement of flipping is backed up by the ability of the lead underwriter to track investors' flipping activity and to penalize syndicate members whose customers flip by withdrawing selling commissions.[10]

Tactics to support aftermarket prices and boost aftermarket demand are unlawful. These include "laddering," in which underwriters require that investors agree to purchase additional shares in the aftermarket at specified prices. In 2005, the SEC settled with Morgan Stanley and Goldman Sachs for unlawful allocation of stock to institutional customers in IPOs underwritten by the firms during 1999 and 2000. Among its complaints, the commission alleged that the firms violated Rule 101 of Regulation M under the Securities Exchange Act of 1934 when they attempted to induce certain customers who received allocations of IPOs to place purchase orders for additional shares in the aftermarket.

After distribution of the new issue, the lead underwriter usually maintains an orderly secondary market in the issue. The lead underwriter keeps the market on an even keel by placing a stabilizing bid at the offer price when the market price drops below the offer price. Meanwhile, the underwriters may sell more shares than the number offered. A "naked short" occurs when the underwriters have to buy the shares in the aftermarket to deliver them. But the underwriters often negotiate the purchase of a number of shares above the planned offering, an overallotment (similar to overbooking of airline flights) known as the "green shoe option." If the stock price goes up, the underwriters exercise the overallotment option and buy shares from the company. If the price begins to drop, the underwriters do not exercise the option and instead buy shares in the open market to support the price of the stock.

The underwriting agreement makes explicit the public offering price, the underwriting spread, the net proceeds to the issuer, and the settlement date.

The underwriting spread, or "gross spread," is the total underwriters' fee. Structured as a percentage applied to the volume of the issue, the gross spread is deducted from the money paid to the firm issuing the IPO. Fees for IPOs were traditionally 7 percent of the deal in the United States, a level that had been holding for decades. (In Europe, the fees have always tended to be more in the 3 to 3.5 percent range.) But with the competition of new underwriters in the United States in the early 2000s, fees have been cut down to the European scale, or 3 to 3.5 percent.

The underwriting spread is typically divided among the multiple lead managers in the following manner:

- A *management fee*, for example, 20 percent of the total spread, goes to the lead managers and comanagers for their "management" of the offering. The management fee is split up among the managers on a fixed basis.
- An *underwriting fee*, also 20 percent of the spread, goes to all underwriters, split up on the basis of underwriting commitments.
- A *selling concession*, 60 percent of the spread in this example, is paid to the underwriter and other syndicate members upon completion of selling the securities. This selling concession is different for the shares sold to institutional investors and those sold to retail investors. The institutional fee is based on the "institutional pot," which is the part of a new issue set aside by the lead underwriter for distribution to institutional investors. This fee is split up on a competitive,

or "jump ball" basis: it depends on the amount of the issue that an underwriter sold to its customers. Lead managers are usually capped to avoid their receiving a disproportionate amount of the fee. Occasionally investors designate the underwriters who should get that part of the gross spread added to their orders. These designated orders usually arise as compensation for research services performed by the particular underwriter. For shares sold to retail investors, underwriters receiving retail allocations are entitled to the entire selling concession for such shares, irrespective of pre-arranged splits for the institutional pot, if any.

Notes

1. Ravi Jagannathan and Ann Sherman, "Why Do IPO Auctions Fail?" Unpublished paper, Northwestern University.
2. Ann E. Sherman, "Global Trends in IPO Methods," SSRN 2005.
3. "Differences between European and American IPO Markets," *European Financial Management*, Vol. 9, no. 4, 2003, pp. 421–434.
4. "In finance and on the internet, uniform price (aka non-discriminatory) auctions are sometimes mistakenly called Dutch auctions. A Dutch auction is an open (rather than sealed bid) descending price auction. A Dutch auction for multiple units involves selling the same item for many different prices and is, in this sense, closer to a discriminatory than to a uniform price auction." Sherman, "Global Trends.
5. In a pro rata allocation, a successful bidder receives a number of shares equal to an allocation percentage multiplied by the number of shares the bidder asked for. The pro rata allocation percentage is found by dividing the number of shares offered by the number of shares represented by all successful bids.
6. Section 5 of the Securities Act requires that a registration statement be filed with the SEC before securities are offered

for sale to the public. It also prohibits the sale of those securities until the registration statement becomes "effective."

7. "It shall be unlawful for any person, directly or indirectly, to make use of any means or instruments of transportation or communication in interstate commerce or of the mails to offer to sell or offer to buy through the use or medium of any prospectus or otherwise any security, unless a registration statement has been filed as to such security, or while the registration statement is the subject of a refusal order or stop order or (prior to the effective date of the registration statement) any public proceeding or examination under section 8." Securities Act of 1933, Section 5, "Prohibitions Relating to Interstate Commerce and the Mails."

8. The syndicate includes both the underwriting syndicate, which bears the risk of ending up with the securities, and the selling group, which does not bear this risk. The lead manager will then sign a letter of intent with the issuing corporation. This formalizes the relationship. However, it is a nonbinding arrangement until the effective date.

9. The underwriting agreement is a contract between the issuer and the book runner that defines the offering price, the underwriting spread, the net proceeds to the issuer, and the closing date.

10. Tim Jenkinson and Howard Jones, "Bids and Allocations in European IPO Bookbuilding," November 1, 2002; ssrn.com/abstract=302206.

11

Strategies in IPOs

The main difficulty in doing an initial public offering, compared to a seasoned equity offering, is determining the price of the newly issued stock. Some people refer to IPOs as "immediate profit opportunities," while others say that IPO stands for "it's probably overpriced." During the 1999–2001 bubble, the dramatic price increases of some IPO shares suggested that they were deliberately underpriced; however, the subsequent dramatic declines in price indicate that they were in fact overpriced.

For an investment bank doing an IPO, there is necessarily a balance that must be achieved between the interests of the investors and the interests of the investment-banking clients (the latter being the company that is about to be listed, its shareholders, or both). After the IPO, the company will probably continue doing business with the lead underwriter, provided the IPO turns out to be a reasonable success. The selling shareholder may be a government offering the stock of a state-owned company to the public in a privatization process. Or it may be a private-equity fund. In short, the client, whether it be the company or the selling shareholders, is always very important for an investment bank. But so are the investing clients; whether they are large institutional investors or private investors for a retail-oriented investment bank, the bank will need them for the next equity offering.

In all IPOs, there is an inherent conflict of interest between issuers and underwriters and between investors and underwriters. In the 1990s, a few banks did not bother to make this distinction. They allocated shares in hot IPOs to chosen investors for the purpose of obtaining their investment-banking business, while making themselves indispensable to issuers by delivering the investors. As a result, some investors paid excessive commissions to obtain these IPO allocations.

So, how should the company doing an IPO select its lead underwriter? How should the latter choose the issuer? What strategy should the investment bank adopt to deal with the conflict between issuers and investors?

Choosing the Lead Underwriter

If the issuing firm already has a strong relationship with an investment bank, it will typically continue working with that bank. Trust is the most important factor in this choice. Otherwise the bank has to go through a "beauty parade" to win the business. According to Paul Myners, "The beauty parade should carry a kind of health warning: it is, at best, a rough and ready process. It tends to place too much emphasis on presentational skills— something for which investment bankers have been thoroughly trained."[1] So with this in mind, a firm should consider three factors when it chooses an investment bank: the bank's experience, its relationship with investors, and its equity analyst.

First, the firm must take into account the bank's experience in the industry in which the firm operates, its knowledge of the industry, and its understanding of the business model. It must also take into account the successfulness of the bank's stewardship of previous IPOs. The league tables are important here, but the quality of the underwriter's performance should matter most.

Second, the firm should inquire about the market presence of the bank with investors, and whether they are institutional or individual investors. For example, if the firm that is about to issue an IPO is in consumer products, it could be attractive to bring in a bank with a large client base of individual investors. (It's easy to see why Ford chose Merrill Lynch for its IPO in 1956.) Finally, it is important to ensure that the relationship manager is going to be personally involved and that he can deliver the bank. The client buys both the bank *and* the banker.

That said, companies often choose a bank as the lead underwriter for their IPO based on the reputation of the particular analyst who will be assigned to follow the newly issued public stock. Underwriters that are competing to be the lead underwriter will each make a pitch to the firm. The "pitchbook" is the set of slides that the underwriter uses when she is making a presentation to the issuing firm explaining why her bank should be hired as the lead underwriter. The pitchbook usually contains the following objectives for the IPO:

- The bank will make sure that the IPO is successful, meaning that it won't have to be pulled out (a big failure), the price won't go south on the first day of trading (an embarrassment), and there won't be "flow back" (investors selling their newly acquired shares on the market at a loss—very costly for underwriters).
- It will maximize the sustainable valuation of a stock.
- It will create "demand tension," or supply/demand imbalance, which gives the company some pricing power. In that respect, the retail-oriented firms like Merrill Lynch and Morgan Stanley will stress the role to be played by private investors, who are less sensitive to the IPO price.
- The bank will allocate the issue to a stable shareholder base.

These objectives must be taken with a grain of salt, however. The foremost measure of an investment bank's success is its ability to sell all of the firm's shares at the offering price. Its strategy is not so much to maximize the sustainable valuation of a stock (as the banks say it is) as to sell the shares as fast as possible. The bank creates demand tension not so much to give the company pricing power (as the pitchbook says) as to be able to place the whole issue. The investment bank says that it allocates the issue to long-term investors. But the post-IPO market trading has to come not from the original shareholders (who can't sell because of lockup clauses), but from the shareholders who bought in the IPO. Often the amount of first-day selling is equal to the amount of the initial offering (this was the case for Google's IPO), which completely defeats the idea of a stable shareholder base!

The underwriters incur the same risk as they would if they were selling a "put" (a contract between buyer and seller that gives the buyer the right but not the obligation to sell the shares). The seller of a put has unlimited risk. This gives the underwriters the creeps, because if the issue does not sell, the market will know that there is an "overhang" (a reserve of unsold shares kept by the underwriters that can be sold at any price). This depresses the price still further, and the underwriting banks then stand to lose an enormous amount of money. That is why their strategy is to turn the shares around as quickly as possible and confirm the IOI (indication of interest) in a matter of hours.

Choosing the IPO Method

According to an IPO advisory committee in a 2003 report to the NYSE and NASD, "The market, and not regulators, should determine whether book building, a Dutch auction, or another method is desirable for a particular IPO."[2] Investment banks the world over have always been in favor of the book-building method for the placement of a bought deal. Why? The key difference between a Dutch auction IPO and a typical firm commitment underwriting is that in the former, the investment banks do not assume financial responsibility for any unsold shares. The other difference is that in an auction, neither the issuer nor the underwriters can choose either the price of the stock or the investors in the stock. It is only natural that banks would prefer the flexibility inherent in book building.

For Ann Sherman, who has studied the two mechanisms, there are two key differences between book building and auctions:

First, the issuer/underwriter has substantial control over information acquisition through book building, but little or no control in the auctions. This control can be used either to maximize expected proceeds from the current offering, or to induce investors to more carefully evaluate the issue, resulting in a more accurate aftermarket price.

The second advantage of coordinating entry to the IPO process is that there is less uncertainty about the number of bidders. The expected number of shares sold is higher because undersubscription is less likely when the number of participants is coordinated. With book building, the underwriter recruits investors. It cannot force investors to like the issue, but it can promise them a reasonable allocation at a sufficiently low price to cover their time and effort, guaranteeing that a number of investors will at least consider the offering. . . . The two advantages of controlling entry help to explain why auctions have not been as useful for IPOs as for other securities, most notably government bonds.[3]

Book building is the fastest way of selling stock in a firm commitment deal. Speed is the key component of success, since the investment bank does not want to take the risk of owning the stock. The true strategic objective of the underwriters is understandable: they want the IPO out the door ASAP.

Choosing the IPO Candidate

Underwriters must maintain a balance between two conflicting interests in IPOs. As a paid representative of the issuer, it is the underwriter's role to present the firm in the most favorable light. But the underwriter also has to be aware of its relationship with institutional investors. Because of the way the fees are paid, the investors command a share of the spoils, either through designated orders or by placing their orders with the book runner in the hope that more shares will be allocated to them.

It is in the interests of the investment bank selected to lead a good IPO, not a bad one. That goes without saying. But what type of company makes a good candidate? Basically, a good candidate is a firm that is growing nicely and will offer substantial profit opportunities to shareholders. In determining the quality of an IPO candidate, the investment bank should ask the following questions:

- What is its management known for?
- What does it do well?
- What is its track record?
- Does the firm have a proven growth story?
- Has the firm shown consistent profitability?
- Is its business model compelling?
- Is it an industry leader?

In the bubble years of the late 1990s, many investment banks underwrote a slew of companies that soon went bankrupt. These firms should have been at best financed by private-equity funds (which won't leave an at-risk company alone to manage itself). Not only had their business model proved not to be viable, but their growth perspectives were largely out of step with the real world. The number of failed IPOs that hit investment banks during that period was a product of the "herd strategy," which goes hand in hand with the herd mentality of investors during a market bubble. What mattered most was the number of firms you could bring to market. IPOs were priced on the basis of inflated prices, and these prices, in turn, were supported by an inflated IPO price.

All IPO projects must be cleared by the commitments committee of an investment bank, which decides what business the bank will do. Research analysts are asked to make assessments of the issuer's prospects. Academic research[4] has found that analysts tend to be more optimistic than objective on stocks underwritten by their affiliated investment banks. This is understandable: no bank can lead an IPO if its analyst is pessimistic about the company. But this raises an important question: will an analyst with a negative view of a company's stock offering be muzzled by its investment bank employer?

In 1987, Merrill Lynch was vying to be selected by the British government to manage the last stage of privatization of British Petroleum (BP). Unfortunately, Merrill's top oil and gas research analyst, the Greek-born Gus Fliakos, thought that the price was too high and did not want to give a buy recommendation on the stock. Fliakos was one of the most prominent research analysts in oil and gas at the time, and his glum assessment of the company created an enormous problem for Merrill's bankers. They asked him to reconsider. But Fliakos wouldn't budge.

Merrill Lynch decided that it had to drop out of the BP privatization. The BP offering was underwritten instead by an international group. It was a huge offering: the equivalent of $12 billion. Four U.S. investment banks agreed to underwrite 22 percent of the issue (505,800,000 shares), but Merrill was not one of them. The offer price was £3.30 a share and the bid £3.265 a share. Thanks to Gus Fliakos, Merrill was losing its potential share in the underwriting spread for the four U.S. underwriters of £17.7 million.[5] Four days later, the October 19 crash cut the market price by 20 percent and the four lead underwriters tried to bargain out of their commitment with the British government, to no avail. By the closing date of the offer, the price of BP stock had fallen to £2.96, and the underwriters had lost more than $1 billion.[6] Gus became an instant hero at Merrill Lynch.

Eighteen years later, it was Jessica Reif Cohen's turn to be a hero at Merrill Lynch. In May 2005, the Warner Music Group went public. Merrill had been listed as one of its main underwriters in its initial prospectus. But, as the *Wall Street Journal* reported,

Merrill decided it had to drop out of the Warner offering after its top media research analyst . . . told her firm's senior bankers that they were overpricing the shares. . . . Her opinion cost Merrill not just a prestigious client, but also millions of dollars in fees. Ms. Reif Cohen, it turns out, was right. In fact, the I.P.O. was such a dud that Warner Music had to lower the planned offering price to $17 a share, down from a range of $22 to $24. The price has generally been flat ever since.[7]

The *Journal* went on to make this blanket statement:

> Clearly, someone in Ms. Reif Cohen's position would have thought long
> and hard before pooh-poohing such a deal in the 1990s. Back then, an
> analyst with a negative view of a company's stock offering would proba-
> bly have kept quiet—bonuses depended on such deals—or have been
> muzzled by investment bankers, who were worried about their own, even
> bigger bonuses.

But this wasn't true in the 1980s, and I can testify from personal experience that this strict behavior was still the norm among good analysts in the 1990s. An investment bank was chosen in large part because of its equity analyst and his or her influence with investors. Therefore, an analyst who wanted to keep his or her reputation valuable would not be tempted to yield to the pressure of investment bankers.

Choosing the Offering Price

There is a conundrum in IPOs: why would the existing share-holders want to sell their shares if the prospects for the stock price are so good? If this is the case, the underwriters have to convince both shareholders and investors that the offering price and buying price, respectively, are good. Their strategy will be directed more toward the investor than toward the seller because they want to make sure that they are not left holding shares after the offering. This is why they will provide for some underpricing to attract investors.

According to Professor Jay Ritter, there are three ways of looking at the pricing of an IPO: the pitchbook view, the academic view, and the profit-sharing view. According to the pitchbook view (so called because it is found in most investment banks' pitchbooks), the initial filing range is found by looking at listed comparables minus a liquidity discount. The academic view[8] holds that the degree of underpricing is based on what it takes to induce investors to spend time on evaluation. This underpricing can be used to persuade investors to evaluate the issue more carefully, resulting in a more accurate issue price.[9] Third, the profit-sharing view holds that underwriters underprice IPOs in order to ingratiate themselves with the investors given allocations in return for favors. To buy these favors, underwriters price the stock below the fair value (which explains why the first-day "pop" occurs).

The offering price is typically 18 percent below the first trading day closing price in the United States and the United Kingdom (and higher in other countries). But the first-day pop can be staggering. The average price increase on the first trading day fluctuated between 10 and 20 percent from 1966 to September 1998 and between 50 and 80 percent from October 1998 to March 1999.[10] While $400 billion was raised in IPOs from 1985 to 2000, almost $96 billion was left on the table.[11]

These days, academic research tends to assume that the market price is the correct one, and the offering price is too low. Perhaps, though, it is the first-day trading price that is too high. Two factors support this view. First, most of the underpriced offerings are IPOs that were priced above the range: 80 percent of the money that is left on the table comes from the 20 percent of IPOs that are offered above their initial price range. Second, many of the hot IPOs subsequently experienced dramatic declines in price.

Could it be that the first-day trading was too high in comparison with the price range determined by the investment banks? Not surprisingly, it does seem that the market can at times be more irrational than the banks. In the end, though, the pricing of an IPO is simply a business decision reached by the issuer in consultation with the underwriter.[12] It is the responsibility of the board of the issuer to use its good-faith business judgment when disposing of the issuer's assets, including its capital stock in an IPO.

Choosing the Investors

Whatever the mechanism used, there is a buyer's curse in IPOs. If the IPO is hot, the buyer will not get any allocation. (If it is a lemon, she will certainly get all she wants!) The book runner retains the discretion to determine the final IPO share allocations while managing the institutional investors' behavior. The strategy is to make sure investors believe that there is reasonable demand for the IPO and that the shares will be allocated giving priority to select investors. So, how are investors selected?

The pitchbook view's answer to this question is that underwriters will use their discretion to allocate shares to institutional investors who are likely to be buy-and-hold investors. By definition, however, trading requires that there first be a seller. Meanwhile, the academic view contends that investors will be allocated shares in return for truthfully revealing their estimate of the share value: bids that were more informative—that came after meeting the management, were submitted early, or were revised upward during the book building—enjoy preferential allocations. Again, the issuing firms could have an influence on which new shareholders they bring into the fold. Finally, the profit-sharing view alleges that underwriters allocate shares in hot IPOs to investors in return for commission business. It's true that underwriters may want to allocate at least some shares to their best customers in order to maintain client relationships. However, underwriters cannot allocate shares as consideration for the payment of excessive commissions on trades of unrelated securities.

These quid pro quo arrangements are abusive and are therefore not a common practice among investment banks. In 2002, the SEC sued Credit Suisse First Boston (CSFB), alleging violations of NASD conduct rules. According to the complaint, "In exchange for shares in 'hot' IPOs, CSFB wrongfully extracted from certain customers a large portion of the profits that those customers made by immediately selling ('flipping') their IPO stock. The profits were channeled to CSFB in the form of excessive brokerage commissions generated by the customers in unrelated securities trades that the customers effected solely to share the IPO profits with CSFB."[13] CSFB settled with the SEC for $100 million—which was considered a slap on the wrist by none other than the former CEO of Salomon Brothers, an investment bank that gained notoriety in the 1980s, John Gutfreund.[14]

The Google IPO

Google decided to use a uniform-price auction[15] to do its IPO in 2004. The company founders, Larry Page and Sergey Brin, stated their goal clearly in the prospectus: "Our goal is to have an efficient market price—a rational price set by informed buyers and sellers—for our shares at the IPO and afterward. . . . Our goal is to achieve a relatively stable price in the days following the IPO and that buyers and sellers receive a fair price at the IPO."[16]

Google's Objectives

Google had several reasons for choosing the uniform-price auction. It wanted to

- *Favor individual investors* and avoid taking care of only the big investors. "By assembling a group of twenty-eight underwriters, many of which deal mainly with private investors, [Google] expected to draw on intense private investor interest and its high brand recognition," wrote the *Financial Times*'s Richard Waters.[17]
- *Avoid leaving money on the table.* An auction before the real auction, as trading starts, would (at least in principle) ensure that the company got the highest possible price for its shares.
- *Obtain better pricing.* The issuer would be able to view all the bids ranked by share price and would know the exact basis for the offering price; therefore, no negotiation would be necessary.
- *Avoid flipping*, since any investor would pay a price lower or at most equal to his bid.
- *Sidetrack Wall Street* and pay a lower underwriting spread.

The Google IPO was a bought deal, where the underwriter buys the securities from the seller/issuer and then resells them to investors. But it was a special case of a bought deal. A bid received by any underwriter involved no obligation or commitment of any kind by the bidder until the underwriters sent a notice of acceptance announcing that the bid was successful. As a result, the underwriters would be buying the shares from Google at the same time that they were sending the notices of acceptance. In a regular bought deal, the remaining unsold securities go onto the underwriter's balance sheet; that wouldn't happen in the Google IPO. Since there was little risk involved for the banks in the Google IPO, the fee was small: 2.8 percent, the third lowest for a big U.S. IPO at the time.

From a regulatory standpoint, auctions are a subset of book building: the issuer precommits to certain pricing and allocation rules. Conversely, in a bought deal, underwriters buy the shares and take the risk associated with distributing the shares at the set price. This gives them significant leverage in allocation and pricing. In an auction, however, the investment banks do not commit to sell the shares to investors at a set price. They have little power, if any, in setting the price and in allocating the issue. Shares are sold at the market-clearing price (the highest price that may be offered to potential investors based on bids in the master order book). Because there is an algorithm used to find this price, underwriters have no power to meddle in the pricing. It's rather simple: each bidder who has a successful bid will be allocated the number of shares he or she bid for.

The road shows are scaled back in auctions, because the process relies on bidding to gauge demand. This is more inclusive of investors, presumably providing a better sense of the clearing price. But the underwriters' equity analysts were not given informal guidance from Google on which to base their earnings models. Therefore, the bids may have been less informed than in normal book buildings.

A Lively Offering

In an auction, once all bids are entered, the firm simply determines the price at which the market clears. This should be the market price observed once trading on an exchange begins. Everything should go smoothly. But this was not to be the case for Google.

Table 11-1. Google's IPO

Dates	Number of Shares (in millions)	Price Range (in dollars)	Proceeds (in billions of dollars)
July 27, 2004	24.6	108–135	$3.30
August 10, 2004	25.7	108–135	$3.47
August 18, 2004	19.6	85–95	$1.86
August 19, 2004	19.6	85	$1.66

The day before the effective date, Google revised the filing range from $108–$135 down to $85–$95. The number of shares offered was also reduced. Table 11–1 indicates the number of shares offered, the price range, and the potential proceeds. While the IPO should have raised $3.3 billion for the company and its shareholders, in the end it raised only half this amount.

So, what happened? The *Wall Street Journal* reported that

> The drama heightened on Monday, August 16, as Google approached its planned deadline to close the bidding. Investors hadn't submitted bids sufficient to buy the planned 25.7 million-share offering at the projected price range. In a conference call, according to someone familiar with it, Google Chief Executive Eric Schmidt told executives and advisers that the auction had failed. . . . Google worked through a revised plan that slashed the expected offering price to $85 to $95 a share. It also made a 24 percent cut in the number of shares to be sold—to 19.6 million—as a few insiders pulled back shares they had planned to sell.[18]

In actual fact, the reduction in the number of shares from 25.7 million to 19.6 million concerned only the shareholders, who were to sell 11.6 million shares at filing, but sold only 5.5 million. The company had filed to sell 14.1 million new shares, and this is indeed what it sold (14.1 + 5.5 = 19.6).

The price range was revised downward when it appeared that the clearing price was going to be below the range and that there was not enough demand at $108–$135. Research shows, however, that Google could have expected to sell the 19.6 million shares at a price of $104.34.[19] Even after slashing the price range the night before, Google priced its IPO at $85 per share, the low end of $85–$95. The $85 offering price was set below the clearing price because the company had reserved the right to do so. This was an effort, according to Google, "to achieve a broader distribution of our Class A common stock or to potentially reduce the downward price volatility in the trading price of our shares in the period shortly following our offering relative to what would be experienced if the initial public offering price were set at the auction clearing price."[20]

Success or Failure?

If you ask James Surowiecki, Google's IPO worked.[21] "Because it used the Dutch auction, [Google] knows it is getting what people were really willing to pay, instead of what a coterie of investment bankers thought their friends and cronies should have to pay." But the auction mechanism itself, which was supposed to provide better pricing and to avoid the need to negotiate the price with the underwriters, did not work. After negotiations, Google and the underwriters set the price at a discount to the clearing price. How different is this from book building, where the underwriters and the firm negotiate on the basis of the order book?

Once the offering price was set below the clearing price, there had to be oversubscription. Setting the IPO price below the clearing price may have achieved a broader distribution of the shares, but it also meant that not all winning bids could be allocated 100 percent. (Winning investors were allocated about 75 percent of their bid.) Consequently, Google shares jumped by almost 18 percent in the first day of trading; they opened at $95 and stood at $100.25 by the close—a rise of $15.25, or almost 18 percent. The money left on the table came to a staggering $300 million. This was dwarfed by the money left on the table during the following two months: the stock price hit $200 in November!

Ironically, the investment banks that were supposed to be sidetracked in the process ended up on top. Three banks—Morgan Stanley, Credit Suisse First Boston, and Goldman Sachs—ended up with 61 percent of the shares. But that was, after all, part of the deal: Google decided on a hybrid offering in which the lead investment banks, Morgan Stanley and Credit Suisse, required the largest U.S. investment firms to place their bids through those two banks exclusively.[22]

Approximately 22 million shares of Google stock changed hands during the first day of trading. This means that either every investor sold his or her allocated stock at least once, or that the Wall Street firms sold their allocations five times. The truth is probably somewhere in between: some investors sold their shares and the acquirers sold them again and again, while others held on to them for the long term. Obviously an auction is not the optimal mechanism for finding long-term investors!

Google's IPO illustrates one of the major risks of the auction mechanism: undersubscription. In an auction, retail investors have a chance to purchase shares in the initial allocation at the clearing price. But they still end up paying the same price that they will pay in the aftermarket. Since an auction does not improve the situation for retail investors, they may not even want to participate in it. This is known as the winner's curse: if the IPO is a success, investors receive partial allocations of shares. However, when the IPO is by a "bad" company, investors receive full allocations. That's why in auctions, it's probably better to wait for the actual trading to take place.

It would have been simpler for Google to use a book-building method—but one that included clear rules for the underwriters:

- Rule 1: reserve a high percentage of the issue for individual investors. In the United States, the way to attract private investors is to include investment banks with retail networks in the syndicate. In other countries, one could open the process to individual investors with a fixed-price offer—either at the price paid by institutional investors or at a discount to this price.
- Rule 2: require that the firm doing the IPO see the book before negotiating the offering price with the underwriters.
- Rule 3: compel the managing underwriter to disclose and explain to the issuer the final allocation of its IPO shares.

Notes

1. Paul Myners, "Guide to Investment Banks: Pick the Bankers Rather Than the Bank," *Financial Times*, June 27, 2006.
2. NYSE/NASD IPO Advisory Committee, "Report and Recommendations of a Committee Convened by the New York Stock Exchange, Inc., and NASD at the Request of the U.S. Securities and Exchange Commission," May 2003.
3. See, for example, Ann E. Sherman, "Global Trends in IPO Methods," December 2004.
4. Two key studies are Hsiou-wei Lin and Maureen F. McNichols, "Underwriting Relationships, Analysts' Earnings Forecasts and Investment Recommendations," *Journal of Accounting and Economics*, Vol. 25, 1998, pp. 101–127; and Roni L. Michaely and Kent L. Womack, "Conflict of Interest and the Credibility of Underwriters Analyst Recommendations," *Review of Financial Studies*, Vol. 12, no. 3, 1999.
5. $(3.30 - 3.265) \times 505.8 = 17,703,000$.
6. Brealey and Myers, *Principles of Corporate Finance*, 8th ed. (New York: McGraw-Hill, 2005).
7. A. R. Sorkin and J. Leeds, "Has Wall Street Changed Its Tune?" *Wall Street Journal*, June 19, 2005.
8. See, for example, Ann E. Sherman, "Global Trends in IPO Methods," December 2004.
9. Alexander Ljungqvist and William Wilhelm, "IPO Allocations: Discriminatory or Discretionary?" *Journal of Financial Economics*, Vol. 65, 2002, pp. 167–201. The authors find evidence that underpricing is "directly related to information production" and that discretionary allocations promote information acquisition.
10. Andre F. Perold and Gunjan Bhow, HBS case, *WR. Hambrecht: Open IPO*, October 20, 1999, Product Number: 9–200–019.
11. Craig C. Dunbar, "Google's Bad Bid: The Search Engine's Founders Believed They Knew Better Than the Thousands of Companies Who Had Preceded Them. The Break with Convention Cost $300M," *Financial Post*, August 25, 2004.

12. NYSE/NASD IPO Advisory Committee, "Report and Recommendations."

13. Securities and Exchange Commission Litigation Release No. 17327, January 22, 2002. *Securities and Exchange Commission v. Credit Suisse First Boston Corporation.*

14. Frank Partnoy, *Infectious Greed* (New York: Profile Books, 2003), p. 284. As CEO, Gutfreund became the icon for the excess that defined the 1980s culture in America.

15. Contrary to what most commentators have said, the Google IPO was not a Dutch auction but a uniform-price auction. In a Dutch auction, the bidders get allocated at their bidding price; thus, each winning bidder may pay a different price. This is the case for Treasuries, which are issued and priced according to a Dutch auction mechanism.

16. Google Prospectus, August 18, 2004, p. 31.

17. "Poor Turnout Mars Google's IPO Democracy," *Financial Times*, August 20, 2004.

18. Kevin J. Delaney, "Google IPO Revisited," *Wall Street Journal*, September 16, 2005.

19. Joyce E. Berg, George R. Neumann, and Thomas A. Rietz, "Searching for Google's Value: Using Prediction Markets to Forecast Market Capitalization Prior to an Initial Public Offering," SSRN-id887562, March 2006.

20. Google Prospectus, August 18, 2004, pp. 38–39.

21. "Ignore Wall St.'s Whining: Google's IPO Worked," *Financial Times*, August 20, 2004. Surowiecki's *The Wisdom of Crowds* (New York: Doubleday, 2004) shows that average forecasts from a group of individuals are frequently more accurate than individual forecasts.

22. John Shinal, "Lifting the Google Lid: Leaders of WR Hambrecht Can Finally Talk about IPO," *San Francisco Chronicle*, September 15, 2004.

12

Fixed-Income Businesses

The role of the investment bank as financier goes back to the beginning of the last millennium, when governments began borrowing as an alternative to tax collection. But when the banks found out how dangerous it was to lend directly to kings and princes, they organized ways to refinance the loans, beginning with the Amsterdam Stock Exchange. Rather than channel resources through a bank, it was more opportune for governments to directly issue government bonds that the public subscribed to.

The Tools of Fixed-Income Businesses

To this day, governments and large corporations issue bonds to finance ongoing projects. Between 1993 and 2003, bonds issued by government and nongovernment entities accounted for nearly half of the overall growth in financial assets in the world.[1] Today, bonds issued by nongovernment entities are the largest component of the global financial stock and the fastest-growing asset class.

Banks are involved in the entire financing process. They provide issuers with advice on financing strategies, participate in the pricing, and distribute securities and loans to investors. When dealing in fixed-income securities, modern-day investment banks still compete with commercial banks. The latter have become very adept at underwriting bond issues. As a rule, a commercial bank would rather use an investment bank to underwrite its own issue, but commercial banks do not hesitate to underwrite big government or corporate bond issues as a matter of course. The very well known and straightforward financing instruments are called "plain-vanilla products," and commercial banks are taking an ever-growing market share of them. This is a factor driving innovation. As commercial banks nibble away at bond financing, they force investment banks to invent complicated financial engineering deals or exotic financial instruments to raise capital. The investment banks' strategy in fixed-income markets is to invent new fixed-income instruments, make them available to issuers and investors, and then move on to new pastures when the commercial banks have started to take over the field.

My Name Is Bond

A bond is a typical plain-vanilla product. It is a fixed-interest instrument for a period of more than one year that is issued by governments, companies, banks, and public utilities for the purpose of raising capital. The profitability of a bond that is retained until repayment is measured in terms of its yield, which is the actual interest rate to be collected by the investor. The price of a bond varies in a manner that is strictly inverse to its yield.

Bond prices rise when interest rates decline. Declining interest rates and tight credit spreads encourage corporations to issue bonds. When bond prices are rising, banks experience unrealized gains on their fixed-income holdings. They also make money on the "carry trade," in which banks borrow short term to invest in (normally) higher-yielding securities with longer maturity.

There are four broad types of markets for bonds: the domestic market, the foreign bond market, the Eurobond market, and the Eurocurrency bond market.

The Domestic Bond Market

The domestic bond market is the market for bond issues governed by the laws and regulations of the country in which the issuer is based. Including all bond issues, the U.S. bond market is the world's largest, and Europe's debt markets collectively make up the second largest. In the United States, as in European countries, large money-center banks are competing (successfully) with investment banks to issue domestic bonds for governments and corporations. The investment banks are still active in bond trading, but they have lost market share in underwriting.

The Foreign Bond Market

The foreign bond market is the market for bond issues governed by the laws and regulations of a country other than that in which the issuer is based. The issue is mainly subscribed by residents of the country in which it is issued and is guaranteed by a syndicate of local banks and financial institutions. A foreign issue is subject to the internal rules governing the issuance of foreign bonds. These rules concern, for example, whether an issue needs to be registered, the possibility of certain bond structures (like zero coupon or convertible), the maximum size and timing of the issue, whether it needs a rating, and the type of disclosure and periodic reporting or the limitation on underwriting banks. In the jargon, these markets bear picturesque names. A Yankee bond is a bond issued by a non-U.S. firm under U.S. law. There are Samurai bonds for non-Japanese issuers in Japan, Bulldog bonds in the United Kingdom, Rembrandt bonds in Holland, and Matador bonds in Spain.

The Eurobond Market

A Eurobond is denominated in a currency other than that of the country in which it is issued under the direction of a syndicate of international banks. Eurobonds are categorized by the currency in which they are denominated, not by the nationality of the issuer. A Eurodollar bond, for example, is an obligation denominated in U.S. dollars and issued in any country other than the United States by a company (American or not). In 2007, euro-denominated debt accounted for over 45 percent of the total outstanding, the U.S. dollar accounted for 36 percent, and the pound sterling for almost 10 percent.[2]

Since it does not use the national currency of the host country, a Eurobond is not governed by that country's laws. Eurobonds are really a global construct, escaping any national regulation. There is no central location where trading in the international capital market takes place. The majority of transactions are still executed "over the counter" under the rules enacted by ICMA (International Capital Market Association), a self-regulatory organization and trade association that represents constituents and practitioners in this global market. ICMA maintains standards of good market practice in the primary markets and has developed standard documentation for new issues, leading to greater efficiencies and cost savings for issuing banks.

The Euro-denominated Bond Markets

Finally, there are euro-denominated bond markets, which are the domestic and foreign bond markets of the countries belonging to the euro zone. The international and foreign bond markets are the fastest-growing markets in the world. Between 1993 and 2002, "international issues of private debt, while still small, have grown nearly three times as fast as domestic issues (20 percent versus 7 percent), reflecting the increasing globalization of capital as companies seek funding outside their domestic borders."[3] This private borrowing spree has continued. From 2004 to 2005, private debt securities posted the second-largest growth levels, after equities—increasing by $3.3 trillion, according to the McKinsey Global Institute. "Just over half of this growth came from international debt issues, which rose by $1.7 trillion, or 15.5 percent, in 2005."[4]

Public and Private Issuers

There are two broad kinds of issuers of bonds, governments and companies, and therefore there are two kinds of bonds, government bonds and corporate bonds.

Government Bonds

Government bonds, or "govvies," comprise bonds issued by central governments, other governments, and central banks. Technically speaking, a state cannot go bankrupt. Yet it may default, failing to settle its debts and leaving interest payments pending. Therefore, even government bonds may present a risk of default. Government yields include a risk premium that is typically positively related to the level of public debt in the country. Under the Basel II accord, which governs the capital adequacy of internationally active banks, the capital charge for specific risk is designed to protect against an adverse movement in the price of an individual security as a result of factors related to the individual issuer. The new capital charge for a government bond is nil for bonds rated AAA to AA−, but it can reach 12 percent for bonds below B−.[5]

U.S. government debt comprises both federal securities and state and local government (or municipal) securities. U.S. government bonds, i.e., Treasuries, are regarded as the highest grade of securities issues, whatever the level of the federal debt. The idea that there is a national coffer somewhere shows up in other countries' name for such bonds as well. In France, for example, they are called "Obligations du Trésor." U.S. Treasury securities, such as bills, notes, and bonds, are debt obligations of the U.S. government. The difference in names reflects the difference in maturity (the life of the issue):

- U.S. Treasury bills have maturities of ninety days to one year.
- U.S. Treasury notes have maturities of more than one year up to ten years.
- U.S. Treasury bonds have maturities of more than ten years, going up to thirty years.

Treasuries are issued and priced using a Dutch auction mechanism. This, as we know, is a multiple-price, sealed-bid auction. Each competitive bidder who has been "awarded" the bid pays the price stated in his or her sealed bid; thus, each winning bidder may pay a different price. Noncompetitive bidders—those who have not specified a price—pay the average of the awarded competitive bids.

The underwriters of a Treasury issue are called "primary dealers." They are licensed to deal directly with the Fed, but are not necessarily investment banks. The more than twenty government securities dealers licensed by the Federal Reserve System include not only the largest U.S. investment banks (Bear Stearns, Goldman Sachs, Lehman Brothers, Merrill Lynch, and Morgan Stanley), but also many money-center banks, not only from America (Bank of America, Citigroup, and JPMorgan Chase), but also from Japan (Daiwa, Mizuho, and Nomura) and Europe (Barclays, HSBC, BNP Paribas, ABN AMRO, Deutsche Bank, Dresdner, Credit Suisse, and UBS).[6] The biggest buyers of these debts are local financial institutions such as banks, insurance companies, and pension funds; but also investors in Japan and in Europe.

Investment banks make a point of being primary dealers, but they do not make much money out of it. One of the advantages of being a primary dealer is the view of dealing flows and other information that this status gives. The other advantage is the relationship with the Treasury and the chance to receive a mandate for less plain-vanilla transactions, such as derivatives transactions or syndicated bond sales for the government.

Corporate Bonds

A company with cash requirements has quite a few sources of financing available. It can either seek out financing on the equity capital market (through a new equity issue or stock market listing) or take on debt. If it chooses debt, the firm may either borrow money from a bank or finance itself through the bond market. Bank debt is typically reset quarterly based on such measures as the London Interbank Offered Rate (LIBOR) or the federal funds rate, and issuers may prefer issuing fixed-income securities. Having made the latter choice, an issuer relies to a lesser extent on banks. With a bond issue, the company is asking investors for a loan, rather than soliciting funds from a bank. Any individual can purchase debentures on the bond market. But not all countries can boast of operating liquid bond markets for corporations. The U.S. market for corporate bonds is the epitome of a well-functioning source of financing for corporations.

Who are the issuers of corporate bonds in the United States? About half of the outstanding U.S. corporate bonds have been issued by firms from miscellaneous industries. The other half is shared about equally by issuers belonging to four sectors: banks, other financial institutions, telecom companies, and utilities, with market shares oscillating between 12 and 14 percent each.[7]

One characteristic of the U.S. corporate bond market is the length of the securities. The average maturity of corporate bonds is 10 years, but maturities can extend to 30 years. There is no other market in the world where a corporation can get funds for such an extended period of time. The shorter bonds are those issued by the banks and other financial institutions sectors, with an average remaining time to maturity of 7.0 years and 7.8 years, respectively. Industrial bonds are slightly longer, with an average remaining time to maturity of 9.8 years. Finally, considering the extended need to fund power plants and communication infrastructure, the longest bonds are found in the utility and telecommunication sectors, with an average time to maturity of 10.1 years and 10.7 years, respectively.

How do the issuers choose which market to tap? Firms that wish to borrow for the short term, or at floating rates, generally issue debt instruments called commercial paper. Some firms that have a preference for long-term, fixed-rate funds will issue bonds in either the public or the private market. They will choose the public market if:

- They have no problem with information and can have a rating.

- The amount is large enough to justify the cost of registration.
- The structure of the financing is straightforward.

More and more, a private placement is a way of issuing a financial asset that is neither debt nor equity, but something in between. The private placement market serves as a testing ground for new types of securities invented by investment banks.

Methods for Issuing Bonds

There are three ways to issue a bond in the United States: by a public offering, by an offering restricted to large investors, or by a private placement. A public offering works pretty much like the equity IPO that we discussed in the previous chapter. The key here (as in an IPO) is the registration with the SEC. There is also an issue mechanism that is a bit less formal because it is restricted to sophisticated investors. This mechanism will provide some liquidity and a secondary market. We call it a 144A issue (after Rule 144A, which was adopted in 1990 for the issuance of private securities like bonds, convertible bonds, preferred stocks, and equity). Finally, there is a private placement, where the issue is limited to a small group of large financial institutions. A private placement is a way of issuing debt or equity securities that are exempt from registration with the SEC by virtue of being issued in transactions "not involving any public offering."

The strategy of investment banks in underwriting corporate bonds is a greyhound chase with the money-center banks. Big commercial banks have leveraged their position in the loan market to become corporate bond underwriters. This holds true in all well-developed national markets, i.e., Bank of America in the United States, Barclays in the United Kingdom, BNP Paribas in France, ABN AMRO in the Netherlands, and Deutsche Bank in Germany. Investment banks compete with them in the fixed-income market on the basis of price and, most importantly, execution. For example, in 2003, Merrill Lynch was awarded the mandate to issue a $1 billion bond for Hong Kong conglomerate Hutchison Whampoa,

Ltd. The issue was completed in just fifteen hours: Merrill launched the deal for $1 billion at 2 p.m. in Hong Kong, and by 5 a.m. the next day, not only was the deal complete, but it had been increased in size by a remarkable 50 percent.

In the early 1990s, as investment banks were chased away from underwriting public offers of corporate bonds by large commercial banks, they came to rely more and more on 144A issues.[8] At the same time, they were prominent in selling private placements. A study of the major agents of U.S. private placements of debt in 1989–1991 found that five investment banks (Goldman Sachs, First Boston, Salomon Brothers, Merrill Lynch, and Lehman Brothers) placed more than 40 percent of the issues in these three years.[9] But, having successfully competed with investment banks in underwriting public offerings of corporate bonds, commercial banks started nipping at the heels of the investment banks in private placements in the United States as well.

Borrowers in the private placement market are domestic issuers that want to issue complex securities, need an amount too small for the public market, or want to avoid the disclosure associated with registration. They can also be foreign firms that want to access a very deep market like the U.S. fixed-income market. Private placements used to be the realm of investment banks, which used their relationship with various corporations in the world to tout a bond issue in the United States. A foreign firm could issue a Yankee bond in the United States for longer terms than were available in its own country. And a private placement saved the issuer the trouble of going through registration. The European and Asian branches of American investment banks in turn combed their large corporate clients for Yankee bond candidates.

In the early part of this century, U.S. investors were even open to buying private placements denominated in foreign currencies. But big commercial banks were competing with one another in the private placement area, and they inevitably drove down margins, pushing investment banks to look elsewhere. With the competition of European banks like Barclays and ABN AMRO, the margin for U.S. private placements, which was 1.5 percent in the late 1990s, plunged to 0.15 percent in the early part of this decade. The European and Asian branches of American investment banks had to look for more profitable businesses elsewhere.

New Financial Products

Investment banks tend to explore new financing structures when commercial banks take their businesses (and margins) away. They have invented a wide variety of such structures, including these:

- Zero coupon convertibles
- Perpetual debt
- Subordinated debt
- Mezzanine finance
- High-yield bonds
- Structured-finance products[10]
- Collateralized debt obligations
- Credit derivatives
- Project finance

Zero Coupon Convertibles

In the early 1980s, Merrill Lynch used a technique known as "stripping"[11] in trading Treasuries. The bank applied the stripping technique to convertible securities and in 1985 invented a new type of convertible bond, liquid yield option notes, or LYONs. These are zero coupon bonds that are convertible at the holder's option into common stock at a put price. Because they do not pay a coupon, LYONs are deeply discounted zero coupon instruments. The put prices are equal to the LYONs' original offering price plus accrued interest to the put dates.

Perpetual Debt

Perpetual bonds have no maturity date and pay regular interest. They are not really perpetual because the issuer has an option to buy them back after any number of years. Perpetual bonds are typically issued by financial institutions with steady cash flow and large capitalizations. In 2004, joint lead managers Citigroup, HSBC, and Merrill Lynch innovatively underwrote a $1.75 billion issue of perpetual bonds for an industrial group, Petróleos Mexicanos (Pemex), Mexico's state-owned oil company. Merrill Lynch recognized that Pemex, though not a financial institution, had steady cash flows and a large capitalization. This was the biggest bond sale ever by a Latin American company, as well as the first issue of perpetual bonds by a borrower in the region.

Subordinated Debt

Subordinated bonds were developed in the late 1980s. They are unsecured debt or preference shares offering interest rates 2 to 5 percentage points larger than those on senior debt. These bonds are "junior" in priority of payment to senior debt—interest is paid out of the cash flow after the interest on the senior bond is paid (i.e., if there is anything left)—but senior to common stock or equity. They are used to finance pools of assets in a securitization.

Mezzanine Finance

Like the mezzanine in a theater, mezzanine securities reside below senior debt on the balance sheet, but above common stock. Mezzanine securities are subordinated debt with an equity "kicker," which usually comes in the form of free warrants for the company's equity securities and/or a "pay in kind" (PIK) mechanism. Equity-related components include warrants to buy common stock, options, or common equity of the debt-issuing company. Interest payments on mezzanine debt securities may involve both a cash payment portion and a PIK. With a PIK, the interest is added back to the loan so that the amount of the loan increases over time. Mezzanine coupons are significantly higher than those on other fixed-income vehicles.

High-Yield Bonds

The category of high-yield debt, or "junk bonds," was invented in the 1980s—to finance the leveraged buyout (LBO)[12] boom—by Michael Milken from the now-defunct bank Drexel Burnham Lambert. High-yield bonds are non-investment-grade bonds; some investors, like pension funds and other institutional investors, are not legally entitled to hold these securities.[13] But other investors can and do hold them. At year-end 2006, the overall median issuer's rating barely hung on to BBB-status, with only 50.7 percent of issuers being at this level or above. During this time, the number of investment-grade issuers stood at 1,589, while there were 1,545 speculative-grade issuers. A large majority (62.1 percent) of nonfinancial issuers were rated "speculative grade." The renewed boom in leveraged buyout activity in the 2000s bolstered sales of junk bonds until the credit crisis of the summer of 2007.

Structured-Finance Products

Asset securitization, a process that converts nontradable loans into tradable bonds, is a major source of structured-finance products. Germany has long used a form of securitization of mortgage loans in the form of Pfandbriefe instruments. But it is in the United States that securitization has been taken up most extensively— through government-sponsored enterprises like the Government National Mortgage Association (GNMA)—to give liquidity to the secondary mortgage market. GNMA, better known as Ginnie Mae, created the first securitization of residential loans in 1970, moving the loans off the banks' balance sheets while allowing them to retain the servicing rights. In a nutshell, Ginnie Mae buys the loans extended to homeowners and secured by mortgages. It pools these loans and issues debt securities backed by them, i.e., mortgage-backed securities (MBS).

Typically, there is a series of bonds of increasing degrees of risk with some degree of uplift from the underlying credit risk of the loans: a very senior secured class A bond, a less senior secured class B bond, and a deeply subordinated note called the "equity tranche." The payment of each obligation is subordinated to the full payment of the forward one. Thus, the equity tranche will be remunerated only if the mortgage loans have generated enough cash flow to pay both the very senior and the less senior debt. (The latter will be paid only after there is enough to finance the former.) The proceeds from these issues are used to buy the loans that constitute the collateral. The "tranching" of claims on the assets in combination with the subordination of junior to more senior tranches reshuffles the risks of the lenders. The riskier bonds pay the highest yields but are the first to lose value if borrowers fall behind in payments.

In the 1990s, banks started issuing MBS, which did not carry the same implicit government guarantee that investors would be protected against unexpectedly high default rates. Securitization of mortgage loans in the United States has increased the available capital for mortgages, which is otherwise constrained by the lending capacity of banks or by their credit limits. The subprime mortgage market refinances the loans of those who are seen as having high credit risk. These loans have allowed credit-constrained homeowners (many of whom are minorities with lower incomes) to borrow against the equity in their homes to meet a variety of needs. This makes home ownership more affordable. Investors benefited as well, from access to new types of securities.

In the early part of this decade, mortgages in the United States reached $9.9 trillion, or 85 percent of GDP, and more than 50 percent ($5.3 trillion) of U.S. mortgages were securitized. According to Susan M. Wachter, professor of real estate and finance at Wharton, "subprime mortgages made up 22 percent of new loans in 2005, compared to 8 percent in 2003, and in 2004 more than 30 percent of all mortgages carried adjustable rates, up from about 10 percent in 2001." When in 2007 home prices leveled off or fell while rising interest rates saddled homeowners with bigger payments, subprime mortgages created the credit crunch of 2007.

After mortgage-backed securities, financial institutions started the securitization of other financial assets, like car loans. Simply put, a financial institution buys car loans from the finance sub-sidiaries of car manufacturers and pools them together in a trust, or some other entity created for this purpose. This entity, called a "special-purpose vehicle" (SPV), is essentially a digital firm. It really does not do anything; nobody works there; it doesn't have a physical location.[14] It simply owns the loans. The SPV is at arm's length from the car manufacturer; its assets cannot be seized if the lender goes bankrupt. Investors in SPV securities are therefore insulated from the risks of the car manufacturer. In a worst-case scenario, the SPV's assets are simply distributed to the investors holding the securities.

This type of SPV issues bonds backed by its assets, which are therefore called "asset-backed securities" (ABS). The proceeds from these securities are used to pay for the car loans. The rev-enue of the bonds comes from the interest paid on the loans. "This contrasts with secured lending, where repayment depends primarily on the company's ability to pay and only secondarily on the liquidation value of the collateral."[15]

Collateralized Debt Obligations

Today, all types of loans could potentially be pooled and securi-tized in the United States: car leases and loans, credit card debt, student loans, equipment loans and leasing, aircraft leases, small-business loans, and other types of bank loans. It is just a matter of creativity on the part of investment banks. The Italians have even securitized the revenues from the television broadcasting rights of soccer clubs.[16] In one of the most innovative cases, singer David Bowie sold $55 million worth of "Bowie bonds," giving investors the right to share in future royalties from his early albums.

A collateralized bond obligation (CBO) refers to the securitiza-tion of high-yield bonds, and a collateralized loan obligation (CLO) to the securitization of bank loans. The risk of the latter is typically lower than that of the former because recovery values on defaulted loans are often higher than those on corporate high-yield bonds. Also, since loans are amortized, they have a shorter duration. In addition, it may be that the risk transfer from banks in a CLO transaction is not complete. Research shows that the portfolio risk is transferred to tranches in a nonlinear way.[17] When a bank issuer retains the equity tranche, most of the risk of the loan portfolio is retained on the bank's balance sheet.

Credit Derivatives

Credit derivatives are a way to redistribute and repackage credit risk to investors, including the insurance sector, investment funds, and hedge funds. On the investors' side, credit derivatives can be used to express a view on credit risk. On the protection buyer's side, a bank, for example, can manage the risk from its loan portfolio by using credit derivatives. If the bank does not want to sell a loan, but simply wants to protect itself, it can hedge the risk by concluding a credit default swap (CDS) with an investor. A CDS operates like insurance: to cover the loss of the face value of an asset following a credit event, a bank purchases credit protection from the other party. A credit event includes bankruptcy, failure to pay, and restructuring. Simply put, a CDS will pay the bank an indemnity if the loan is not paid. The bank makes quarterly payments to the investor until a credit event or maturity, whichever occurs first. These payments are known as the "premium leg." Conversely, the "protection leg" is the payment to compensate the bank for the loss if a credit event does occur before the maturity date of the contract.

Investment banks package CDSs and sell them to investors. The investment bank may also structure a CDO to be the counterparty in the CDS. This CDO issues the usual pancake of bonds to finance a risk-free investment. If the event occurs, the indemnity will be paid out of the risk-free investment. Otherwise, the bondholders will share the investment among themselves, together with the premium paid by the bank to protect its risk.

Project Finance

Project finance belongs to the category of asset financing. The debt used to finance the project is paid back from the cash flow generated by the project, rather than by the project owner. Project finance has always been the province of commercial banks. But investment banks are charting new territories, and they are promoting public-private partnerships to finance infrastructure. Not only the European markets but also the Australian and Canadian markets have a history of dedicated infrastructure investors financing airports, ports, waterways, railways, roads, bridges, and even water-supply plants. Funding by a concessionaire can provide more capital at a lower cost than municipal bonds, and the leverage (debt/equity) can be as high as 80/20.

Notes

1. McKinsey Global Institute, "$118 Trillion and Counting: Taking Stock of the World's Capital Markets," February 2005.
2. International Capital Market Association, January 2007.
3. McKinsey, "$118 Trillion and Counting."
4. McKinsey Global Institute, "Mapping the Global Capital Markets," January 2007.
5. Each rating agency has its own nomenclature or "investment grade" that ranks the default risk of issuers. There are roughly ten different credit ratings or grades that each agency publishes. The ratings range from Investment Grade to In Default. "A" are high credit quality (AAA is the highest, AA very high credit quality, and A high credit quality); "BBB" is good credit quality. These ratings are considered to be investment grade. Ratings that fall under "BBB" are considered to be speculative.
6. The complete list is available from the New York Fed.
7. About 50 percent of the U.S. corporate bonds outstanding have been issued by the industrial sector. Four specialized industries

share the other half among themselves: banks (12.3 percent), financial institutions (14.6 percent), telecommunications (11.9 percent), and utilities (14.4 percent). From Standard & Poor's, "Refunding of U.S. Corporate Bonds in 2004 and 2005," August 31, 2004.

8. Public issues of bonds are typically managed by an underwriter on the basis of a firm commitment. Private placements are sold on a best-efforts basis by an agent, but many Rule 144A transactions are firm commitment underwritings.

9. Mark Carey, Stephen Prowse, John Rea, and Gregory Udell, "The Economics of the Private Placement Market," Board of Governors of the Federal Reserve System, December 1993.

10. These come with a whole range of acronyms: ABS, MBS, CDO, CLO, and CBO, to name a few.

11. In bond stripping, the holder of a bond strips off the coupon payments and sells the structured interest-rate stream while retaining the principal redemption payment upon maturity.

12. An LBO is an acquisition of a firm by a private group using debt financing.

13. About three-fourths of outstanding U.S. corporate bond debt in 2007 is investment grade (i.e., above B+, or BB− and above). Within the investment-grade category, about two-thirds of all issuance comes from the two rating categories BBB and A, which are well above noninvestment grade. From Standard & Poor's, "Refunding of U.S. Corporate Bonds in 2004 and 2005" and "U.S. Ratings Distribution: Expanding High-Yield Clout," March 2007.

14. "Enron Aside, Special Purpose Vehicles (SPVs) Are Legal, Innovative and Widely Used," Knowledge@Wharton, May 17, 2006. Legally, SPVs can be limited partnerships, limited-liability companies, trusts, or corporations. They have no decision-making powers, and all their actions are governed by strict rules written by the sponsor. In addition to securitizations, they may be formed to conduct research and development, engage in lease transactions, or perform other functions.

15. Alexander Roever and Frank Fabozzi, "A Primer on Securitization," *Journal of Structured and Project Finance*, Vol. 9, no. 2, Summer 2003, p. 5.
16. The securitization of Italian soccer club revenues is not very different from the securitization of the Rentes sur l'Hotel de Ville of the 1500s in France mentioned in chapter 2.
17. See Jan Pieter Krahnen and Christian Wilde, "Risk Transfer with CDO and Systemic Risk in Banking," Frankfurt University Center for Financial Studies, May 30, 2006.

13

Strategies in Fixed Income

The key to success in fixed-income businesses is to understand intimately the strategies of two types of clients: the issuers and the investors. The two types of customers are not covered by the same team, but coordination between the two teams is essential.

Understanding the Investor Community

A successful investment bank will always understand its clients' investment styles. In today's global economy, investors in different parts of the world do not have the same interests. Asian investors are often interested in yield, even if they have to invest longer term. When Merrill Lynch, with HSBC and Citigroup, launched the perpetual bond deal for Pemex, they placed most of the issue in Asia. Pemex received bids of about $5 billion for the bonds, which had a 7.75 percent coupon. Yield-hungry Asian investors, who were specifically targeted by the underwriters, purchased about 65 percent of the issue.

The strategies of different types of investing institutions, such as mutual funds, pension funds, finance companies, and insurance firms, are different because these institutions have different needs, specifically for securities with varying maturity and price-volatility characteristics. In the early part of this century, mutual funds had sought protection against interest-rate hikes by investing in the collateralized debt obligation (CDO) market. In this market, investors can buy into pools of loans with variable rates. Investment banks developed a sort of secondary market for CDOs called "arbitrage CDOs." To distinguish the arbitrage CDOs from the ones where a bank securitizes its own loans, the latter are called "balance sheet CDOs." While balance sheet CDOs are initiated by commercial banks that want to sell assets to free up regulatory capital, arbitrage CDOs, in contrast, are inspired by asset managers. An investment bank buys loans and/or bonds from the market instead of purchasing them directly from the originator of the obligations. The investment bank will then pool these obligations in a special-purpose vehicle (SPV) and securitize them as before, with the intent of gaining an advantage on the rates. Balance sheet CDOs allow a reduction of regulatory capital, while arbitrage CDOs provide arbitraging profits.

In 2003, when California money manager Trust Company of the West wanted to take advantage of opportunities in the asset-backed bond market, Merrill Lynch assembled a $1 billion CDO fund from across eight countries on five continents. The asset manager invested in this CDO in order to boost its return for a fixed-income risk. During the past decade, pension funds needed to generate higher fixed-income returns, since they were falling short of their actuarial assumptions. However, many pension funds had charters preventing them from investing in high-yield bonds. Sponsors often found mezzanine securities to be more attractive than many alternative asset classes, given their risk/return profiles. Finance companies have also traditionally participated in the mezzanine market. Finally, insurance companies, with their longer-term liabilities, purchased fixed-rate longer-term assets with low risk. For insurance companies, asset-backed securities have offered a superior risk/return profile compared with other corporate bond sectors because they are backed by rather substantial assets of the obligor.

Understanding Issuers' Businesses

The wisest strategy for a successful investment bank is to develop a detailed understanding of a client's business interests so that it can deliver the best advice on financing. There are four types of issuers of fixed-income assets: banks, insurance companies, corporations, and governments and agencies.

Banks

Commercial banks manage their portfolios very actively. Typically, an investment bank will structure a special-purpose vehicle to purchase commercial and industrial loans that the bank does not want to keep on its balance sheet. In the years 2005–2006, corporate lending in the United States and the United Kingdom had risen sharply as companies refinanced their credit facilities on increasingly advantageous terms. Banks tried to boost their return by lending to less creditworthy borrowers, a marketing strategy that completely changed their financing strategy. Under the previous business model (known as "originate and hold"), commercial banks would find an obligor, lend it money, and keep the loan on their books while maintaining the ongoing customer relationship. They would normally refinance these loans by issuing bonds.

After 2000, however, banks started abandoning the originate and hold strategy for a new one, "underwrite and distribute." As Michael Crouhy, Dan Galai, and Robert Mark note, "The old *originate and hold* business model where bank loans reside where they are originated is not viable anymore. It is too capital intensive and produces too low adjusted return on economic capital."[1] Under the new strategy, banks keep the customer relationship with the obligor, but they manage their loan portfolios actively. However lending risk is passed on to investors rather than being held in the institutions that originate the loans.

The resulting transformation of the credit business gave rise to new strategies for investment banks. With underwriting and distribution being the main forte of investment banking, the strategy was to get back the commercial lending business that they had lost to commercial banks by catching up on underwriting and distributing collateralized loans. So, come 2005, the chairman of Merrill Lynch was able to boast, "In CDO's, collateralized debt, we were almost non-existent in 2000—ranked 13th. Today we're ranked number one."[2] Unfortunately, Stan O'Neal had to leave the firm in 2007 when Merrill Lynch was struck badly by the credit crunch because of its prominence in CDOs.

Commercial banks also started to compete with investment banks in underwriting and distributing financial assets, using their solid distribution network. After 2000, for example, Bank of America (BofA) moved to a new model combining commercial banking and investment banking in order to make its products available to more clients, on both the investor and the corporate sides.

Insurance Companies

Insurance companies do not have a sufficient level of equity to cover the effects of certain extreme risks, like the damage resulting from natural or human disasters. The traditional solution, reinsurance, is also not enough to cover the appalling damages that can result from these risks. Investment banks can structure and underwrite insurance derivatives, offering insurance companies the opportunity to limit some sources of risks by outsourcing them to investors. Such risks range from life and car insurance risks to earthquake, storm, and other such catastrophe risks. These insurance derivatives work on the same principle as a credit-default swap. An insurance company sponsors a bond, called a "catastrophe bond," underwritten by an investment bank. The bond pays a high coupon if no disaster strikes. But if a predefined event occurs and triggers the bond, the principal that was initially paid by the investors is forgiven, and the funds are used by the sponsor to pay its claims to policyholders.

Investment banks are in a good position to structure financing for regulatory capital relief. For example, Regulation XXX, issued in 2000, required insurance companies to hold reserves that were deemed to be well in excess of a reasonable estimate of policy liabilities. For insurance companies, securitization provided the largest economic benefits as a way to fund their peak reserve requirements. For example, in 2005, Goldman Sachs arranged the securitization of defined-term life policies for Scottish Re, a global life reinsurance specialist and issuer of customized life-insurance-based wealth management products for high-net-worth individuals and families. An SPV sponsored by Scottish Re issued $455 million of 30-year-maturity securities backed by cash flows from a defined block of insurance contracts. The transaction was structured in such a way that the securities had recourse only to the SPV.

Corporations

The corporate world is also a potential seller of many types of assets to be securitized. For a corporation, securitization is a cheap way of financing because the creditworthiness of the assets is separated from the general credit of the company. The cash flow generated by these assets can be used to support securities that may be of higher credit quality than the company's debt. These arrangements typically benefit from legal and structural enhancements that enable the ratings on the debt issued to have some degree of uplift from the underlying corporate credit rating on an operating company and mitigate aspects of operating risk that would otherwise exist. In addition, the assets are removed from the balance sheet (which does wonders for the company's return on assets!).

When issuers cannot find any cheaper source of funds, they may have to access more expensive financing, such as high-yield bonds. For example, Hong Kong–listed Panva Gas Holdings Ltd., which supplies liquefied petroleum gas and natural gas in China, raised $200 million of 8.25 percent seven-year bonds with a non-investment-grade rating in September 2005. A month before, Toronto-listed Sino-Forest Corp., which operates plantations in southern China, raised $300 million of 9.125 percent seven-year bonds. Both deals received strong investor demand and were increased from their original offering sizes.

Finally, issuers may want to diversify their sources of financing. In September 2004, in its $1.75 billion issue of perpetual bonds, Pemex had a goal of moving beyond its traditional American and European investor base. As we saw, Asian investors purchased about 65 percent of the issue. The other attraction of perpetual bonds for an issuer is the option to buy back the bonds. Pemex is likely to exercise the option after five years if it is able to borrow at a lower rate, which could very well be the case if its credit ratings continue to improve.

Governments and Agencies

Raising taxes is the traditional source of funding for a government. In some countries, the state can subsidize financing, allowing municipalities to issue bonds. In the United States, for example, the traditional way to finance transportation infrastructures is to issue municipal bonds that are exempt from taxes. These bonds can be secured by some form of municipal income, for example, by gas taxes, license fees, or registration fees. When the infrastructure being constructed charges a toll, the revenue can be used to enhance the remuneration of the bond, as is the case for highway revenue bonds or toll revenue bonds.

An alternative to the traditional method of financing is to create a public company with its own financing structure. The typical public company uses moderate leverage, with debt/equity being 50/50. Another way is to create a private company. For example, the Tangier-Mediterranean Special Agency (TMSA) is a private company, operating under an agreement with the Government of Morocco, that implements, coordinates, and manages the Tangier-Med Project. The project involves the construction of a new deep-sea port thirty-five kilometers east of Tangiers on the strait of Gibraltar, and the creation of logistic-, industrial-, and commercial-free zones and a tourist zone. The project was completed in 2007. The TMSA allotted the concessions for many activities, such as the hydrocarbon terminal, to private corporations.

The Value-Creation Conundrum

There is a conundrum in securitization and, more generally, structured finance. These techniques must indeed create value for both the users and the investors. If they did not, they would cease to exist rather than continuing to multiply! However, for the academic world, structure should not matter, because in theory one cannot create value by structuring financing.

The Pizza Theory

Merton Miller, the author with Franco Modigliani of the Modigliani-Miller proposition,[3] used an aphorism attributed to the New York Yankees Hall of Fame catcher Yogi Berra. One day the great left-handed slugger was asked if he preferred his pizza to be sliced into four or eight pieces. Because he was hungry, Yogi said, he'd rather have eight. Miller added, "If you find that funny, you understand the Modigliani theorem." Of course, the number of portions does not change the size of the pizza. Likewise, the way in which liabilities are cut up does not alter the value of the company.

If one splits a company or project into two pieces, the cost of capital for the two parts should be the same of that of the whole. If this were not the case, there would be an opportunity to earn arbitrage profits by buying the whole and selling the parts, or vice versa. This is, however, exactly what one does in securitization: one splits the assets and the debt of a company into two pieces. This off-balance-sheet financing arrangement is less expensive than traditional financing because it is backed by assets of the firm, and thus presents less risk for the lender. The Modigliani-Miller proposition says that if you spin off a well-diversified pool of assets generating stable cash flows, you increase the risk of the remaining assets.

The validity of this proposition depends on three assumptions: homogeneous expectations, homogeneous business risk, and perfect capital markets (the latter includes equal access to all relevant information). But these three hypotheses are not always met in practice.

Let us start with the third assumption. In the real world, markets are not perfect. Business risks (or the perception of business risks) become more homogeneous with securitization. Securitization can reduce the myopia of lenders who might not have correctly appreciated the real risk of the securitized assets when these were part of the company. Above all, the real world does not function according to the first assumption, homogeneous expectations. Investment banks will therefore strive to exploit the reality of this world to create value for the investor. Through structured finance, arrangers create new assets with desired return/risk characteristics that are better adjusted for the nonhomogeneous expectations of issuers and investors.

Nevertheless one cannot measure the risks of a security paying many basis points over the money market if one has forgotten the pizza theory of Modigliani-Miller. Around 2005 and 2006, before the subprime crisis, investors were eager to buy subprime securities because of their higher yields. The higher yields came from the higher mortgage rates charged to riskier borrowers. According to the pizza theory, these higher yields were the price of the risk taken. In the summer of 2007 this risk materialized. Investors who bought securities backed by subprime loans apparently did not understand the risks.

Illustration: Dolly the Sheep

Dolly the Sheep was a clone created in 1996 out of frozen udder cells from an adult ewe. In November 1998, French wool and fabric company Chargeurs Wool completed an innovative $200 million deal combining a securitization and a revolving loan facility, via lead manager Merrill Lynch. The CDO was aptly called Dolly, and the idea was to create a clone wool maker. Sources praised the deal because it allowed a company that had previously financed itself with bank debt to raise money at tight spreads rather than having to borrow from local banks. Chargeurs Wool was able to raise $115 million of long-term notes with an A1 credit rating by Moody's, although the parent company Chargeurs then had a Baa3 rating, the lowest investment-grade category.[4]

Chargeurs manufactured wool tops (a stage in yarn making), interlining, fabrics, and protective film. With twenty subsidiaries in many different countries, Chargeurs Wool was a global leader in the wool tops business, with a 25 percent market share. Its competitors were mainly niche players, and the larger ones were generally downsizing their wool business. The wool industry is a commodity industry, with a relatively small number of major geographically concentrated producers and numerous geographically diverse buyers.

Dolly departs dramatically from more traditional securitizations. The main difference, which has to do with the nature of the receivables, is twofold. First, the risk associated with Chargeurs Wool's trade receivables is obviously affected by the nature of the industry. While the atomistic structure of the downstream sector allows some risk reduction through diversification of the pool of receivables, the casual observer can see right away that Chargeurs Wool's trade receivables are much more risky than the usual receivables. This is because the degree of diversification is less than that achieved when telephone bill or credit card collections are bundled together. Default risk for industrial customers can be deemed to be higher than that exhibited by individual consumers on amounts that are relatively small compared to their income. Furthermore, while the fortunes of individual customers are not closely tied to one another, risk factors in an industry like the wool industry have a tendency to work together. Also, wool price volatility is huge, and exchange risk is a concern.

Second, the risk associated with the underlying instruments is magnified by the fact that close to 30 percent of such instruments are not trade receivables, for wool tops that have been delivered and invoiced to the customer, with collection being due within approximately four months. Instead, they are contract receivables, for which the industrial transformation process has not even begun, the customer has not been invoiced, and collection therefore will not take place for up to a year. The contract receivables are exposed to the risks of contract cancellation by the buyer or the seller, and to simultaneous adverse price movements of foreign currency and wool prices, as well as to the risk of bankruptcy of the tops maker.

Despite these characteristics of the underlying assets, which made a securitization seem highly implausible, Merrill Lynch and Chargeurs still managed to sell mid-investment-grade-rated securities to investors. Their innovative structure was as follows. They created two SPVs: one for financing (Wool Finance), and the other for managing cash flows (Chargeurs Wool Partners). Both were bankruptcy-remote corporations, insulated even from the consequences of Chargeurs Wool's insolvency. The first one, Wool Finance (WF), issued five-year senior notes for $115 million backed by receivables originated by Chargeurs Wool's worldwide sale of wool tops. And the second, Chargeurs Wool Partners (CWP), had $7.5 million in preferred shares privately placed.

The $115 million bond issue was rated A+ by Duff & Phelps and A1 by Moody's Investors Service, thanks to credit enhancements made up of a $17.5 million loan to Chargeurs Wool Partners from the parent, the $7.5 million private placement of equity, and a $1.25 million reserve account that was expected to rise to $2.5 million with excess spread. Merrill Lynch, the sole manager of the issue, said at the time that the securitized paper was sold to twelve investors, mostly banks.[5] In addition, a $60 million revolving loan, standing pari passu with the senior notes, was put in place to purchase additional receivables and conduct foreign exchange and commodity hedging transactions. The issuer then lent the proceeds of the $115 million senior bond issue to CWP, which used the funds to purchase trade (existing) receivables and contract (future) receivables from Chargeurs Wool's operating subsidiaries. When the initial receivables were collected, the proceeds were applied to the purchase of an equivalent amount of new receivables, until the notes began to be paid off four and a half years after they had been issued.[6] Contractual agreements, pledges of CWP shares, and transfer-ability of insurance contracts and letters of credit ensure that WF has access to the receivables owned by CWP.

To summarize the structure:

- Chargeurs Wool remained in charge of operations (prospecting and sales; designs and manufacturing; guaranteeing product quality; logistics) and sold trade receivables to CWP without recourse.
- CWP signed the contracts with customers, financed the purchase and storage of raw materials, invoiced customers, and collected customer receivables.
- WF financed the working capital requirements by raising funds in the markets.

The $115 million bond issue paid a return of 80 basis points over three-month LIBOR. Chargeurs could not even contemplate raising plain-vanilla debt that cheap with its Baa3 rating.

In its 2005 annual report, Chargeurs indicated the impact of securitization on its activity: "Over the last few years, Chargeurs has taken steps to refocus all its resources on its core businesses. To achieve this refocusing, the Group has outsourced certain operations previously performed internally to external companies that are legally and financially independent from Chargeurs."[7]

The Dolly model also helped the company to change its way of managing risks:

The Dolly model is all about managing risk and has been a driving force in establishing a strong risk-containment culture and discipline across the entire Chargeurs organization. . . . The Dolly model is based on obtaining accurate information about risks so that they can be actively managed. . . . For the Dolly financial structures to operate effectively, it is essential for us to analyze and eliminate a large number of risks. The transactions, put together with risk management professionals such as insurers, banks and investors, automatically bring with them the controls that are a standard feature of securitizations.[8]

Notes

1. Michael Crouhy, Dan Galai, and Robert Mark, *The Essentials of Risk Management* (New York: McGraw-Hill, 2005).
2. Stan O'Neal, "The 2005 Merrill Lynch Banking and Financial Services Investor Conference," November 15, 2005.
3. Miller and Modigliani demonstrated that in an ideal capital market, the value of a firm would hinge exclusively on its activities and investment decisions, no matter how the latter were financed—that is, no matter what the structuring of its permanent capital might be. All the good corporate finance books explain the logic very clearly. See, for example, Ross Chesterfield Jaffe, *Corporate Finance*, 7th ed. (New York: McGraw-Hill, 2005), Chapter 13.
4. In 2001, Moody's Investors Service downgraded the long-term rating of the Class A notes issued by Wool Finance 1998–2001 Limited from A1 to A2. The rating action followed the downgrade of Chargeurs Wool's issuer rating from Baa3 to Ba1, announced by Moody's on March 20, 2001.
5. "Wool Company Spins Deal," *Asset Sales Report International,* November 30, 1998.
6. The early repayment in full of the five-year notes occurred on June 11, 2003.
7. Chargeurs, 2005 annual report, p. 45.
8. Ibid., p. 14.

14

Mergers and Acquisitions: Getting the Deal

Put simply, mergers and acquisitions (M&A) refers to the consolidation of companies. Most firms grow their business in four ways: organically, via bolt-on acquisitions, by way of alliances, or through strategic acquisitions. Organic growth includes investing in technology, creating new products, and hiring new people—all of which are outside the M&A division's province. Alliances, joint ventures, strategic acquisitions, and mergers are the turf of the M&A division of an investment bank. Bolt-on acquisitions are those that are within the realm of a company's existing operations. Investment banks with local knowledge might be helpful, but most firms will manage these acquisitions by themselves or with the help of consultants. Alliances, joint ventures, and acquisitions of another business can provide access to a new set of clients or penetrate a new geography more effectively. Larger strategic mergers lead to the consolidation of businesses.

Types of M&A

An M&A transaction involves an acquirer and a firm that has been targeted by another firm for a takeover. The acquirer's purpose is to gain control of the assets of the target company in order to generate synergies[1] between the acquirer's assets and those of the target. These transactions are often called mergers, even if they are technically acquisitions. On the other hand, the term *acquisition* may be used in the context of a financial transaction, a buyout,[2] when no consolidation of businesses is involved. So what is the precise legal difference between a merger and an acquisition?

There are four basic legal procedures that one firm can use to acquire the assets of another firm:

- Acquisition of the assets of the target only.
- Acquisition of the shares of the target to get control over the assets. These acquisitions just need the shareholders of the target to agree to sell their shares.
- A merger including the target company as part of the acquiring company.[3] This requires the authorization of both groups of shareholders:
  - The shareholders of the target to approve its extinction
  - The shareholders of the acquirer because mergers usually result in additional shares being issued at the time of the combination
- Consolidation of the two companies. A consolidation is like a merger except that both companies disappear to form a new company. Consolidation is a combination of two companies to form a new company with shares to be issued.

In these four types of M&A, the price will be key for the finalization of the transaction. The price is the total amount of consideration paid in all forms in order to acquire the target company or its assets. Acquisitions of the assets or of the target shares can be paid for in cash or in shares. When cash is paid, an acquisition is often called an *outright acquisition*; when shares are used, it is called a *stock swap* or an *all-equity transaction*. A merger is always paid in shares. In all cases, there needs to be a valuation of the consideration.

M&A and Value Creation

In physics, critical mass is the minimum mass of fissionable material necessary for a nuclear explosion to take place. In M&A, critical mass is the minimum size a company must reach to better negotiate its purchases of raw materials, to impose selling prices for its products, or to produce at a better unit cost. Mergers create value only when the association of the companies involved makes it possible to reach critical mass—to offer the best products and services, to manufacture them at the best cost, to reach new customers, or to develop new know-how.

Many studies by academics and consulting firms, not to mention tons of articles in the business press, explain that mergers are just as likely to destroy shareholder value as to create it. While many acquisitions fail to create value for the acquirer, some do not even create value for the target. Do shareholders of acquiring firms gain from acquisitions?

According to a celebrated book on valuation published in 1990, as many as two-thirds of all transactions failed to create value for the acquirers.[4] One study of 12,023 acquisitions by public firms from 1980 to 2001 found that the shareholders of these firms lost a total of $218 billion when acquisitions were announced. Small firms gain from acquisitions, so shareholders of small firms gained $8 billion when acquisitions were announced, and shareholders of large firms lost $226 billion.[5] On average, acquisitions are profitable, but in the aggregate they are not.

In research published by McKinsey in December 2006, Richard Dobbs, Marc Goedhart, and Hannu Suonio reviewed nearly 1,000 global M&A transactions from 1997 to 2006, comparing share prices two days before and two days after each deal was announced in order to assess the financial markets' initial reaction to the deals. They showed that deals during the boom, which began in 2003, created proportionally more value than those before it and that acquiring companies were keeping more of that value for their shareholders: "In the current boom, the proportion of acquirers that the market believes to be overpaying for deals has averaged 57 percent, decreasing annually from 63 percent in 2003 to 56 percent in 2006. In contrast, from 1997 to 2000, the overall average was 65 percent, with the level of overpayment increasing significantly, from 54 percent in 1997 to 73 percent in 2000."[6]

The Boston Consulting Group explains that on average, contrary to academic opinion, acquisitive growth strategies create superior long-term shareholder returns. The BCG has discovered the secret of successful M&A, the "method in the madness."[7] The most experienced M&A players will treat the process in a systematic, "industrial" manner, pursuing a deal only when the expected returns are above the cost of capital. Three key ingredients for success are strategic focus (on growth areas, not targets), valuation discipline, and early cross-functional integration planning. While these might seem like obvious imperatives, many companies ignore them.

The M&A disaster, which lasted for three years (1999–2001), included massive write-offs for AOL Time Warner,[8] massive losses for shareholders of JDS Uniphase[9] and Tyco,[10] the ruin of WorldCom,[11] and the collapse of Enron. But these wreckages may be the result of inadequate management, not of the deal per se. According to Wharton accounting and finance professor Robert W. Holthausen, "Some of the findings on WorldCom indicate that the board sometimes spent only 20 to 30 minutes reviewing a multibillion-dollar acquisition." Meanwhile, many companies, like General Electric and Cisco, benefited from acquisitions.

Takeover Defenses

Acquirers can be friendly or hostile. If the board of the target firm resists a takeover attempt, and if the bidder continues to pursue it, the bid is hostile. The resistance of the target's management and board starts with press releases and communications to shareholders. It presents a negative view of the target's management.

The resistance can involve many different defense tactics. If the aggression has been anticipated, a potential target may have amended its corporate charter to make a hostile bid more difficult. In the United States, for example, a firm could ask its shareholders for measures like staggering the terms of the board of directors or requiring a supermajority shareholder approval of an acquisition (for example 67 percent to take control). According to Arturo Bris, associate professor of corporate finance at Yale School of Management, "The most effective defense against hostile takeover bids in the U.S. today is called 'staggered boards,' and practically every company has them. Every year, you can only replace, for example, 10 percent of the members of the board. This means that a competitor can only acquire effective control after five years have passed."[12] In Europe, amending corporate charters to change majority rules is forbidden, and the line of defense would instead be to increase the equity of the company or to propose to shareholders a share buyback.

Once it has become the target of a hostile bid, the target can use defense tactics that read like pages from Harry Potter.

The target tries to find a "white knight," or it uses a "poison pill," or it sells the "crown jewels," or it provides "golden parachutes," or it finally succumbs to "greenmail." A *white knight* is a competing bidder—which can work if the target's board believes that such a dialogue is likely to result in a superior proposal. *Poison pills* are provisions in the corporate charter that go into effect when there is a hostile takeover. For example, shareholders have the right to buy shares in the company at a big discount, which would make the hostile takeover extremely expensive for the company making the acquisition.

Golden parachutes grant generous compensation to the outgoing management of the target firm. *Crown jewels* are major assets that the target firm's management sells off to keep the bidder away. Finally, with *greenmail,* the target firm buys back its own stock from a potential acquirer at a premium in order to stay independent. Historically, in the United States, about half of hostile bids have been successful and the target firm has been sold to the hostile bidder. The other half have been unsuccessful and the target remained independent or was sold to a white knight.[13]

Hostile bids can turn out to be very expensive. The premium over the target's closing price one day prior to the announcement between 1999 and 2003 was close to 43 percent on average,[14] whereas friendly acquirers pay just slightly more than 20 percent to win their target acquisitions.[15] But when they succeed, the shares of hostile cash acquirers often outperform those of friendly cash acquirers.[16] This is a curious result because "going hostile" makes it difficult to gain information and do due diligence in evaluating the deal. According to Ross, Westerfield, and Jaffe, one explanation is that unfriendly cash bidders are more likely to replace poor management.

Merger Waves

If there is one thing on which everybody can agree, it is that mergers happen in waves. When a consolidation takes place in an industry, it is hard for a competitor not to follow suit. Merger waves can engulf the whole economy. According to Dr. Neil H. Jacoby, former dean of UCLA and a member of President Eisenhower's Council of Economic Advisors, merger waves can come along with a market boom, but also with new technology developments. They are, in his words, "an accumulation of perceived but unexploited, profit-making opportunities for enlarging the scale of enterprises, which have arisen from basic technological and social changes and a buoyant capital market with a strong demand for new securities."[17]

Nearly thirty years later, Andrei Shleifer and Robert W. Vishny give a quite similar explanation.[18] They present a model of mergers and acquisitions based on stock market misevaluations of the combining firms. The key ingredients of their model are the relative valuations of the merging firms, the planning horizon of their respective managers, and the market's perception of the synergies from the combination.

The first wave of M&A in the United States took place from 1897 to 1902, beginning in 1895 along with a strong stock market rise and peaking in 1899, when there were 1,200 mergers. The focus of this early merger wave was on transportation (railroads) and communications (telegraph and telephone companies), as well as steel and rubber. These were integration deals merging many one-plant manufacturing companies into multiplant entities—for example, U.S. Steel, U.S. Rubber, and American Can.[19]

The second merger wave in the United States built up between 1924 and 1930, peaking in 1929 with 1,250 mergers. The basis of the second merger wave was the same, but in different forms: transportation (cars and roads) and communications (radio and national advertising, which involved brand names and chain stores). These coincided with a booming stock market, which lasted from 1921 to September 1929.[20]

The third merger wave arose between 1965 and 1968, with 2,500 mergers. This was the zenith of diversification, and it was driven by a sense of managerial control, leading to the foundation of large-scale conglomerates (ITT, Gulf and Western, Fiat in Italy, Schneider in France). With the help of computers, management had become a science (at least, this is what Jacoby believed at the time).[21] The large conglomerates paid for most of these acquisitions in overvalued shares.

The fourth wave occurred between 1986 and 1989, and is generally seen as the unraveling of the third. Financial acquisitions and LBOs (driven by Hanson in England, KKR in the United States, and other financial acquirers) broke up the conglomerates created in the late 1960s. These acquisitions were driven by the failure of the conglomerates to deliver value, and they occurred when the value of the conglomerate was deemed inferior to the value of its components. Two-thirds of them were paid for in cash and financed by debt. This wave was associated with a rise in stock prices.

The fifth wave was the Internet stocks and the new-economy bubble of 1997 to 2000. According to an article published by the Wharton Business School, companies spent $3.5 trillion on acquisitions between 1992 and 2000, making those eight years the most active M&A period in history.[22] Most of the mergers took place in the same industry. In large part, M&A transactions involved transportation of data and telecom companies. Some 58 percent of the mergers (by value) were paid for in stock.

There is little that an investment bank can do to make a market upbeat. But the lesson of the past three merger waves is that a merger must provide synergies if it is to have a chance to be successful. Thus, the strategy of investment banks nowadays is to focus on the strategic rationale for the contemplated merger (or at least it should be).

The Role of Matchmaker

The investment bank acting on the buy side of an acquisition will spend a lot of time analyzing the strategic setting of the buyer and of the target, to identify potential strategic motives for the deal. The banker tries to identify how a deal might fit in with the company's strategy. Typically, the banker will focus on the following six essential questions:

- What is the client's M&A strategy?
- How does each specific target enhance our client's strategic objectives?
- What does our client need from a potential partner?
- What does the target need from our client?
- Where are the synergies?
- What are the risks?

If he is convinced that a deal would make sense, the banker will have to consider how to approach the potential client.

First off, it's important to figure what is the best contact point for the target firm: the shareholders? top management? the corporate development team?[23] the operational executives at a subsidiary? Once the banker has honed in on the contact point, a meeting can be organized. The banker then needs to find an angle for the target (access, knowledge) or a special know-how (trusted advisor on negotiating and/or on structuring). Why might the target be "in play"? There may be, for example, a favorable ownership structure, or the company may have signaled that it is looking for a buyer. Finally, how should the bidder approach the target, as friend or foe?

The Timetable for an M&A Transaction

The 2003 merger between two biotech companies, IDEC and Biogen, illustrates the typical timetable for a merger. In the fall of 2002, the chairmen and CEOs of IDEC and of Biogen discussed the possibility of exploring a potential strategic collaboration between their two companies. During the course of the collaboration negotiations, IDEC asked its financial advisor, Merrill Lynch, to assist it in evaluating whether a possible business combination with Biogen or with one or more other entities would enhance stockholder value. On the surface, it appears that it was the senior management of the two firms that first discussed the possibility of exploring a potential strategic collaboration. But actually the deal may first have come from a banker's imagination.

The investment bank retained by a client in an M&A transaction will typically start assessing the strategic rationale for the merger and deliver its analysis to the board.

On December 18, 2002, IDEC's board of directors was presented with a preliminary analysis of a business combination with Biogen, prepared by Merrill Lynch. The presentation included background information about Biogen and strategic rationales for a combination with Biogen.

If the analysis confirms that the deal's business rationale makes sense, the board gives the green light to expand the discussions.

IDEC's board of directors agreed that members of IDEC's executive management should expand discussions with Biogen. IDEC also began consulting with its legal and financial advisors about a possible business combination with Biogen. Consultations with these advisors by IDEC continued throughout the remaining business combination discussions.

The first meetings between the two companies' representatives and their advisors are held to exchange information relating to the organizational structure of a combined company and to discuss the strategic rationale for a potential business combination.

On January 31, 2003, Biogen retained Goldman Sachs as its financial advisor in connection with a possible strategic transaction between Biogen and IDEC. At a regularly scheduled meeting of Biogen's board of directors on February 7, 2003, there was a general discussion of the strategic rationale for a possible business combination between IDEC and Biogen.

In order to exchange meaningful information, the parties sign a nondisclosure agreement.

A nondisclosure agreement was signed by the parties on February 11, 2003, and representatives of IDEC and Biogen and their outside legal, accounting, and financial advisors met on February 11 and February 12 to present information relating to their products, manufacturing operations, and finances.

Then the discussions concerning alternative merger structures and valuations—the financial and market implications of a transaction—begin. The two teams discuss the potential business combination, including management organization and structure. The two boards independently keep close control of the discussions. They meet regularly, often every two or three weeks. The financial advisors present their view to the respective firm's board of directors. There can be joint meetings between the two firms.

Between March 17 and March 20, 2003, members of IDEC's and Biogen's executive managements met with certain members of the other company's board of directors. The meetings focused on the strategic rationale for a potential business combination and the ramifications of structuring the transaction as a merger of equals.

A merger of equals is a combination of two firms that have approximately the same premerger market capitalization. Ownership of the new entity is to be split approximately 50/50 by each company's shareholders, and it is characterized by approximately equal board representation in the merged firm. The due diligences process is conducted by the buyer to investigate and review the operations of the seller. Unfortunately, extensive due diligence may not be done in those situations where it is most needed, or in hostile takeovers. For a merger of equals, the due diligence is reciprocal.

IDEC's management and its financial and legal advisors met on March 5, 2003, to discuss due diligence topics and the due diligence process, financial terms, and possible structures of the potential business combination. At the same time, members of IDEC's executive management toured Biogen's manufacturing facilities and discussed manufacturing, financial, and other integration issues with members of Biogen's executive management.

A data room where all economic, financial, and legal information concerning the target company is available is usually set up.

Each company made available to the other party a data room containing legal and business due diligence materials beginning on April 2, 2003.

The final phase is the negotiations between the two parties leading to the pricing of the transaction (or the determination of an exchange ratio if it is a merger proposal). The price will depend on the synergies resulting from the combination.

During the remainder of April and continuing through May, the parties and their legal and financial advisors continued their due diligence and engaged in negotiations with respect to a merger agreement, during which the discussions focused on organizational matters and possible synergies that could result from a business combination.

The purpose of the discussions is to determine the price to be paid, the mode of payment, and other terms of the deal. Here the bank may play an active role in the negotiation, or it can act as a backup to prepare the field on valuation, for example, or on the structuring of the transaction.

During the next two weeks (in early June), the parties negotiated the final terms of a merger agreement and, in particular, the final share exchange ratio.

These discussions prepare for the special board meetings to consider adoption of the merger agreement and approval of the transactions contemplated by the merger agreement. At these meetings, which are held separately, each bank will render to the board of directors its oral opinion, subsequently confirmed by delivery of a written opinion, that—as of that date and based upon and subject to the factors and assumptions set forth in the opinion—the price of the acquisition or the exchange ratio in the proposed merger is fair from a financial point of view to the holders of its client's common stock.

Following the approvals of the merger and related transactions by their respective boards of directors, IDEC and Biogen executed the merger agreement on June 20, 2003.

How to Identify a Prospective Client

So far we have considered the case of a banker acting for an acquirer. But a banker can act for a seller as well. In addition, she may have asked for the deal, or she may have been asked by the client. From an origination perspective, one can position any M&A transaction in a two-by-two matrix. In the matrix in Table 14–1, the rows identify the role the bank played in getting the mandate. Did the banker have to persuade the client that there was a worthwhile M&A transaction to be done (a *push*),

Table 14-1. The M&A Origination Matrix

	Buy Side	Sell Side
Push	Need an angle	Offer strategic getaway to shareholders
Pull	Value/deal structure	Strategic review Auction, dual track

or did the client come to hire the banker to do a transaction (a *pull*)? The columns in the matrix refer to which side of the deal the bank was involved with in the transaction. Was the bank working on the buy side, helping a client to acquire a business, or on the sell side, advising on the disposal of assets?

The strategies in each quadrant are clearly very different.

Push on the Buy Side

The top left quadrant in the matrix refers to the situation where the investment bank approaches a prospective client with the suggestion that it take over a company. The bank may have an existing relationship with the client, or the client may be a new client. It is easier to push an idea if there is a relationship of trust between the banker and the client (although one can certainly jeopardize a good relationship with a bad idea!). Normally knowledge of the industry will not be enough; the client knows the story better. The banker needs to know something that the client does not know, or that he does not appreciate fully. The bank may have information about a target—for example, why the company is in play.

Or the banker can have a piece of news that the client has not fully understood. When Westinghouse Electric Corporation made public its interest in the media company CBS in 1995, it became quite obvious that it would dispose of its other assets in the power-generation industry. An industrial giant for much of the twentieth century, Westinghouse was seeking to transform itself into a major media company with its purchase of CBS. That was a good angle for a banker to use in testing the appetites of the various potential acquirers in the power-generation businesses. He needed to approach the European nuclear and energy manufacturing companies (British Nuclear Fuels, Siemens A.G. from Germany, and GEC Alsthom and Framatome from France). Indeed, Westinghouse changed its name to CBS Corporation in late 1997 and began to sell all of its nonentertainment assets. It sold its nonnuclear power-generation business to Siemens and its nuclear business to British Nuclear Fuels.

Pull on the Buy Side

This is an easier situation to be in. The client comes to the investment bank and asks whether it should go for an M&A, or for help with an acquisition.

The client may recognize the need for an acquisition search, but not be able to do it alone. So the investment bank searches for a suitable partner, based on both the profile of the client and its ideas and ambitions regarding growth.

The client may come because of its relationship with the bank. Or it can be the bank's strategy to develop a relationship that will lead to its being selected as advisor in an M&A transaction. We saw the case of Merrill Lynch being asked by the drug company Sanofi to be its exclusive advisor in 2002. We also discussed the development of the relationship between Goldman Sachs and some of its Chinese clients.

There may be occasions when the trusted long-term advisor has a conflict. In this case, the client may hold a beauty parade, with each pitch being evaluated against well-articulated criteria. We will see later how Renault chose Merrill Lynch to help it work on the acquisition of Nissan through an informal beauty parade.

Sometimes the client will choose the bank so that the target does not take that bank as an advisor. This often happened in the late 1990s and the early part of this century with Goldman Sachs or Lazard. This is when the reputation of the bank is the best wedge for M&A. More recently, many clients have come to an investment bank or a large commercial bank, asking it to commit capital.

Push on the Sell Side

The top right quadrant includes approaches to a prospective client with the suggestion that it sell its company (or part of it). More frequently, the push sell strategy will apply to the sale of a subsidiary. It is, as a rule, quite difficult to go to a company's management and suggest it sell the entire company! Often the client is a shareholder of the company to be sold. The bank will lose the client after the sale, and it may not get the acquirer. It may also be a good strategy, when one learns that a firm is looking for a target, to go and see one of the possible targets and propose to help that firm in case it is contacted by the potential acquirer.

Pull on the Sell Side

This quadrant covers the cases of a possible sale, acquisition, merger, or joint venture. The client comes to the investment bank and asks whether it should look for a partner. In the financial press, this is tactfully described as a strategic review. The firm is looking for strategic partners, but the decision to sell has already been made. The focus will be on the valuation of the company with a view to establishing the appropriate price.

Investment banks may propose to organize an auction sale or dual track arrangement. A dual track arrangement is an attempt to sell a company to another firm or to financial investors while preparing to have shares offered and listed on the stock exchange as a backup. You may remember that this was what MGM (Morgan Stanley, Goldman Sachs, and Merrill Lynch) proposed to Elf for the disposal of its U.S subsidiary Texas Gulf.[24]

Transaction Fees

For some mysterious reason, there is very little documentation on M&A fees. One may mention the famous 5–4–3–2–1 Lehman Formula.[25] But this formula is used only in the middle market (if it is used at all). In research published in 2005, Terry Walter, Alfred Yawson, and Charles P. W. Yeung discovered interesting statistics for all deals where an advisor is hired, using a comprehensive sample of 15,422 M&A transactions announced in the United States between January 1980 and December 2003.[26]

On average, M&A fees represent about 1 percent of the value of the deals, whether the bank is on the sell side or the buy side. The difference between the mean (around 1 percent) and the median

Table 14-2. Transaction Fees

	Acquirer Advisor	Target Advisor
Fees (millions of dollars)		
Mean	2.89	3.06
Median	1.00	1.13
Deal Value (millions of dollars)		
Mean	1,345	898
Median	177	143
Fees (as a percentage of deal value)		
Mean	0.91%	1.06%
Median	0.52%	0.76%
N	1,996	3,932

N denotes the number of observations.

(around 0.5 percent) suggests that the fee level for acquirers diminishes steeply in proportion to the size of the deal (see Table 14-2). It may be more profitable for a bank to do ten small deals than one big one. Here's an example. A bank may garner a 1 percent fee on a $200 million merger, whether it is on the side of the acquirer or that of the target. In a $2 billion deal, that drops to 0.4 percent. Thus, ten $200 million deals can generate more than twice the fees earned from a single $2 billion transaction. On megadeals (above $25 billion), the fee may drop to 0.001 percent.

These skewed statistics illustrate three deficiencies in the fee structure:

- Ideally, the fee should motivate the bankers to do their best for their client: to help acquirers to pay the smallest price and targets to get the highest price. Of course, identical fee structures for the buyer and the seller cannot provide the right incentives in both cases. The fee as a percentage of deal value should be different on the buy and sell sides. The statistics, however, show that this is not the case (on average).
- The fee should be based not on the total value of the transaction, but on the value produced by the bank. This is far from being the case in practice.

- Finally, and this is the most important, the fee is due even if it would have been in the best interests of the client not to do a transaction. All incentives work to push the banker to close a transaction: his reputation, his bonus, and his instinct. Unfortunately for the clients, it would often be in their best interests not to do a transaction.

Notes

1. Synergy results from a reduction in charges or an improvement in sales that leads to the value of the whole being greater than the sum of the values of the parts.
2. A feature of a buyout is the use of a lot of debt to acquire a company, backed by the assets of the purchased company, which will be paying the interest on the debt with the cash it will generate.
3. This is the definition in corporate law. In practice, the word *merger* is also used when a company takes over another company through the acquisition of its equity capital. This is the case, for instance, in many competition regulations.
4. Tom Copeland, Tim Koller, and Jack Murrin, *Valuation: Measuring and Managing the Value of Companies* (Hoboken, N.J.: Wiley, 1990), pp. 318–321.
5. Sara B. Moeller, Frederik P. Schlingemann, and René M. Stulz, "Do Shareholders of Acquiring Firms Gain from Acquisitions?" National Bureau of Economic Research, Working Paper 9523, February 2003.
6. Richard Dobbs, Marc Goedhart, and Hannu Suonio, "Are Companies Getting Better at M&A? The Latest Boom in Merger Activity Appears to Be Creating More Value for the Shareholders of the Acquiring Companies," *McKinsey Quarterly*, December 2006.
7. BCG's long-term analysis of 705 U.S. companies shows that the most experienced M&A players produced a median total shareholder return of 12.4 percent over a ten-year period

(1993–2002), compared with 9.6 percent produced by organic-growth firms. See Boston Consulting Group, "Growing through Acquisitions," 2004, and "Successful M&A: The Method in the Madness," December 2005.

8. AOL Time Warner was a new company created by a consolidation announced in 2001 between the Internet company AOL and the media conglomerate Time Warner. AOL Time Warner reported a loss of $99 billion in 2002 (at the time, the largest loss ever reported by a company) as a result of a goodwill writedown for AOL.

9. JDS Uniphase, known as JDSU, a fiber-optic company based in California, was formed by the 1999 merger between two fiber-optic companies, JDS FITEL and Uniphase Corporation. The company tanked in 2001, and many people lost their shirts.

10. The conglomerate Tyco International adopted an aggressive M&A strategy between 1991 and 2001, acquiring more than a thousand other companies. Unlike the other companies mentioned here, Tyco was never bankrupt, but it had to split into three separate companies in 2006.

11. In the 1990s, the telecom company WorldCom grew essentially by acquiring other telecommunications companies, the largest being MCI in 1998. WorldCom went bankrupt in 2002. It emerged from bankruptcy in 2004, changed its name back to MCI, and was acquired by Verizon Communications in 2006.

12. Knowledge@wharton, February 23, 2005.

13. Houlihan Lokey Howard & Zukin, "Hostile Takeovers: Will Governance Trends Keep Barbarians at the Gate?" 2004; www.hlhz.com.

14. Ibid.

15. Dobbs, Goedhart, and Suonio, "Are Companies Getting Better at M&A?"

16. S. Ross, R. Westerfield, and J. Jaffe, *Corporate Finance*, 7th ed. (New York: McGraw-Hill, 2005), Chapter 9.

17. Neil H. Jacoby, *Corporate Power and Social Responsibility: A Blueprint for the Future* (New York: Macmillan, 1973).

18. Andrei Shleifer and Robert W. Vishny, "Stock Market Driven Acquisitions," NBER Working Paper 8439, National Bureau of Economic Research, 2001.

19. Jacoby, *Corporate Power and Social Responsibility.*

20. Ibid., p. 75.

21. Ibid., pp. 78–79.

22. "The Innovation-through-Acquisition Strategy: Why the Payoff Isn't Always There," Knowledge@Wharton, November 18, 2005, Wharton School Publishing.

23. Does the client have an internal M&A team (typically called "corporate development")? Increasingly, clients have their own acquisition teams. Thus the role of investment banks in finding a candidate for an M&A deal is less significant than it may have been in the last century.

24. See Chapter 6.

25. The Lehman Formula provides that the advisors get 5 percent of the first million, 4 percent of the second, 3 percent of the third, 2 percent of the fourth, and 1 percent of all the consideration above $4 million.

26. Terry Walter, Alfred Yawson, and Charles P. W. Yeung, "Does a Quality Premium Exist in M&A Advisory Fees?" www.docs.fce.unsw.edu.au/banking/workpap/wp_06_2005.pdf.

15

Synergies in M&A

Investment banks are becoming more involved in the kind of detailed, bottom-up estimation of synergies that is needed to produce a successful transaction. It is generally believed that the combination will not create value if the value of synergies is zero or negative. There is synergy when the value of the merged entity is more than the sum of the values of the two original entities taken separately. Two simple equations illustrate synergy:

- $2 + 2 = 5$. On the revenue side, the goal is to sell the same products to more clients, more products to the existing client base, or both.
- $2 + 2 = 3$. On the cost side, the combination of two firms permits the reduction of operating costs and expenditures.

More precisely, these synergies can come from economies of scale and scope, best practices, the sharing of capabilities and opportunities, and, often, the stimulating effect of the combination on the individual companies.

How Are Synergies Estimated in Financial Terms?

Synergies are measured by the difference between the value of the combined entity and the sum of the values of the two entities taken independently.

So, how do investors estimate synergies? Let's look at the share prices of the companies involved in the transaction, in particular the share prices two days before and two days after a deal has been announced. As long as the announcement is a true surprise (with no leaks beforehand) and there is no uncertainty over execution risk (e.g., opposition by certain shareholders or a possible veto by antitrust authorities), the difference between the cumulative value of the two organizations before and after the deal announcement, adjusted for market variations in the interval, corresponds to the value of the synergies estimated by investors, irrespective of whether the buyer or seller captures them.[1] McKinsey defines the *deal value added* (DVA) index as the aggregate change in value across both companies at the time of the announcement as a percentage of a transaction's value (adjusted for market movements). According to McKinsey's research, the market's estimate of the value that deals created from 1997 to 2006 for the buyer and seller combined (as measured by the DVA index) averages around 3.4 percent of the transaction value. During the boom beginning in 2003, however, the average DVA has been 6.1 percent, with the annual numbers trending upward to +10.6 percent, from +2.1 percent. In 2006, in fact, the DVA index was at a ten-year record high. "Those numbers stand in stark contrast to the previous boom's, when the DVA averaged only 1.6 percent for the whole period—and trended downward from +8.6 percent in 1997 to -5.9^2 percent in 2000."[3]

How do the parties involved in a deal estimate synergies? A little bit of math is called for. In the following equation, S is the value of synergies and V is the value of the firm; CF is the free cash flow available for distribution among all the security holders of a company in year t. Suppose that a company (A) acquires a target company (T). The value of the combined entity is V_{AT} the value of the acquirer on a stand-alone basis is V_A, and the value of the target on a stand-alone basis is V_T. Thus $S = V_{AT} - (V_A + V_T)$.

Classically the value of a firm is determined on the basis of the present value of the free cash flows. The value of the combined entity V_{AT} is the present value of the free cash flows of the combined entities. The value of each company, V_A and V_T, is the present value of the free cash flows of each entity independently. Therefore, the synergy is calculated by the present value of the incremental cash flow associated with the deal.

For each year, one calculates the difference ΔCF_t between the free cash flows $CFAT_t$ of the combined entities AT and the sum $CFA_t + CFT_t$ of the free cash flows of each entity A and T independently: $\Delta CF_t = CFAT_t - [CFA_t + CFT_t]$. The value of the synergies from the deal is the present value of incremental cash flows ΔCF_t, $S = \Sigma \Delta CF_t / (1+r)$. In turn, ΔCF_t (the incremental free cash flow in year t) is equal to the increments of its components. Free cash flow is the cash from operations less the amount of capital expenditures required to maintain the firm's present productive capacity. The cash from operations is derived by taking net income or loss and adjusting it for both noncash transactions and changes in working capital. The incremental free cash flow in year$_t$, ΔCF_t, is therefore equal to:

ΔRev_t,	(incremental revenues resulting from the combination)
$- \Delta Costs_t$	(incremental operating costs)
$- \Delta Taxes_t$	(incremental taxes)
$- (\Delta Capex_t + \Delta WCR_t)$	(amount of capital expenditures required to maintain the firm's present productive capacity plus changes in working capital requirements)

These increments can be positive or negative and are direct consequences of the transaction. Finally, the value of the synergies is the present value of these incremental yearly cash flows: $S = \Sigma \Delta CF_t / (1+r)^t$, where r is the appropriate risky discount rate.

The sources of synergies (and value creation) come from the following sources:

- Increase in *revenues* resulting from the combination
- Diminution in *operating costs* as a result of the combination
- Diminution in *taxes* as a result of the merger
- Diminution in the *working capital requirements* of the combined entity
- Diminution in the *capital expenditures* and *working capital* required to maintain the combined entity's present productive capacity.

Categories of M&A

In a well-known article published in the *Harvard Business Review*, Professor Joseph L. Bower analyzed all M&A deals over $500 million in the United States between 1997 and 1999.[4] His sample contained 1,036 deals. Bower identified six distinct varieties of M&A transactions:

- Overcapacity deals
- Product-line extension
- Financial deals in which a multibusiness company sold a division to a financial acquirer
- Geographic roll-ups
- M&A as R&D
- Industry convergence deals

This study gives investment banks very important information concerning the advice they can give in evaluating synergies, since the chances of success of these different types of deals are poles apart. In Bower's findings, overcapacity and product-line extension deals were the most common, with, respectively, 37 percent and 36 percent of the transactions. These two types of deals are illustrative of the two simple equations we just discussed. Product-line extension deals belong to the 2 + 2 = 5 synergy equation on the revenue side (more clients or more products sold to clients).

Overcapacity deals illustrate the other equation, $2 + 2 = 3$, on the cost side (the combination of two firms permits the reduction of operating costs and capital expenditures).

The third-largest category, with 12 percent of the sample, was deals in which a multibusiness company sold a division to a financial acquirer. Geographic roll-ups were next, with only 8 percent. Finally, the last two categories, M&A as R&D and industry convergence deals, were still uncommon.

Overcapacity M&A Deals

Overcapacity M&A deals are aimed at reducing capacity and duplication in mature industries through consolidation in order to obtain cost synergies. The acquiring company (part of an industry with excess capacity) will eliminate capacity, gain market share, and create a more efficient operation. "They happen when the giants must be trimmed down to fit shrinking world markets," according to Bower. He provides two examples: one in the banking industry (Chemical Bank merging with Manufacturers Hanover and then with Chase in the early 1990s), and the other in the car industry (Daimler-Benz merging with Chrysler in 1998).

On paper, this looks perfect. And that explains why this is the largest rationale for acquisitions. However, according to Bower, few of these deals have been judged successful after the fact. The reason that so few are successful comes from the fact that they "are usually win-lose games: the acquiring company keeps open more of its own facilities, retains more of its own employees, and imposes its own processes and values. Employees of the acquired company don't have much to gain. As with any win-lose scenario, the loser doesn't make it easy for the winner. And because these are often megamergers, they tend to be onetime events, so the acquirer doesn't learn from experience."

But the investment bank has precisely this type of experience. Part of the strategy of a successful investment bank is to try to avoid a win-lose scenario. This is what Merrill Lynch did with its client Renault in the acquisition of Nissan (see the section below entitled "Illustration: Success and Failure in the Car Industry"). While it was in fact an acquisition of the Japanese company Nissan by the French company Renault, the word *acquisition* was never mentioned. Instead, the deal was always (and still is) presented as an "alliance." Bower's findings are not completely in line with other results from consultants. Whereas he considers few of these deals to have been successful after the fact, the principal objectives of these deals—cost synergies—are obtained in most of the cases.

In a very interesting study published in 2004, three McKinsey consultants created a database of estimated and realized merger synergies based on their experience as consultants in 160 mergers. The important objectives of overcapacity deals entail reducing duplication and therefore creating cost synergies. From the McKinsey data, "managers in about 60 percent of mergers deliver the planned cost synergies almost totally." In fact, 36 percent delivered more than was expected, and 25 percent delivered 90 percent or more. True, in about a quarter of all cases, the cost-based synergies were overestimated by at least 25 percent, "a miscalculation that can easily translate into a 5 to 10 percent valuation error." In short, 60 percent of the mergers delivered more than 90 percent of the expected cost synergies, but this type of merger also generated heavy losses when the merger did not work.[5]

Geographic Roll-Up M&A

Geographic roll-ups are the traditional "big fish swallowing the small fish" in order to gain access to a target's customers, channels, and geographies. Like overcapacity M&A deals, roll-ups are designed to achieve economies of scale and scope by rolling up competitors in geographically fragmented industries.

According to Bower, this is how industry giants get built:

Many industries exist for a long time in a fragmented state: local businesses stay local, and no company becomes dominant regionally or nationally. Eventually, companies with successful strategies expand geographically by rolling up other companies in adjacent territories. Usually the operating unit remains local if the relationship with local customers is important. What the acquiring company brings is some combination of lower operating costs and improved value for the customers.

Not only that, but roll-ups (unlike overcapacity acquisitions) are often a win-win proposition; consequently, they're easier to pull off. Being acquired by a larger company can help a smaller company solve a broad range of problems. For the acquirer, the deal solves problems of geographic entry and local management. For the target, it solves the problems associated with size and scarcity of resources. "The large accounting firms were assembled this way. So were the super-regional banks, the large chains of funeral homes, many hotel chains, and the emerging large Internet consulting companies," says Bower. An example in the United States would be Banc One's acquisitions of scores of local banks in the 1980s.

In their study, the three McKinsey consultants discuss the synergies expected from consolidating branch networks in retail banking. They stress that "when one large U.S. bank acquired a competitor with a substantial geographic overlap, the acquirer suffered unusually high losses among the target company's customers, rendering the deal unprofitable and exposing the merged entity to a takeover. . . . This experience may be relatively extreme, but our experience indicates that the average merging company loses 2 to 5 percent of its combined customers."[6] Of the 124 mergers for which they have relevant data, 50 percent lost between 2 to 5 percent of their customer base. Some even lost more than 30 percent of their customers!

Product/Market Extension M&A

These acquisitions extend a company's product line or its international coverage. For Bower, "Sometimes these are similar to geographic roll-ups; sometimes they involve deals between big companies. They also involve a bigger stretch (into a different country, not just into an adjacent city or state)." In his assessment, he mentions three telling acquisitions: Snapple by Quaker Oats, Peoples Department Stores (Canada) by Marks & Spencer, and Nuevo Pignone (Italy) by GE. The first two were failures; the latter, though, was a real success. For Bower, the chance of success of these deals hinges on the relative sizes of the acquirer and the target. It also depends on the experience of the acquirer: serial buyers have a better chance to be successful in integrating the two cultures.

In the late 1980s, a noncarbonated drink, Snapple, was invented in New York; between 1989 and 1993, its sales shot from $24 million to $516 million. A new category, dubbed "New Age" or "alternative beverage," was born. Quaker Oats Company had already bought Gatorade in the 1980s, a beverage associated with athletes and athletic people in general. So Quaker Oats bought Snapple on December 6, 1994, believing that pairing the established Gatorade brand with Snapple would generate significant synergies. Quaker's initial plan was to exploit the seemingly straightforward synergies between New Age cornerstone Snapple and sport drink dominator Gatorade. The real challenge, however, was to integrate the two distribution systems. Coordinating them proved not to be feasible, so in 1997 Snapple was sold to Triarc Company for $300 million. The Snapple mistake cost Quaker upwards of $1.5 billion, and PepsiCo eventually acquired Quaker in December 2000 for $13.4 billion in stock.

According to the three McKinsey consultants, the expectations for revenue synergies in product/market extension deals are usually substantially overstated:

> *Wall Street wisdom warns against paying for revenue synergies, and in this case it is right. The greatest errors in estimation appear on the revenue side—which is particularly unfortunate, since revenue synergies form the basis of the strategic rationales for entire classes of deals, such as those pursued to gain access to a target's customers, channels, and geographies. Almost 70 percent of the mergers in our database failed to achieve the synergies expected in this area.*

Of their 124 mergers, 70 percent captured less than 90 percent of the anticipated synergies. Not only are these mergers often unsuccessful, but the failure is frequently dismal; 23 percent achieved less than 30 percent of the expected top-line synergies!

M&A as a Substitute for R&D

Bower defines innovation-through-acquisition deals in the following way: "Acquisitions are used in lieu of in-house R&D to build a market position quickly in response to shortening product life cycles." He provides the examples of Cisco and Microsoft. Between 1996 and 2002, Cisco acquired 62 firms in the Internet server and communication equipment fields. However, Cisco bought only two firms in 2001, after Bower's article. Cisco, once the leader in innovation through acquisition, has adopted a wait-and-see approach to technology acquisitions since then. But Oracle, the top supplier of database software, spent more than $24 billion between 2005 and 2007 to buy more than forty companies.

These deals are extremely difficult, which probably explains why they are not very frequent—they represent only 1 percent of Bower's sample, even though it covers the last three years of the tech boom days of the 1990s, when innovation was moving at such a frantic forward pace that even industry leaders like Cisco had to buy firms to keep up with the latest advances. According to Wharton management professor Saikat Chaudhuri, the innovation-through-acquisition strategy presents four major challenges at the product, organization, and market levels:

- Integrative complexity as a result of technological incompatibilities
- Integrative complexity as a result of the "maturity" of a target company
- Unpredictability of a product's performance trajectory ("technical uncertainty")
- Unpredictability of that product's market ("market uncertainty")[7]

Chaudhuri's contention that "buying companies with early-stage products and entering uncertain markets had substantially adverse effects" flies in the face of the notion that buying these "uncertain" products and companies is a good strategy simply because it might pay off down the road. Purchasing firms can help themselves by buying only those companies that bring along limited uncertainty. The nice thing about this is that the strategy is reversible: either you grow by acquisition, or you sell if you fail in your strategy. It gives more business to the investment banks!

Industry Convergence M&A

The purpose of deals of this kind is nothing less than "to exploit eroding industry boundaries by inventing an industry." For Bower, "Success depends not only on how well you buy and integrate but also, more importantly, on how smart your bet about industry boundaries is." Needless to say, these deals are not often successful. It takes a lot of nerve to justify a merger, with all the risks of integration and disruption to people's lives, on one's bet about industry boundaries.

Bower gives as examples AT&T's convergences—AT&T/NCR, AT&T/McCaw, and AT&T/TCI—which have not precisely been a string of successes. He mentions also Sears, Roebuck, which thought that financial services was a natural extension of retailing, but later chose to divest Discover and Dean Witter (another failure). Even the marriage of investment bank Morgan Stanley and Dean Witter Discover, which seemed to be doing well at the time of Bower's writing, is not going so well three years later. And the main example of a failed convergence is, of course, AOL Time Warner.

Viacom, though, seems to be enjoying success as a global-branded entertainment content provider (but with what convolutions!). You remember that Westinghouse Electric merged with CBS in 1995, then changed its name to CBS after having sold its traditional activities. In 1999, CBS was purchased by Viacom, a cinema company that had initially been created by none other than CBS! Six years later, Viacom decided to split into two publicly traded companies, undoing the Viacom/CBS merger of 1999. The existing Viacom was renamed CBS Corporation, and a new spin-off company called Viacom was created. Viacom includes a movie studio

(Paramount), two cable networks (MTV and Nickelodeon), and (until 2004, that is) a video distributor (Blockbuster). The example of Viacom shows how difficult it is "to exploit eroding industry boundaries by inventing an industry."

When they work, these are said to be "industry convergence deals." If they don't work, they simply create conglomerates with unrelated business units.

Basically, these deals are the old vertical M&A, where a corporation buys a supplier or a customer. They are not usually successful because the combined entity will compete with customers of the former supplier or with suppliers of the former customer. For instance, cable networks outside of Viacom might have wanted to buy Paramount movies in competition with MTV and Nickelodeon. The same held true with suppliers and the video distributor Blockbuster, because the latter needed Disney films. These are therefore very difficult deals to justify for investment banks, which usually do not emerge victorious from industry convergence transactions.

Procter & Gamble/Gillette

While this classification may seem relatively simple on paper, real life is not as simple as Bower's typology seems to indicate. We will illustrate the difficulty of identifying the synergies in two very similar mergers, Daimler-Benz with Chrysler and Renault with Nissan. But for the time being, let us take a simple example. In 2004, the global manufacturer of laundry and dish products Procter & Gamble (advised by Merrill Lynch) acquired fellow consumer-products company Gillette (advised by Goldman Sachs and UBS) for $57.5 billion.[8] What type of deal was it?

A. Cost-based synergies
B. Extension into new product lines
C. Access to international markets
D. Access to the target's customers, channels, and geographies

The answer is A and D. The transaction created a company with the power to fight for shelf space at a time when gigantic retailers such as Wal-Mart were calling the shots. The combination enabled both companies to distribute their products more cheaply and to remove duplicate costs. P&G expected to achieve revenue and cost synergies with a present value of about $14 to $16 billion. This deal was aimed at capturing the benefits of both scale and focus, creating a business that would be both larger and more reliant on a smaller portfolio of stronger brands.

Illustration: Success and Failure in the Car Industry[9]

The rearview mirror was invented by a Frenchwoman in 1897. Miss Davy de Cussé attached a mirror to the front of her car to "see what's going on behind." She even filed a patent for the first rearview mirror. It seems that the strategy of the German firm Daimler, the company that produces Mercedes cars and trucks, was seen from the rearview mirror when it acquired the U.S. firm Chrysler. But such was not the case for the French car company Renault when it acquired the Japanese firm Nissan! Both mergers were announced in marriage terms: that of Daimler and Chrysler as a merger of equals and that of Renault and Nissan as an alliance. Both mergers took place at about the same time, that of Renault and Nissan (1999) coming a year after that of Daimler and Chrysler (1998). Both were in the same sector. Both were overcapacity mergers. But the results could not have been more different.

The Marriage between Daimler and Chrysler

On May 7, 1998, Juergen Schrempp, the CEO of Daimler, and Bob Eaton, the CEO of Chrysler, announced a merger of equals between Daimler-Benz, the German maker of Mercedes-Benz luxury cars, and Chrysler Corp., the American producer of minivans, Jeeps, and Chrysler automobiles. The deal created a new giant in the auto industry, with $155 billion in sales. The key problem in the automotive sector at that time was an estimated overcapacity of nearly 25 percent, which had reduced the profitability of car manufacturers to 3 to 5 percent. Based on production figures at the time, there was a leading group of five global actors that commanded almost 60 percent of the worldwide total: GM, Ford, Toyota, Volkswagen, and DaimlerChrysler after the merger. Five other manufacturers represented less than a quarter of the world's production: Fiat, Nissan, Honda, Renault, and PSA.

Overcapacity tends to trigger a wave of M&A. As Bower explains,

The rationale for overcapacity deals is the old law of the jungle: eat or be eaten. This kind of deal makes strategic sense, when it can be pulled off. The acquirer closes the less competitive facilities, eliminates the less effective managers, and rationalizes administrative process. In the end the acquiring company has greater market share, a more efficient operation, better managers, more clout, and the industry as a whole has less excess capacity.[10]

With the merger, DaimlerChrysler achieved an 8.4 percent market share worldwide. The biggest manufacturers at the time were General Motors and Ford, with a market share of about 15 percent each, followed by Toyota with 10 percent.

In their book on the DaimlerChrysler merger, Bill Vlasic and Bradley A. Stertz said that many praised the transaction: "The marriage of Daimler and Chrysler promised to rock the global auto industry and provide a blueprint for international consolidation on an epic scale."[11]

On paper, the fit was indeed perfect. Chrysler lacked the infrastructure and management required to be a truly global automobile company. Daimler-Benz wanted to diversify its product line and distribution channels. The two carmakers were complementary by region and by product. They expected a cost reduction of $1.3 billion in 1999 alone, and an increase in cross-selling by integrating Daimler-Benz's competencies in technological innovations with Chrysler's ability to rapidly introduce products into the marketplace.

But DaimlerChrysler's share price lost around 50 percent within a year and a half following the merger. Why? Because in this kind of merger, it is important to integrate well and quickly: "You can't run the merged company until you've rationalized it, so figure out how to do that quickly and effectively. . . . Impose your process quickly. . . . Don't try to eradicate differences associated with country, religion, ethnicity, or gender."[12] Daimler and Chrysler do not seem to have been able to integrate their very different cultures and processes quickly enough. The German management culture could not be imposed on the American processes. Nobody ever said that the first was better than the latter.

While Daimler was an engineer-centered company, Chrysler was focused on sales and marketing. The sources of Chrysler's energy, the top leaders of Chrysler's manufacturing, engineering, and public relations departments, left quickly when they learned that their fate was to be subordinated to the functional bureaucracy in Stuttgart.

Another reason the merger failed was the lack of due diligence directed at valuing the synergies precisely during the merger discussions. The parties spent more time on the transaction structure and the governance structure for the combined company than on a precise and detailed analysis of the potential synergies. The major points of discussion involved providing a tax-free transaction for both companies' stockholders, how best to meet the requirements of a cross-Atlantic transaction, and sharing of management roles consistent with the parties' conception of a "merger of equals."[13] The valuation teams devoted more effort to considering the structure of the transaction than to identification of the synergies and their valuation. The background of the transaction shows this point clearly.

In mid-January 1998, while he was attending the Detroit International Auto Show, Juergen Schrempp visited Robert Eaton to discuss the possibility of a business combination, given the likelihood of consolidation in the worldwide automotive industry. Toward the end of the month, Eaton telephoned Schrempp to suggest a meeting. On February 5, 1998, the Chrysler board was briefed on the discussions between Schrempp and Eaton. A week later, Eaton and two colleagues met with Schrempp and a Daimler-Benz management board member. After a discussion concerning the consolidation that was likely to take place in the automotive industry and the complementary nature of the companies' respective product lines and markets, they decided to consult with their respective financial advisors.

On February 17 and 18, 1998, representatives of Daimler-Benz and Goldman Sachs met with representatives of Chrysler and Credit Suisse First Boston (CFSB) to discuss various transaction structures. The simplest structural solution, a direct merger of Daimler-Benz and Chrysler, was not possible under German law. During the course of that week and the next, representatives of the two companies and their respective financial advisors and legal counsels met to discuss the transaction structure. They agreed on five objectives:

- The transaction should maximize value for both companies' stockholders.
- It should be tax-free to Chrysler's U.S. stockholders and tax-efficient for Daimler-Benz AG.
- It should have the postmerger governance structure of a "merger of equals."
- Optimally, it should be able to be accounted for as a pooling of interests.
- The surviving entity should be a German stock corporation.

During these meetings, various tax, corporate, and management issues were discussed with a view to developing a transaction structure that would accommodate the parties' objectives. On March 2, 1998, the two CEOs met in Lausanne, Switzerland, to discuss governance and business organizational structures for a possible combined entity. Over the course of their discussions, the parties considered various alternative transaction structures for the combination of the two enterprises. On March 5, 1998, the Chrysler board was updated concerning the status of the discussions with Daimler-Benz, and it was informed every two weeks thereafter. The two executives in charge of the project, Gary Valade for Chrysler and Eckhard Cordes for Daimler-Benz, met on March 6 to conclude that the working teams should continue to meet in an effort to refine the structural alternatives that were then under discussion. In addition, Valade requested that Daimler-Benz provide Chrysler with its preliminary thoughts on valuation.

On March 5 and 17, representatives from each party's legal and investment-banking teams met in New York to continue their discussion with respect to alternative transaction structures. On March 19, representatives of Chrysler and CSFB met with representatives of Daimler-Benz and Goldman Sachs to discuss valuation matters. On March 23, the Chrysler board was updated concerning the status of the discussions with Daimler-Benz. On March 26, representatives of Chrysler and Daimler-Benz met at the offices of CSFB to discuss the progress of the working teams, valuation analyses, governance, and structural matters. During late March and throughout April, the legal and investment banking teams continued to discuss and refine their analysis with respect to the appropriate business combination structure.

On May 3, the Daimler-Benz management board unanimously approved the combination agreement and the transactions. The Chrysler board did the same on May 6. Late in the evening, in London, all constituent parties signed the combination agreement. The next morning, the signing was publicly announced, less than four months after the first contact between the two chairmen. The "merger of equals" had been consummated.

The Alliance between Renault and Nissan

While the predeal discussions between Daimler and Chrysler lasted four months and focused on the transaction structure, the negotiations between Renault and Nissan lasted nine months and assessed the potential for synergy in great detail. On March 27, 1999, Renault and Nissan Motor Co. announced that they had signed an agreement for a total partnership, "which will create the fourth largest automobile manufacturer in the world, while providing growth and profitability to the two partners." Renault invested 605 billion yen (US$5.1 billion) to acquire 36.8 percent of the shares of Nissan Motor. By April 2004, Nissan's share price was 3.3 times its price in 1999!

Renault and Nissan were unlikely candidates for success: both were large, bureaucratic organizations, and many of their executives were former civil servants or graduates of elite schools without entrepreneurial talent (or so it seemed). They were both a bit sclerotic, and they both suffered from the increased competition in the auto industry. Both had permanent employment systems. Neither company's management model was clearly better than the other's. The goal of the alliance was to set up a powerful binational group within a balanced partnership focused on performance. In 1990, Renault had tried to create an alliance with Volvo, which had gone down the drain. This time the two companies made it work.

In 1998, Renault was a company with total sales of €37 billion; it produced 2.2 million vehicles of all types, from passenger cars to light commercial and industrial vehicles. Nissan was the second-largest carmaker in Japan, with total sales of €51 billion and producing 2.7 million vehicles annually, of which 2.2 million were passenger cars. Renault had no debt and €1.9 billion in cash available. The biggest shareholder was the French state, with around 44 percent; the remaining 56 percent was held by private shareholders and Renault employees. All told, the company was valued at €8 billion in 1999.

Nissan had more advanced technology and higher quality; nevertheless the company had run into trouble in the 1990s when demand for cars flattened. Overcapacity and a lack of new models led to decreasing profitability. Since the company was highly leveraged, with debt that was 2.5 times equity, its huge debt ($21 billion) resulted in serious financial difficulties. From January 1997 to October 1998, Nissan's share price had declined around 60 percent. Meanwhile, Renault wanted to become a major player in the consolidating automotive industry. The firm had achieved better balance in Europe, but it had no presence in Asia or North America. Nissan was an ideal target: a global firm with twenty-two subsidiaries in eighteen countries and a strong presence in Asia and the United States as well as Europe.

In early May 1998, Renault sounded out a few investment banks for their view of the Asian market. Many international banks had already worked with competitors (i.e., Goldman Sachs and DaimlerChrysler), while others did not have the wherewithal in Asia. Merrill Lynch presented Renault with ideas about potential alliances in Asia; Nissan came out on top, over smaller companies like Hyundai and Kia. In June the bank organized meetings between Renault and potential Asian candidates for an alliance, and in July the first meetings between the Renault and Nissan management teams took place. On July 9, convinced of the potential opportunities offered by a tie-up with the Japanese car manufacturer, Renault appointed Merrill Lynch as its exclusive financial advisor on a potential transaction.

Renault said later that it had started working closely with Nissan's management in July. In actual fact, if Renault was very committed, Nissan was only lukewarm. It turned out that Goldman Sachs had approached Nissan on behalf of Daimler, and the Japanese had much preferred the German. In 1998 Nissan's sales had reached $49.7 billion for 2.75 million units of a full range of automotive products. The Japanese firm was bigger than the French. But Nissan was losing not only money but also market share; the firm had a very low capacity utilization (about 50 percent) and poor financial performance, including very high leverage. It was clearly heading toward bankruptcy.

On September 10, 1998, Renault and Nissan signed a commercial and industrial *memorandum of understanding* (M.O.U.) to analyze the potential synergies between the two firms. Nissan was still talking to Daimler. From the outset, Renault wanted to forge an alliance of equals, contrary to the win-lose strategy imposed by Daimler on Chrysler. This approach was better suited to the

Japanese. In any case, Renault could not afford to take on all of Nissan's debt, so it had to be content with a minority investment in the Japanese firm. Thus, with the help of Merrill Lynch, Renault worked closely with Nissan to thoroughly flesh out Nissan's strengths and weaknesses and the synergies of the alliance.

"We have been working closely with Nissan's management since July of last year. I must say that it became apparent from the outset that the fit between us was promising," said Renault's chairman when he announced the deal. "Throughout these last eight months, at each stage of our discussions, there grew a spirit of mutual understanding which drove our teams towards a comprehensive and global alliance which we believe will produce significantly enhanced value to our shareholders. Since last summer, the common work that we have done has allowed us to assess in great detail, the potential for synergy. We have reached today a good understanding of Nissan's businesses and current situation having completed an extensive phase of due diligence."

From August to December 1998, twenty-two working groups involving more than two hundred people from the two firms and their advisors, Merrill Lynch and CSFB, were formed to assess specific projects and potential synergies. It turned out that there was an excellent fit between the two firms in terms of markets, products, and production sites. By combining forces, Renault and Nissan created the number four player in the world automobile industry, with a 9.1 percent market share. Nissan was the answer to Renault's scale problem. Not only did Nissan have a broader international base than Renault, but the footprints of the two companies were complementary: Nissan had a strong position in Japan and a significant share in North and Central America and Europe; Renault was essentially a European manufacturer with a presence in three international markets of consequence: South America, Turkey and the Middle East, and Eastern Europe. The product lines of each firm were strong in key volume segments and complementary in all categories. Finally, there was a fit in industrial production, with the possibility of common platforms and cross-supply of products in given markets.

As the end of the year approached, there were three contenders vying for a merger with Nissan: Renault, DaimlerChrysler, and Ford. Renault was still the underdog in the eyes of Nissan compared to DaimlerChrysler. In December, Carlos Ghosn, then deputy COO of Renault, presented in Tokyo his concept of cross-company teams, which was to be powerful in facilitating the integration between the two firms and resolving cultural issues. On December 23, 1998, Renault and Nissan signed an M.O.U. opening a due diligence period of three months, with the goal of determining the terms of a final agreement.

On February 17, Merrill Lynch presented to Renault its views on the valuation of Nissan and the financial implications of the deal for Renault. The following day, Renault decided to make an offer to Nissan. The negotiations between the two firms and their bankers started on March 1 and continued until March 15. DaimlerChrysler was still involved in the discussions with Nissan. According to Michael A. Hitt, R. Duane Ireland, and Robert E. Hoskisson, "An adequate evaluation of the target firm through Daimler-Chrysler's due diligence process appears to be the cause of the company's decision not to acquire Nissan."[14] Thomas T. Stallkamp, Chrysler's president, composed a three-page memo to the board saying, "Nissan is going to go bankrupt and would be better off going bankrupt. The world doesn't need it." Adding Nissan to the already faltering union between Daimler and Chrysler was too much to ask. The DaimlerChrysler management board convened on March 10 at the Hotel Beau-Rivage outside Lausanne, almost a year to the day from Eaton and Schrempp's discussion of their merger in the same hotel. And they killed the deal.[15] The following day, Schrempp went to Tokyo to announce to the top managers of Nissan that DaimlerChrysler was withdrawing.

Renault was left as the only contender. On March 16, Renault made a definitive and exclusive offer to Nissan, which was accepted by Nissan the following day. It took nine days to finalize the negotiations and set up a draft of the merger agreement with the representations and warranties and covenants. On March 27, Nissan's board accepted the Renault offer. On that same day, Louis Schweitzer, CEO of Renault, and Yoshikazu Hanawa, CEO of Nissan Motor Co., announced that the agreement would create the fourth-largest automobile manufacturer in the world, while providing growth and profitability to the two partners.

Delivering the Synergies

Despite the good fit, it was clear to both sides that there would be many barriers to overcome, starting with language and cultural differences. How could they merge the individualistic nature of a French company with the group orientation of a Japanese company? The two groups created a transnational structure to define the joint strategy and to develop the synergies of the alliance. A Global Alliance Committee, headed by Renault's CEO and Nissan's president and including five senior executives from each firm, was put in charge of the strategy. Carlos Ghosn was appointed chief operating officer of Nissan in May 1999. He brought with him twenty other Renault managers, and he began revolutionizing the workings of the "bureaucratic and sleepy" Japanese company. In July 1999, Ghosn established eleven cross-company teams (CCTs) to "identify, study, propose, decide and implement all the possible synergies between Renault and Nissan."

The areas covered by the CCTs included five functions: vehicle engineering, power trains (the mechanism that transmits engine power to the wheels), purchase and supply, product planning and related strategy, and marketing and sales. Except for the product planning and related strategy CCTs, which were comanaged by the two partners, each CCT was directed by a manager from one company or the other, who was recruited using specific competency criteria. The manager's deputy necessarily came from the other company, and the members were from both companies. These synergies covered procurement, product strategy, and research. That way, common platforms and mechanical components would be codeveloped. The synergies also included geographical complementarities. Renault and Nissan expected to save $3.3 billion from these synergies in the 2000–2002 period alone, and $3 billion annually thereafter.

It was the alliance of Renault with Nissan, not the marriage of Daimler and Chrysler, that would "rock the global auto industry and provide a blueprint for international consolidation on an epic scale." Meanwhile, on May 14, 2007, DaimlerChrysler AG announced that U.S. private equity investment firm Cerberus Capital Management would take over an 80.1 percent stake in newly founded Chrysler Holding. Analysts expected the business risk profile of the remaining group, Daimler AG, to benefit from the separation of its Chrysler operations.

Notes

1. See "How Much Are Synergies Actually Worth?" www.Vernimmen.com, 2007.
2. The DVA is negative when the stock market's reaction to a deal announcement is so unfavorable (possibly because of the loss of credibility for the management team) that the decline in the acquirer's market capitalization more than offsets the increase in the acquired company's share price.
3. Richard Dobbs, Marc Goedhart, and Hannu Suonio, "Are Companies Getting Better at M&A? The Latest Boom in Merger Activity Appears to Be Creating More Value for the Shareholders of the Acquiring Companies," *McKinsey Quarterly*, December 2006.
4. Joseph L. Bower, "Not All M&A Are Alike—and That Matters," *Harvard Business Review*, March 2001, p. 93.
5. Scott A. Christofferson, Robert S. McNish, and Diane L. Sias, "Where Mergers Go Wrong," *McKinsey Quarterly*, no. 2, 2004.
6. Ibid.
7. Saikat Chaudhuri, "The Multilevel Impact of Complexity and Uncertainty on the Performance of Innovation-Motivated Acquisitions," research paper, Wharton, 2005.
8. However, this deal fell short of being the largest merger in 2004. That honor went finally to French pharmaceutical company

Sanofi-Synthélabo's purchase of Aventis at the end of April 2004 for $72.7 billion.

9. Sources: For Daimler/Chrysler, SEC filings. For Renault/Nissan, the March 29, 1999, presentation by Louis Schweitzer, CEO of Renault, and the book *Citoyen du Monde* by Carlos Ghosn and Philippe Riès (Paris: Grasset, 2003).

10. Bower, "Not All M&A Are Alike—and That Matters," p. 93.

11. Bill Vlasic and Bradley A. Stertz, *Taken for a Ride: How Daimler-Benz Drove Off with Chrysler* (New York: HarperCollins, 2000).

12. Bower, "Not All M&A Are Alike—and That Matters."

13. See the background of the transaction on pp. 57–58 in www.sec.gov/Archives/edgar/data/942666/0001047469–98–0 35292.txt.

14. Michael Hitt, R. Duane Ireland, and Robert E. Hoskisson, *Strategic Management: Competitiveness and Globalization*, 4th ed. Cincinnati, Ohio: South-Western College Publishing, 2001), p. 291.

15. Vlasic and Stertz, *Taken for a Ride.*

16

Getting the Deal Done

An M&A transaction is complete once the parties have agreed on a price. Investment banks spend a lot of time developing valuation models for a transaction. Typically, the advisors first value the firms on a stand-alone basis. Then they check and value the synergies. Finally, they prepare the final negotiations and help negotiate the purchase price: the total amount of consideration paid in all forms in order to acquire the target company or substantially all of its assets. Acquisitions can be financed by cash, shares, or a combination of the two. Even though many commentators play down the dissimilarity, cash-financed acquisitions are different from stock-financed acquisitions.

The Difference between Cash-Financed and Stock-Financed Acquisitions

In a cash-financed acquisition, the target's shareholders leave with cash in exchange for their shares. In a stock-financed acquisition, the selling shareholders join the purchasing shareholders as owners of the acquiring company. They receive shares of the acquiring company in exchange for their shares in the target company.

A merger is a stock-financed acquisition in which the acquired entity disappears.[1] Unlike in an acquisition, where the acquiring firm gets control of the assets without having to deal with minority shareholders, the acquirers become shareholders of the combined company in a merger. The acquired firm disappears, all of its businesses are transferred to the acquiring company (or to the new corporate entity), and the selling shareholders receive shares in the combined company in exchange for their shares in the defunct acquired firm. By contrast, when the acquisition is paid in cash, the selling shareholders leave the scene.

If stock-financed acquisitions and mergers resemble marriages, cash-financed acquisitions are more akin to divorces. In a cash-financed acquisition, everything hinges on the acquisition premium, which is like alimony. All of it is given to the "divorcing" shareholders, who take the money and run and are not entitled to any downstream synergies. In a merger, by contrast, the shareholders of the target company have a continuing interest in the ongoing concern and share in the synergies.

Since the selling shareholders share in the synergies, it should not come as a surprise that the postmerger stock performance is related to the method of payment. In the debate over whether there is an abnormal return after a merger, Professors Tim Loughran and Anand Vijh found that acquirers in cash offers earn positive long-run abnormal returns, whereas acquirers in stock-financed mergers earn negative returns.[2] It seems that acquirers in stock deals overpay more often than in cash deals. This observation is confirmed by a 2006 study by McKinsey that we discuss below (see note 11).

The M&A Conundrum

The strategy of investment banks for getting the deal done centers on valuation. In principle, the investment bank advising the acquirer will estimate the best price at which the shares of the target can be acquired by its client. For the acquisition to create value, the purchase price should be less than the value for the acquirer.

A transaction destroys value when the bidding firm pays more than what the shares are worth; the value for the buyer should therefore be higher than the price it pays. The opposite holds true for the seller. The bank advising the seller will want to make sure that the price is above the value for its client. The value for the seller ought to be lower than the price it receives.

However, the value for the buyer should be lower than the value for the seller because of the former's lack of confidence. Since the seller knows the business better, the business plan that it deems achievable might not be realistic for the less knowledgeable buyer. Thus, the discount rate that a buyer applies to the expected cash flows should be higher simply because the purchaser takes all the risk of an impossible forecast. The present value of future cash flows is normally higher for the seller than for the buyer.

Thus, the M&A conundrum is this: there should never be an M&A transaction because the buyer and the seller will never agree on a price that creates value for them. There will be a transaction only if the value for the buyer is above the negotiated price and this price is above the value for the seller. But the value for the buyer is normally below the value for the seller because of uncertainty. Therefore, it stands to reason that the buyer and the seller should never be able to agree on a price. Nonetheless, there are many, many M&A transactions!

To resolve this conundrum, one needs to conclude that there can be a transaction in two cases only: (1) when the seller is obliged to sell and (2) when the firm is worth more to the buyer than to the seller.

When the seller is obliged to sell for personal reasons, the price he receives may be lower than the value he gains for his own firm—but a transaction might take place anyway.

A transaction can still take place if, and only if, the firm's value to the buyer is higher than its value to the seller. The firm is worth more to the buyer if (1) the buyer can manage the concern better than the seller or there is some hidden value that the buyer has discovered. This is the case with financial buyers, and it explains leveraged buyouts (see Chapter 17). Or (2) the buyer discovers ways to generate synergies that the seller could not obtain by itself. This is the case for strategic buyers when there are synergies between the two businesses, so that the buyer has higher expectations of cash flows.

The successful investment banks will discover real value for strategic buyers by discovering real sources of synergy and valuing them precisely. Hence the significance for an investment bank advising a bidder when it identifies and evaluates the synergies that can make the negotiations successful. Granted, the investment bank advising the seller will also try to ensure that the selling firm gets as large a share of the synergies as possible.

An Ultra-Short Valuation Theory

There are at least three different views of value: (1) the fair value, (2) the financial buyer's view, and (3) the strategic buyer's view. In general, the fair value is lower than the value to the financial buyer, which in turn is lower than the value to the strategic buyer.

The Fair Value

Accounting standards require firms to carry assets and liabilities on the balance sheet at "fair value." In the United States, the fair value of an asset is the amount at which the asset could be bought or sold in a current transaction between willing parties.[3] In international accounting, it is the amount for which an asset could be exchanged, or a liability settled, between knowledgeable, willing parties in an arm's-length transaction (a transaction in which the buyer and seller act independently and have no relationship to each other).

The "fair market value" of a going concern (also called a value-in-exchange) is different from the investment value of a going concern, which is the value of a property for a specific use or to a specific user, reflecting the expected utility and/or profitability of the property, including synergies arising from a merger or acquisition.[4] It is exclusive of any element of value arising from the accomplishment or expectation of a merger or acquisition.

The fair market value approach leads the practitioner to use the method of *valuation by comparables*. The market value of the concern is determined based on comparisons with the market capitalization of comparable listed companies and their various multiples (cash flow multiples, earnings multiples, and so on). Ideally, one should consider other M&A that have occurred in the same field, but the valuation must be based on a reasonable number of meaningful transactions (which is not always available). In addition, one could argue that M&A comparables do not give a fair market value, but rather an *investment value*. The financial market is obviously a better basis of comparison to give a fair market value of a company, except that this market value is a minority interest value.

The Value to the Financial Buyer

The financial buyer's view recognizes that the ability of a controlling shareholder to improve operations "might cause the fair value of a reporting unit as a whole to exceed its market capitalization."[5] It takes into account the improvements in operations that may arise from control, but not from industrial synergies. The financial buyer value is the present value of the enterprise's free cash flows, determined by the business plan of the acquirer.

The Value to the Strategic Buyer

The strategic buyer's view takes into account the synergies resulting from the combination of two firms. The only valuation method compatible with the strategic buyer's (or financial buyer's) view is a discounted-cash-flow valuation (DCF valuation), which provides a valuation of the synergies. Investment banks will apply a DCF valuation to the cash flows forecasted by management, including all synergies resulting from the business combination, to justify the value of the acquisition for the acquirer.

The Method of Valuation by Comparables

The method of valuation by comparables is based on observed prices for comparable companies that have a value either because they are listed or because they have been a recent M&A target. Ideally, one should look at the value given to a comparable company during an M&A process. Because mergers happen in waves, one can often find comparable M&A transactions ("comps"). However, the analyst working on comps should be careful: it has been shown that when mergers happen together (on the wave), they lead to lower shareholder value relative to off-the-wave mergers.

In the absence of comps, one must use the listed price of comparable companies: the fair market value. The market value is based on a comparison with companies that are operating in the same sector or are in a similar type of business, and that are of similar size and with a similar commercial positioning. The difficulty is finding comparable companies. In heavily populated economic sectors, analysts will establish certain criteria for comparability. Often the criteria are the geographical distribution of the activities performed, the size of the company, and the activities carried out along the value creation chain.

Within the sample of comparable companies, the market value of each company (estimated on the basis of its current stock exchange price) is divided by selected key financial figures. To find these key figures, the analyst should research what the financial parameters are that explain the differences in quoted values between the companies in the sample. The differences in stock price can reflect differences in sustainable growth or in profitability measured by the return on capital employed, but they can also reflect differences in marketing policy or advertising, R&D, or any other parameter of performance.

Take the price/earnings ratio (P/E ratio), for example. If the market thinks that the company will grow considerably in the future, it is ready to pay a higher P/E. This growth is not eternal, however, and the company's sustainable rate plays a role in the level of the P/E.

The multiples of turnover, cash flow, and EBITDA are calculated from the enterprise value (stock exchange capitalization plus financial debts and minority interests). The average values of stock market capitalization divided by these various key financial indicators are applied to the corresponding indicators of the firm to be valued in order to find its fair market value.

The Discounted-Cash-Flow Method

This method involves estimating the value of the financial flows that will be generated by the firm and available for capital contributors (shareholders and lending bankers), based on the predictive business plan. The latter is a forecast for a given period of the future free cash flows that the company is likely to bring into being.

The forecasting horizon is generally five years, but it may eventually be prolonged, and it should be for new undertakings that will be profitable only in the long term. At the end of this period, an end value (or residual value) has to be calculated. The weight of the latter in the total value is inversely proportional to the number of projected years. Often end value is an essential element in the forecasted value.

The usual questions from investment-banking analysts are two-pronged: what future operational cash flows will there be, and what will be the discount rate? The answer is: it depends on the purpose. If the goal is to determine the maximum price to be paid for the target, then future operational cash flows must include all synergies from the combination. The discount rate should therefore reflect not only the opportunity cost, but also the risk premium reflecting the degree of uncertainty of these flows. The result is the maximum intrinsic value of the target. But if the purpose is to find the target's minimum price without the transaction, the future operational cash flows must not include any synergies from the combination, and the discount rate is the target's own cost of capital. The result is the minimum sale price.

Valuing Synergies

There are many methods that investment banks use to value synergies, but the theory is simple: the synergy from a merger or an acquisition is the value of the combined firm minus the fair value of the two firms as separate entities. Remember that the fair value is the true or intrinsic value of the property interest exclusive of any element of value arising from the accomplishment or expectation of a merger or acquisition.

$$(1) \ S = V_{AT} - (V_A + V_T)$$

The sources of synergies (and value creation) come from the following sources:

- Increase in *revenues* resulting from the combination
- Diminution in *operating costs* as a result of the combination
- Diminution in *taxes* as a result of the merger
- Diminution in the *working capital requirements* of the combined entity
- Diminution in the *capital expenditures* and *working capital* required to maintain the combined entity's present productive capacity

To identify the sources of synergy, Ross, Westerfield, and Jaffe find it useful to decompose the cash flows arising from the transaction.[6] The gain in value of the combined firm is the present value of the synergy cash flows. Synergy may arise from:

- The size of the expected future cash flows (the additional cash flows resulting from the combination of assets)
- Their timing
- A reduction in the risk of the cash flows

As was explained in Chapter 15, the additional cash flow for a given year may arise from:

- Revenue enhancement resulting from the combination of assets
- Cost reductions thanks to complementarities and economies of scale
- Reduction in taxes
- Reduction in capital requirements (capital expenditures and working capital)

The value of synergies is the present value of the additional cash flows resulting from the combination of the firms:

$$\Delta CF_t = \Delta Rev_t - \Delta Costs_t - \Delta Taxes_t - \Delta Capital\ Requirements_t$$

1. ΔRev_t is the revenue enhancement in year t, which is the result of revenue synergies (2 + 2 = 5, remember?). There are two sources, volume and price. First, in what Bower calls the "product or market extension M&A" (a merger in which the acquirer tries to gain access to the target's customers, channels, and geographies; see the previous chapter), the postmerger entity is expected to sell more than the two merged firms. Second, the merged entity may get a larger market share that enables it to raise the price of its products.

   An example of joint product extension in the Renault Nissan alliance was the common platforms developed to keep pace with the renewal of the two partners' model line-ups. Market extension was based on the principle that the stronger partner in each market would promote the other partner's development through active support in sales and marketing and/or production.

2. $\Delta Costs_t$ are the cost-reduction synergies (2 + 2 = 3). Better operating performance leads to a reduction in the cost of goods sold. Significant cost reductions have been achieved in the Renault Nissan alliance through joint purchasing and a common supplier base for 72 percent of the two companies'

purchasing turnover. Renault and Nissan aimed to share ten common platforms in 2010. In 2006, they used their first common platform for eight models. They codeveloped three gasoline engines, one diesel engine, and one transmission between 2004 and 2005. Reduction in overhead expenses and economies in marketing and distribution led to an improvement in selling and general and administrative expenses.

3. $\Delta Taxes_t$ is the tax gains. This includes the amalgamation of net operating losses with taxable profits and unused debt capacity. Investment banks use the adjusted present value method (the APV method) to value leveraged buyouts (LBOs), where a large amount of debt is used to purchase a target. The reduction in the target's taxes results from the deductibility of the interest expense related to borrowed funds.

4. $\Delta Capital\ Requirements_t$ are the incremental new investments in working capital and fixed assets that are required. Reducing investment in working capital requirements (WCRs) means reducing this investment to a level justified by the combined operations. With the Renault Nissan alliance, combining the two companies' logistics functions shortened delivery times and reduced the WCR. After a merger, the combined entity may be able to use its combined assets more efficiently by cross-using factories on a regional basis. For example, Renault's South American facilities were used to assemble Nissan products, and Nissan's ASEAN and Mexican plants assembled Renault vehicles.

Timing is important. As a McKinsey study points out,

Deal teams often make simplistic and optimistic assumptions about how long it will take to capture synergies and how sustainable they will be. As a result, important deal metrics, such as near-term earnings and cash flow accretion, can end up looking better than they deserve, which leads companies to overestimate the net present value of synergies substantially. . . . We have found evidence to suggest that unless synergies are realized within, say, the first full budget year after consolidation, they might be overtaken by subsequent events and wholly fail to materialize.[7]

The deal teams in the Renault Nissan alliance did not make this mistake; projects had been carefully classified as "ready for implementation" or "medium/long-term objectives."

The net present value of synergies can then be valued with the usual discounted-cash-flow model. Theoretically, one should use a discount rate that takes the risk of the cash flows into account. The determination of the discount rate is a matter of policy in each investment bank. Typically, banks will make one of two mistakes. Some banks will use a weighted-average cost of capital (WACC), with the capital structure of the merged entity being used for the weights of the costs of debt and equity. There is, of course, some circularity in these calculations, which can be resolved by spreadsheet approximations. But this method does not take into account the sizable risk of not delivering the synergies in time. The other mistake is worse: banks will apply a price/earnings multiple to the cash flows (usually the multiple of the acquirer). This method overvalues the synergies.

Valuing Synergies in the Real World

Investment banks should be more demanding when they estimate revenue enhancement. These improvements usually come from revenue economies of scope (attributable to the cross-selling that arises when the overall cost to the buyer of purchasing multiple products from a single supplier is less than the cost of purchasing those products from separate suppliers). In the Renault-Nissan deal, it was relatively simple to measure the sales from cars that Renault could sell in markets opened by Nissan—Mexico, the Mercosur market, and Japan—and, conversely, expansion in Europe for Nissan. Given the relatively small market share, there was little chance of competitors responding successfully. This is not always the case. Sometimes the revenue enhancement can be achieved only if the competitors are not in a position to retaliate successfully.

Revenue enhancement often comes from qualitative efforts that are more difficult to measure (the exchange of best practices, for example).

Finally, there can be revenue deterioration resulting from the disruption caused by the merger itself. Many mergers fail as a result of not paying enough attention to the existing businesses.

The second consideration should be cost reductions, which usually come from economies of scale[8] and/or cost economies of scope.[9] For the period 1999 to 2002, Renault and Nissan's joint efforts resulted in total savings of $1.9 billion. These were again easy to size up: the two companies started using two common platforms for the B and C segments (types of passenger cars) that they were starting to sell in Japan and in Europe in 2002. Often one neglects the cost involved in reducing expenses. Renault and Nissan did take the onetime cost of moving from an existing platform to the new one into account in their computations. They precisely identified procurement savings by setting up a common purchasing subsidiary. And they precisely assessed the savings associated with swapping power trains (engines and transmissions).

Sharing the Synergies

Once the synergies have been evaluated, there is the problem of dividing the spoils. With a cash transaction, the target firm's shareholders are not entitled to share in any downstream synergies, because they left the combined entity. Therefore, all synergies should go to the buyers. But sellers often negotiate an acquisition premium, which is the difference between the price paid to the selling shareholders and the value of the acquired firm. In a cash transaction, the acquisition premium corresponds to the share of the synergies that the sellers take upon leaving.

In a merger, the selling shareholders have a continuing interest in the ongoing concern because they share in the synergies. Much as in a marriage, the spouses share in the common wealth, but in a merger the two groups don't share 50/50 as they would in a marriage—the breakdown depends on the exchange ratio.

This ratio is the number of shares of the acquiring company that a selling shareholder will receive for one share of the acquired company. It also defines the share of the synergies that the selling shareholders will be entitled to.

Sharing the Synergies in Cash-Financed Acquisitions

Suppose firm A acquires target firm T for cash. The synergy S (the total gain in value to the shareholders of A and T) is the difference between the value of the combined business and the sum of the values of the two entities:

$$S = V_{AT} - (V_A + V_T)$$

Because the selling shareholders are not entitled to any downstream synergies in a cash transaction, they try to extract a premium on top of the fair value. The acquisition premium AP is the difference between the acquisition price and the target's fair value:

$$AP = P_T - V_T$$

The gain to the acquirer's shareholders is equal to the synergies minus the acquisition premium. Thus, no acquirer should pay an acquisition premium in excess of the synergies. The problem is that this premium is paid immediately as part of the price, whereas the synergies will materialize only over time. This is why the discount rate used to value these synergies should take into account the risk that they won't materialize. Another way to account for the risk of synergies is to structure the transaction as an all-stock merger.

Sharing the Synergies in Stock-Financed Mergers

Suppose firm A acquires firm T in an all-stock transaction. Typically, firm A will issue new stock to finance the acquisition. The shareholders of the target company T receive stock in the acquiring company A in exchange for each share of the stock of

T they hold. The number of shares they receive depends on the exchange ratio, which indicates how many shares of A they will receive in exchange for one of their shares.

In this case, the shareholders in A keep their shares, but their equity participation is diluted: the percentage of the equity capital that they own is smaller because of the issuance of new shares. If no synergies are created through the combination of A and T, then the merger is a zero-sum game and the gain to T shareholders is equal to the cost to A shareholders. The acquisition premium is the value that the shareholders in A lose to the shareholders in T in the event that there are no positive or negative synergies.

One can show that the acquirer's shareholder value decreases with the acquisition premium and increases with the acquirer's percentage of the synergy from the merger.[10] The acquirer's shareholders will lose when their share of the synergies is smaller than the acquisition premium. But they are not harmed by a merger if the acquisition premium is equal to their percentage of the synergies from the merger. In other words, if the percentage ownership of A's shareholders after the merger is equal to the pre-merger value of A divided by the value of the postmerger entity (synergies included), then A's shareholders are just as well off as they were before the deal. Under the assumption that the synergies equal the acquisition premium, A's shareholders do not lose value, but T's shareholders get all the synergies.[11]

In order to get a percentage of the synergies, A's shareholders should get a percentage ownership of the new entity that is higher than the premerger value of A divided by the value of the post-merger entity (synergies included).

What happens when the synergies turn out to be negative? The value of the merged entity falls below the predeal values of the two companies. Not only will the acquirer's shareholders lose the acquisition premium in the merger, but they will also lose the amount represented by their share of the negative synergies. The target shareholders, on the other hand, may not lose because the acquisition premium from the acquirer to the target implicitly insures the target's shareholders.

Why Do Acquirers Tend to Overpay More in Stock Deals Than in Cash Deals?

In 2006, Richard Dobbs, Marc Goedhart, and Hannu Suonio from McKinsey[12] reviewed nearly 1,000 global mergers and acquisitions from 1997 to 2006, comparing share prices two days before and two days after each deal was announced in order to assess the financial markets' initial reaction to the deals. They measured the proportion of all transactions in which the initial share price reaction for the acquirer was negative (adjusted for market movements). This represents the proportion of acquirers that the market perceives as having transferred more than 100 percent of the value created in their deal to the sellers. The study found that in all-cash deals, an average of around 49 percent of acquirers overpay, compared with 69 percent for all-stock deals—a difference that has remained fairly constant from 1997 to 2006. The research also showed that cash deals received a more favorable market reaction than stock deals: cash deals generated an average deal value added[13] of +13.7 percent, compared with −3.3 percent for all-stock deals.

Acquirers in stock deals are deemed to overpay more often than in cash deals because of the risk that their share of the synergies be smaller than the acquisition premium.

Illustration: The Merger between Alcatel and Lucent

In 2006, the two communications equipment companies Alcatel and Lucent decided to merge. Upon completion of the merger, Lucent's shareholders received shares in the combined company, which was renamed Alcatel-Lucent. Lucent shares were exchanged for Alcatel American depositary shares[14] (Alcatel ADSs) at an exchange ratio of 0.1952 Alcatel ADS for one Lucent share. The exchange ratio corresponded to parity for the Lucent and the Alcatel share prices over a period prior to the market rumors of the merger.

Goldman Sachs was financial advisor to Alcatel. Morgan Stanley and JPMorgan were financial advisors to Lucent. The

Alcatel board of directors mandated that the bank BNP Paribas deliver a fairness opinion. We therefore have four opinions of investment banks on the values of the transaction.

Goldman Sachs's Methodology

a. *Historical stock trading analysis.* Goldman Sachs reviewed the historical trading prices for Lucent common stock for the twelve-month period that ended March 23, 2006, the day before news of a potential combination was reported in the press. The relative share price performance of Lucent was examined in relation to the selected companies (as hereinafter defined) and Alcatel and in relation to the S&P 500 Index and the S&P 500 Telecom Index.

b. *Selected companies analysis.* Goldman Sachs reviewed and compared estimated enterprise value to estimated calendar year 2008 revenue ratios and estimated price to estimated calendar year 2008 earnings per share ratios for Alcatel and Lucent to corresponding financial information, ratios, and public market multiples for six publicly traded corporations in the communications technology industry.

c. *Historical exchange ratio analysis.* For the period from March 23, 2005, through March 28, 2006, Goldman Sachs computed the daily implied exchange ratios of the closing stock market prices of Alcatel ADSs to Lucent common stock and compared them to the fixed exchange ratio of Alcatel ADSs to Lucent common stock of 0.1952.

d. *Contribution analysis.* Goldman Sachs reviewed the estimated future operating and financial information, including, among other things, sales; earnings before interest, taxes, depreciation, and amortization (or EBITDA); earnings before interest and taxes (or EBIT); and net income of Alcatel, Lucent, and the combined entity resulting from the merger. The information was based on Alcatel management's assumptions for Alcatel and Lucent, and, in the second instance, on the median of estimates from the Institutional Brokers Estimate System (I/B/E/S). The analysis also indicated that, at share prices as of March 23, 2006, holders of Alcatel ordinary shares represented

61.6 percent of the combined outstanding common equity and 58.5 percent of the combined enterprise value.

e. *Synergies analysis.* Goldman Sachs reviewed the impact of the estimated pretax operating synergies, including revenue synergies and cash restructuring costs, for calendar years 2007, 2008, 2009, and 2010 (estimates were provided by the managements of Alcatel and Lucent). The bank analyzed the value of 100 percent of the synergies using discounted-cash-flow analysis and multiples analysis.

f. *Accretion/dilution analysis.* Goldman Sachs analyzed the pro forma financial effects of the merger on Alcatel's estimated earnings per share, using (1) estimates of earnings for Alcatel and Lucent based on the views of Alcatel management using the fully diluted number of shares and (2) estimates of earnings for Alcatel and Lucent based on I/B/E/S estimates. For calendar years 2007, 2008, and 2009, Goldman Sachs compared the projected earnings per share for Alcatel common stock on a stand-alone basis to the projected earnings per share for the combined company.

JPMorgan's Methodology

a. *Historical common stock performance.* JPMorgan's analysis of the performance of Lucent common stock and Alcatel ADSs involved a historical analysis of their respective trading prices over the period from December 30, 2005, to March 31, 2006, the last trading day prior to the public announcement of the merger.

b. *Exchange ratio premium analysis.* JPMorgan calculated the exchange ratio premium/(discount) for twenty-two M&A transactions between listed companies in various industries (telecom, pharmaceuticals, finance, oil and gas, and food and beverage) relative to the implied exchange ratio based on average prices over the thirty-day period before the official announcement of the transaction. For the selected transactions, the average thirty-day exchange ratio premium was 2 percent and the median thirty-day exchange ratio premium was 1 percent.

c. *Relative contribution analysis.* JPMorgan reviewed the relative contributions of Lucent and Alcatel to the historical and forecasted revenue, EBITDA, and net income of the combined company for the calendar years ending December 31, 2005, and December 31, 2006. The calendar year 2006 forecasted revenue, EBITDA, and net income for both Lucent and Alcatel were based on management estimates.

d. *Publicly traded comparable company analysis.* JPMorgan compared the financial and operating performance of Lucent and Alcatel with publicly available information on seven publicly traded companies engaged in businesses that JPMorgan deemed relevant to Lucent's and Alcatel's businesses.

e. *Discounted-cash-flow analysis.* JPMorgan calculated ranges of implied equity value per share for both Lucent common stock and Alcatel ADSs by performing discounted-cash-flow analysis based on management projections for the calendar year ending December 31, 2006, for both Lucent and Alcatel and using extrapolations of such projections for the calendar years ending December 31, 2007 to 2010, which were based on publicly available estimates of certain securities research analysts.

f. *Value creation analysis.* JPMorgan analyzed the pro forma impact of the merger on the equity value per share of Lucent common stock. The pro forma results were calculated as if the merger had closed on December 31, 2006, and were based on the unaffected price per share of Lucent common stock on March 23, 2006, prior to the public disclosure by Lucent and Alcatel that they were in merger discussions. JPMorgan calculated the potential increase/decrease in the equity value per share of Lucent common stock.

Morgan Stanley's Methodology

a. *Historical common stock performance.* Morgan Stanley's analysis of the performance of Lucent common stock consisted of a historical analysis of trading prices over the period from December 30, 2005, to March 31, 2006.

b. *Comparative stock price performance.* Morgan Stanley performed analyses of the historical closing prices of Lucent common stock, the Alcatel ADSs, and an equally weighted index of communications equipment companies consisting of L.M. Ericsson Telephone Co. and Nortel Networks Corp.

c. *Exchange ratio premium analysis.* Morgan Stanley reviewed the ratios of the closing prices of Lucent common stock to the corresponding closing prices of the Alcatel ADSs over various periods ending March 31, 2006.

d. *Relative contribution analysis.* Morgan Stanley analyzed the relative contributions of Lucent and Alcatel to historical and estimated revenue; earnings before interest, taxes, depreciation, and amortization (EBITDA); and net income of the combined company for the calendar years ending December 31, 2005, and December 31, 2006, based on available management estimates by Lucent and Alcatel.

e. *Present value of equity research analyst price targets analysis.* Morgan Stanley performed an analysis of the present value per share of Lucent common stock and Alcatel ordinary shares by analyzing the twelve-month target prices based upon publicly available equity research estimates.

f. *Comparable company analysis.* While noting that no comparable public company was exactly identical to Alcatel or Lucent, Morgan Stanley compared selected financial information for Alcatel and Lucent with publicly available information for comparable communications equipment companies that shared certain product characteristics and similar customer bases with Alcatel and Lucent, respectively. The bank selected the price/earnings multiple and the aggregate value divided by the estimated EBITDA for calendar years 2006 and 2007. The aggregate value of a company was defined as the market value of equity minus cash and cash equivalents plus the value of any debt, capital leases, minority interests, and preferred stock obligations of the company.

g. *Discounted-cash-flow analysis.* Morgan Stanley calculated ranges of implied equity value per share for Alcatel and

Lucent as of March 31, 2006, based on a discounted-cash-flow analysis utilizing management projections for the calendar years 2005 and 2006 and extrapolations of such projections for the calendar years from 2007 to 2010. The unlevered free cash flows from calendar years 2006 through 2010 and the terminal value were then discounted to present values using a range of discount rates from 10.0 percent to 11.0 percent. Morgan Stanley incorporated a risk premium into Alcatel's and Lucent's predicted weighted-average cost of capital to take into account unique risks for the companies and for the communications equipment industry as a whole.

h. *Pro forma analysis of the merger.* Morgan Stanley analyzed the pro forma impact of the merger on estimated earnings per share for Lucent for calendar years 2007 and 2008. The bank performed the analysis assuming no synergies as well as with the realization of annual pretax synergies during calendar years 2007 and 2008.

BNP Paribas's Methodology

a. BNP Paribas first compared the proposed parity of 0.1952 Alcatel ADS per Lucent share with the parity resulting from the performance of the Lucent share price and that of the Alcatel ADS (which correlates exactly with the price of the ordinary Alcatel share) over several periods prior to market rumors on March 24, 2006. The proposed parity is lower than the averages recorded on March 23, 2006 (one-month, three-month, six-month, and one-year). It is higher than the parity of the last share prices only on March 23, 2006 (0.1848). The proposed parity was also compared to the parity resulting from the target share prices of financial analysts prior to March 24, 2006. For each twelve-month period preceding this date, it is lower than the parity resulting from the average target share prices for Alcatel and Lucent.

b. BNP Paribas then performed a valuation of the Alcatel shareholders' share in the value of the combined company's equity, synergies included, and compared this value with the value of Alcatel's equity prior to the rumors of March 24, 2006 (the market capitalization of Alcatel calculated on the basis of the one-month average share price on March 23, 2006, was used as a reference). The value of the combined company was determined using two separate methods:

1. By discounting the free cash flows of the group resulting from the merger, synergies included. The bank extrapolated the free cash flows after 2009, the last year of the financial projections prepared by Alcatel, on a normalized basis, assumed to grow at 2 percent per year (inflation included). A discount rate of 9.7 percent, corresponding to its estimate of the weighted-average cost of capital of the combined company, was used.

2. Through a comparison of the multiples of Alcatel, Lucent, and comparable companies (Avaya, Cisco Systems, Ericsson, Motorola, Nokia, and Nortel Networks). The most relevant multiple is the value of capital employed over EBIT, which factors in the earnings power and capital intensity of the companies, without factoring in the impacts of different financial structures. This multiple was calculated for 2007 and 2008, as financial analysts' estimates were unavailable for 2009. This multiple was applied to projections of the EBIT of the combined company for 2007 and 2008.

Expected synergies for 2007 and 2008 representing only 30 percent and 70 percent, respectively, of the synergies expected over the long term, discounted at the weighted-average cost of capital, were factored in so as to provide a truer image of the earnings power of the combined company.

c. The two methods were applied both on the basis of the consensus of financial analysts' forecasts for both companies and on the basis of projections prepared by Alcatel. The cost of implementing the synergies resulting from the merger was deducted from the asset value in order to determine the equity value in the multiples approach, but they were included in the flows in the discounted-cash-flow approach.

Regardless of the method used to value the equity of the combined company, and given the expected synergies, Alcatel's shareholders' share in the equity of the combined company (60 percent) was substantially higher than the value of Alcatel's equity prior to the announcement of the merger (calculated on the basis of the Alcatel one-month average share price on March 23, 2006).

The value creation for Alcatel shareholders, calculated using the discounted-cash-flow method, is positive when the actual synergies realized represent approximately half of the expected synergies. With the financial projections for Lucent drawn from analysts' consensus estimates for 2006, 2007, and 2008 only, the percentage of the value created by the merger that the Alcatel shareholders would get would be close to the percentage of their share in the capital of the combined company (60 percent). Additionally, also on the basis of the financial projections for Lucent drawn from the analysts' consensus, the creation of value for Alcatel shareholders, calculated using the discounted-cash-flow method, was positive when the actual synergies realized represented approximately one-third of the expected synergies.

BNP Paribas analyzed the impact of the merger on Alcatel's forecasted earnings per share. This analysis was based on projections made by Alcatel for Alcatel and Lucent (factoring in only the service cost) and expected synergies from the merger in 2007, 2008, and 2009. Earnings per share were calculated before depreciation of intangibles and excluding the cost of implementing the synergies. This analysis reveals, given the expected synergies, a slight increase in Alcatel's earnings per share for 2007, and an increase of over 30 percent in 2008 and 2009.

Notes

1. There are two kinds of mergers: a *statutory consolidation*, in which a new corporate entity is created from the two merging

companies, and a *statutory merger*, in which the acquirer continues to exist as a legal entity. In both cases, the target company disappears.

2. Tim Loughran and Anand Vijh, "Do Long-Term Shareholders Benefit from Corporate Acquisitions?" *Journal of Finance*, Vol. 52, no. 5, December 1997, pp. 1765–1790.

3. *Fair value* is defined in Appendix F of *Statement of Financial Accounting Standards (SFAS) 142* as "the amount at which an asset (or liability) could be bought (or incurred) or sold (or settled) in a current transaction between willing parties, that is, other than in a forced or liquidation sale."

4. Internal Revenue Service Revenue Ruling 59–60 defines *fair market value* as "the price at which property would change hands between a willing buyer and a willing seller when the former is not under any compulsion to buy and the latter is not under any compulsion to sell, both parties having reasonable knowledge of relevant facts."

5. *SFAS 142*, Appendix B, Paragraph 154.

6. S. Ross, R. Westerfield, and J. Jaffe, *Corporate Finance* (New York: McGraw-Hill, 2005), Chapter 29.

7. Scott A. Christofferson, Robert S. McNish, and Diane L. Sias, "Where Mergers Go Wrong," *McKinsey Quarterly*, no. 2, 2004.

8. Economies of scale are the gains on unit costs resulting from higher overall physical volume produced.

9. Cost economies of scope are achieved when the joint production of two or more products or services is accomplished more cheaply than producing them separately.

10. Let a be the percentage ownership of A shareholders in their company after the completion of the merger. The selling T shareholders get $1 - a$.

$$m = \text{Number of old A shares}$$
$$n = \text{Number of new A shares issued}$$
$$a = m/(n + m) \text{ and } 1 - a = n/(n + m).$$

For acquiring shareholders not to lose value, the postmerger value per share of A should be superior or equal to the premerger A stock value:

(Premerger value of both firms + synergies)/$(m + n) \geq$ premerger A stock value

Alternatively, the stake of A's shareholders in the value of the combined company's equity, synergies included, should be superior or equal to the premerger value of the acquirer's equity:

(Premerger value of both firms + synergies) $\times m/(n + m) \geq$ pre-merger A stock value $\times m$

Let us write the value of the combined company's equity, synergies included as

$$V_A + V_T + S$$

and the premerger value of the acquiring company as V_A. For the A shareholders not to lose value,

$$a \times (V_A + V_T + S) \geq V_A$$

For the T shareholders not to lose value,

$$(1 - a)(V_A + V_T + S) \geq V_T$$

The acquisition premium is the gain for T shareholders in the event that there are no synergies:

$$PA = (1 - a)(V_A + V_T) - V_T$$

It is also the loss to A shareholders in the absence of synergies:

$$PA = a(V_A + V_T) - V_A$$

Gains for the A shareholders are written $aS - PA$, and gains for the T shareholders as :

$$(1 - a)S + PA.$$

11. When gains for the A shareholders are zero, $aS = PA$, and gains for the T shareholders are $(1 - a)S + aS = S$.

12. Richard Dobbs, Marc Goedhart, and Hannu Suonio, "Are Companies Getting Better at M&A? The Latest Boom in Merger Activity Appears to Be Creating More Value for the Shareholders of the Acquiring Companies," *McKinsey Quarterly*, December 2006.

13. Deal value added measures the aggregate change in value at the time of the announcement across both companies as a percentage of a transaction's value (adjusted for market movements). It tracks the financial markets' assessment of how much total value a deal will create, irrespective of whether the buyer or seller captures it.

14. An American depositary share, or ADS, is a security that allows shareholders in the United States to hold and trade interests in foreign-based companies more easily. ADSs are often evidenced by certificates known as American depositary receipts, or ADRs.

17

The Business of Asset Management

Managing pools of savings is known as asset management, investment management, or money management.

Andrew Carnegie wrote that "the problem of our age [the end of the nineteenth century] is the proper administration of wealth, so that the ties of brotherhood may still bind together." He argued that the accumulation of riches should be invested in the interests of the greatest number. And he felt that to further the spread of wealth, the state should tax inheritances "in condemnation of the selfish millionaire's unworthy life." Putting philosophy into practice, Carnegie went on to found TIAA-CREF, a not-for-profit company whose purpose was to assist retired professors. It was a pension fund before the term existed, and it is one of the greatest success stories in the field of asset management.

Almost every investment bank in the United States owns or operates an investment management division and/or a private-banking business for affluent investors. A "high-net-worth individual" is defined by Merrill Lynch as a client with any and all liquid financial assets over $1 million. For these wealthy investors, the investment bank will set up an individual account. It can be managed directly by the bank, or it can simply be advised by the bank. Private banking and private wealth management cater to the complex needs of high-net-worth clients, their families, and select institutions.

To the less wealthy, the bank offers mutual funds. A mutual fund is an entity operated by an investment company that collects funds from investors (both individual and institutional) and invests them in a variety of securities. Mutual funds, as a whole, constitute the second-largest financial intermediary in the United States, behind commercial banks. According to the 2007 S&P survey of investment services, there were more than 8,000 mutual funds operating in the United States as of January 2007, with total assets under management valued at $10.6 trillion, up from $1 trillion in 1990. But this is not true of the rest of the world. While mutual fund assets in the United States have fluctuated between 9 and 12 percent of the total financial stock since 1997, in Europe they have stagnated in the region of 4 percent of the financial stock since 1995.[1]

For investment banks, asset management businesses provide a relatively steady flow of management fees, which contrasts nicely with the instability of investment-banking income. Asset management provides not only a management fee, but often also a performance fee. The management fee is based on a percentage of assets under management. Revenue from these fees flows more smoothly and predictably than revenue from other sources. Initial public offering (IPO) and M&A investment-banking income are very volatile; trading for the firm's own account is precarious; and trading commissions depend on investors' eagerness to trade. All these incomes go up when the market goes up and down when the market is down. In order to develop a more stable source of income, the strategy of investment banks has been to grow their assets under management, either by obtaining more inflow of savings from their clients or by new acquisitions. The consequences of lower earnings volatility should include higher debt ratings and therefore lower costs of financing for investment banks. For them, the cost of financing is the bread and butter of their overall strategy.

Baby Boomers and the Mutual Fund Industry

In many regions, the mutual fund industry has experienced spectacular growth in assets under management over the past several
decades, driven by market appreciation and consistent net inflows.
The primary driver of this growth has been the need to save for
retirement. The aging of the baby-boom generation (approximately 77 million Americans were born between 1946 and 1964)
should reinforce this trend in the years to come. If an average person's saving phase begins around age forty, the first baby boomers
probably began to save around 1986. As for those born in 1955, at
the height of the baby boom, they started saving around 1995 and
will continue until 2015, their predicted year of retirement.

Retirement pensions are financed by contributions, capitalization, or both. In the first system, active employees contribute to
pay the pensions of the retired; the contributions for a given year
finance the pensions paid that same year. This system is known
as pay-as-you-go. Most countries, including the United States and
the United Kingdom, include in their retirement systems a contribution scheme insured by the state (the first instance of this was
in 1889 in Bismarck's Germany). Nearly everywhere, the pay-as-
you-go system is hitting a brick wall (see, for example, the situation in the Detroit auto industry). This explains the turn toward
capitalization, more commonly known as the pension system.

Some countries have given preference to a system of retirement
by capitalization, otherwise known as pension plans. A pension
plan is a system for self-funding a greater portion of retirement
income. Acquired rights are managed according to the principle
of capitalization; they are accumulated, and the gains are rein-
vested up until the date of effective retirement in an account
opened in the name of the beneficiary. There are two types of
pension plans: defined benefit and defined contribution.

Defined-benefit pension plans promise to pay a specified amount
to each person who retires after a set number of years of service.
In some cases, employees contribute to these plans; in others, the
employer makes all contributions. The Pension Protection Act of

2006, which laid out more stringent requirements for companies offering defined-benefit plans, may speed the decline of these plans as more companies move toward less costly schemes.

In *defined-contribution pension plans*, contributions are fixed at a certain level, while benefits vary depending on the return from the investments selected. Unlike defined-benefit pension plans, defined-contribution pension plans give the employee investment options. A 2007 fact sheet from the nonpartisan Employee Benefit Research Institute (EBRI) shows that coverage by both types of plans had stagnated at about 30 percent of American workers since 1979.[2] Participation in "traditional" defined-benefit plans and defined-contribution [401(k)-type] plans has basically reversed since 1979 (a year in which participation in defined-benefit plans was 62 percent and defined-contribution 16 percent, compared to 10 percent for defined-benefit plans and 63 percent for defined-contribution in 2005). In the last twenty-five years, 401(k) plans have become the dominant form of retirement plan adopted in the for-profit sector. The Pension Protection Act of 2006 may further the advance of these funds. This act allows employers and their plan sponsors to offer advisory services to employees. It also provides an automatic enrollment in defined-contribution pension plans. The year before the act, 16.9 percent of respondents in the survey on practices and trends in profit sharing and 401(k) plans had automatic enrollment, up from 10.5 percent in 2004.[3]

According to the AXA Retirement Scope 2007[4] (AXA is a global leader in financial protection), Americans lead the world in preparing for their retirement, saving more than people in any other country and beginning preparations earlier than most. Pension funds and company pension plans play an important role for Americans, while the government's role is more minimal. Americans, along with the Dutch and Germans, were best informed about their retirement conditions. And just as in the other English-speaking countries, the United Kingdom and the Pacific region countries, Americans turned to financial advisors for information about retirement. However, the private pension system in America faces numerous problems.

Employees with low wages and those who work for small businesses have extremely low rates of coverage.

Pension funds are also growing fast in countries that recently have engaged in pension system reforms—for example, Chile, South Korea, Japan, and Australia. They are still small relative to GDP in many regions of the world: in Europe, in spite of its aging populations, but also in Latin America and in China. For example, Mexico, Argentina, and Brazil all have less than 15 percent of GDP in private pension fund assets, compared with 63 percent of GDP in the United States.[5]

Growing Assets under Management

In the years 1995–2005, U.S. investment banks adopted two very different strategies for growing their assets under management: internal growth and acquisitions of other money managers. Goldman Sachs and Lehman Brothers have aggressively expanded their asset management businesses since 2000. Goldman Sachs did this largely to service ultra-wealthy clients. The bank started with assets under management of some $50 billion in 1995. At the end of 1997, it still had not even a third of the assets under management at Merrill Lynch and less than one-half of what Morgan Stanley had. In 2005, however, Goldman Sachs Asset Management had ten times more than when it started, with assets under management about equal in size to the figures at Merrill Lynch and Morgan Stanley (both around $500 billion). Revenues from assets under management represented 12 percent of the firm's net revenues in 2005.

Lehman did a few add-on acquisitions (Neuberger Berman and the Crossroads Group, a leader in fund-of-funds private-equity investments, both in 2003), but essentially the bank grew internally.

The former chairman and CEO of Goldman Sachs Henry Paulson liked to say that the key drivers for success in asset management were the bank's performance (which drives inflow), the quality of the bank's relationship with its clients, and a wide-ranging product offering (which attracts investors).

In its annual survey of the industry, Standard & Poor's mentions the same three factors. These factors are key in attracting customers' money.

Performance Drives Inflow

In the specialized press, funds are often classified on the basis of their annual performance. These rankings are taken quite seriously by the collective management industry, because investors tend to invest in funds whose performance has been superior to that of others in the same category. However, one year's performance cannot predict the fund's performance in the following years. Except for low-ranked funds that are perennially found at the tail end of the ranking and stay there (fees and high expense ratios appear to explain the underachievement of some perennially low-rated funds), past performance does not foretell future results.

Traditionally, investment banks like Merrill Lynch marketed their own funds through their own sales force. The investor had to pay a sales charge for investing in the fund; hence the name "load funds." In the early 1970s, some companies started to sell their funds directly to investors without a sales charge. Since that time, the popularity of no-load funds has been tremendous. Today, most mutual funds are no-load funds.

The strategic response of investment banks selling load funds through their own marketing force has been to sell other firms' funds through their network. What we call "open architecture" is the possibility of selling funds through third parties' marketing networks. In an open-architecture system, broker/dealers, bank trust departments, defined-contribution record keepers, third-party administrators, and variable-annuity insurance companies offer products from many competing asset managers, as opposed to selling only proprietary funds. For example, Deutsche Bank offers Merrill Lynch investment funds to its clients outside the

United States. The strategy of Merrill Lynch Investment Managers has been to grow revenues and better meet client needs through international, third-party distribution, with more than 1,300 outlets in Europe and Asia. Deutsche Bank wins the distribution fee as a result.

The third response is to generate stellar performance. This is the current strategy of Goldman Sachs. As a result, the net inflows (excluding money market funds) at Goldman Sachs have grown from $15 to $20 billion per year in 2000–2003 to more than $50 billion in 2004 alone, and again in 2005.[6] The strange thing is that the public results of the mutual fund business at Goldman Sachs were not very good. It might be that the bank has been able to attract so many assets because a few of its private funds have done particularly well.[7]

Growing Client Relationships

Investors can come to the funds on their own, through independent advisors, or through financial consultants working for big brokerage houses. The Internet has made it easy for investors to shop around. There are platforms that allow real-time linkages to multiple financial services vendors. For Professor Ingo Walter at NYU,

> *Absent the need for continuous financial advice, such a business model could reduce information costs, transactions costs and contracting costs while at the same time providing client-driven open-architecture access to the universe of competing vendors. Advice could be built into the model by suppliers who find a way to incorporate the advisory function into their downlinks, or through independent financial advisers. If in the future such models of retail financial services delivery take hold in the market, then some of the rationale for cross-selling and revenue economies of scope could become obsolete.[8]*

Independent advisors often steer their clients away from investment banks' in-house funds and toward those of the free-standing fund companies. Third-party sales through other banks' networks have not worked very well. It is understandable that financial consultants would be reluctant to recommend funds bearing rivals' names. In 2006, Merrill Lynch changed the name of the U.S. mutual funds it sells through third parties to Princeton Portfolio Research. Merrill hoped that changing the funds' names might eliminate investors' worries about conflicts of interest.

There are two strategies regarding client relations. One strategy is to use the reputation of the bank and its expertise. The bank's franchise can help to land big mandates from institutional investors and to generate inflows from retail clients. You may remember that Goldman Sachs Asset Management was one of only three firms, and the only non-Japanese firm, selected to provide money management services to Japan Post's $3 trillion savings system in 2005 (a mandate that the firm later lost).

The other strategy for generating inflows is to exploit cross-selling, the process of selling complementary products to a customer. With cross-selling, the banks hope to steer retail customers to their in-house funds and other products.

A Broad Range of Products

A wide-ranging product offering attracts investors. Goldman Sachs Asset Management offers a broad range of investment strategies in order to address all possible client needs. In 2005, its assets under management were 20 percent in alternative investments,[9] 30 percent in equity, 20 percent in money markets, and 30 percent in fixed income.

There are two philosophies of portfolio management: active and passive.[10] Goldman Sachs, for example, is an active manager. Active investors seek out what they consider to be better-than-average opportunities. As early as 1968, academic researchers scrutinizing the results of mutual funds showed that money managers cannot systematically beat the market. The efficient market theory dismisses the possibility of superior returns through investment selection. Launched in the mid–1970s, the passive management strategy has seduced some major players in the United States, like Vanguard and State Street. Passive management seeks to match the return and risk characteristics of a market. But passive management could not exist without active managers keeping the markets efficient.

There are two families of passive management: indexed investing, which aims to faithfully reproduce the performance of an index, and quantitative funds and enhanced indexing, which represent an attempt to obtain, over a medium- or long-term horizon, results superior to that index through strategic asset allocation.

Enhanced indexing attempts to add value by taking risk relative to an assigned benchmark. The excess return relative to the benchmark is called *alpha*, and the risk relative to the benchmark is called *active risk*. For instance, at Goldman Sachs, the fixed-income portfolio management teams seek to add value through research, sector selection, and security selection, rather than taking large bets on the direction of interest rates. In equity, they aim to deliver excess return through superior stock selection rather than from sector rotation. They capitalize on proprietary quantitative models and risk management expertise like the Black-Litterman Global Asset Allocation Model, a key tool in Goldman Sachs Asset Management's asset allocation process. (It could be said that this is just active management plus a computer.)

The active management process is often split into two steps so as to allocate the funds managed among asset classes first (*strategic allocation*), and then to pick up the specific securities in each class (*tactical allocation*). Strategic allocation consists of deciding on asset allocation in accordance with the investment horizon and risk tolerance in the customer's profile. It is the risk limit imposed by the institutional customer (which is the risk style displayed by the fund or the management style in accordance with the investor's time horizon) that governs strategic allocation. Asset allocation remains subject to a certain number of constraints aimed at minimizing risk; they hinge on the rules adopted by the funds. For example, there could be a requirement for sector-based diversification in the composition and performance of the security price index. A fund may provide its managers with a limit on maximum deviation from the stock index of 3 percent for each share and 5 percent for each sector.

Tactical allocation adapts strategic choices to market realities. Let's take an example. If strategic allocation suggests that the manager should invest 60 percent of the portfolio in stocks, tactical allocation consists of prioritizing the stocks of this or that country, but also avoiding bank sector stock given the interest-rate forecasts. As for fixed-income securities, tactical allocation leads to investing short term rather than long if a rate increase is anticipated.

In active management, there are two ways to choose stocks: top down and bottom up. With the former, the manager proceeds from the general to the particular. First, she analyzes the economic fundamentals of the main worldwide investment zones in order to decide on the proportion of the different markets in the portfolio. Then she decides on the sectors, and finally on individual stocks. According to the bottom-up method, the manager takes the opposite tack: he selects the stocks company by company by comparing them with one another in their sectors of activity. This approach is also known as stock picking. The manager analyzes the attractiveness of the sectors to which the stocks belong in accordance with their situation in the economic cycle.

Other methods pick stocks on the basis of their specific characteristics, not the sector that the stocks belong to:

- Growth
- Value
- Cyclical
- Income
- Small-cap
- Large-cap

"Growth stocks" are those of companies that grow substantially faster than others. Some securities benefit from sustained growth and high visibility in a buoyant market. The capitalization multiple is high. This type of stock had its heyday in the late 1990s when the TMT companies (technology, media, and telecommunications) displayed spectacular rates of progress and shot up.

"Value stocks" are those of firms that appear to be underrated in the stock market. These firms offer reduced visibility accompanied by mediocre results. Their price is low, but their value is good, and they are fundamentally sound; a strategic change, a modification in management, or an alliance may improve their prospects. As the market becomes aware of the company's true value, its stock price should mount.

"Cyclical stocks" are those that tend to move strongly higher and lower along with the overall business cycle. They are stocks of companies situated upstream in the productive sector and typically close to fixed investment and capital goods such as auto manufacturing and residential construction. Other cyclical groups include transportation, oil services, and mining.

"Income stocks" provide a steady stream of income to shareholders by paying a solid dividend. The dividend yield measures the actual return that a dividend gives the owner of the stock by dividing the annual dividend per share by the share price. Income stocks are typically stocks with high dividend yields.

The definitions of "small-cap" and "large-cap" can vary. In general, the former have a market capitalization lower than $2 or $3 billion. Institutional investors cannot buy a large portion of any one issuer's outstanding shares, and therefore are excluded from small-cap investing. Large caps are companies with a total stock value of over $10 billion.

Categorizing stocks is not a very easy task. Growth stocks should grow faster than value stocks. The problem is that they don't. Research by McKinsey in 2006 shows that growth stocks, characterized by higher market-to-book ratios, had revenue growth rates virtually indistinguishable from those of value stocks.[11] Value stocks may end up having high dividend yields and tend not to be very different from income stocks.

Nevertheless, many investment banks offer funds specialized by style. Take, for example, the myriad funds offered by Goldman Sachs in 2007: Goldman Sachs Concentrated Growth Fund, Goldman Sachs Small Cap Value Fund, Goldman Sachs Mid Cap Value Fund, Goldman Sachs Growth Opportunities Fund, Goldman Sachs Strategic Growth Fund, Goldman Sachs Capital Growth Fund, Goldman Sachs Large Cap Value Fund, Goldman Sachs Growth and Income Fund, Goldman Sachs CORE Small Cap Equity Fund, Goldman Sachs CORE Large Cap Growth Fund, Goldman Sachs CORE Large Cap Value Fund, Goldman Sachs CORE U.S. Equity Fund, Goldman Sachs Asia Growth Fund, Goldman Sachs Emerging Markets Equity Fund, and Goldman Sachs International Growth Opportunities Fund. In all likelihood, offering this wide range of types of funds has been a successful strategy in attracting new investors.

Acquiring Assets under Management

Instead of attracting new customers, some investment banks have adopted a strategy of acquisition. In the 1990s, many American investment banks like Merrill Lynch and Morgan Stanley acquired asset management organizations in order to increase their fee income and to reduce the earnings volatility of their investment-banking activities. Merrill bought Mercury Asset Management in 1996, and Morgan Stanley acquired Dean Witter a few years later. In Europe, after its merger with Swiss Bank Corporation at the end of 1997, the present UBS AG[12] announced the acquisition of Bermuda-based Global Asset Management (GAM) for its private-banking division, with assets under management of nearly $14 billion, and the U.S. broker Paine Webber in July 2000 (Paine Webber has since been renamed Wealth Management USA).

Ten years later, investment banks have been breaking away from their asset management activities. In 2005, Citigroup traded its asset management group, which counted $460 billion in assets under management, for Legg Mason's 1,540-person brokerage operation and about 15 percent of equity. In 2006, Merrill Lynch sold its asset management operation to BlackRock, an investment management firm.

The main reason for acquiring funds management outfits was to exploit synergies: economies of scale (the reduction of per unit costs as output increases), cost economies of scope (the reduction of per unit costs through the production of a wider variety of services), and revenue economies of scope (selling more products to the same customer). Obviously, this does not always work; a few years later, the same investment banks chose to outsource this service to industry-leading managers.

Economies of Scale

As in any industry with high fixed costs, there are economies of scale in asset management. Increasing the volume of sales augments the profitability, since the fixed costs do not change. The converse is diseconomies of scale attributable to increases in size, which create administrative overhead and problems of complexity. As Ingo Walter pointed out at the Hamburg Institute of International Economics, "There is ample evidence ... that economies of scale are significant for operating economies and competitive performance in areas such as global custody, processing of mass-market credit card transactions, and institutional asset management. Economies of scale may be far less important in other areas such as private banking."[13] But it does not suffice to add two pools of savings to reap synergies. The resulting entity should be able to improve operating efficiency (usually reflected in improved cost-to-income ratios).

Economies of scale were what Robert C. Doll, the then president and CIO of Merrill Lynch Investment Managers, called the "Boutique with Backing" approach.[14] According to Doll, "This approach combines the best of big and small: the performance focus of a small boutique with the critical, overarching investment and support structure afforded only by the depth of a large organization." A year later, Merrill Lynch sold Merrill Lynch Investment Managers to BlackRock.

Revenue Economies of Scope

On the revenue side, economies of scope attributable to cross-selling arise when the overall cost to the buyer of purchasing multiple financial services from a single supplier is less than the cost of purchasing them from separate suppliers. Economies of scope justify the concept of a supermarket. Using the appeal of one-stop shopping to attract and retain customers, who would be there to buy all sorts of financial products, is an old idea in finance. It has never worked.

Cost Economies of Scope

Cost economies of scope mean that the joint production of two or more products or services is accomplished more cheaply than producing them separately. Asset management is largely based on information. Information can be reused over a broad range of financial products, thereby avoiding cost duplication. Unfortunately, most empirical studies have failed to find significant cost economies of scope in the banking, insurance, or securities industries.[15]

Illustration: Merrill Lynch's Acquisition of Mercury Asset Management

In 1998, Merrill Lynch purchased U.K.-based Mercury Asset Management (MAM) for $5.3 billion in cash. Naturally it was said that "the combination of the two companies would create one of the world's largest asset management groups." At the time, analysts said that the combined entity had a comprehensive product line, a valuable brand image (Merrill Lynch), and an extensive client list—in short, a foundation for a new global money management model. They said that the profile of Mercury's business was complementary to that of Merrill's, as Mercury's focus lay mainly with managing equity investments for an international institutional clientele, whereas Merrill Lynch was a known quantity to the American middle class. It was an expensive acquisition, however: Merrill Lynch paid a 32 percent premium over Mercury's closing price the day before the announcement, a multiple of 25 times earnings, and 3 percent of Mercury's total funds under management of $176.7 billion. But was it a good strategic move?

The Strategic Reasons for the Acquisition

In 1997, Merrill Lynch had just completed a strategic review of the asset management industry to identify the opportunities for growing its asset management activities, Merrill Lynch Asset Management (MLAM). MLAM had focused mainly on providing mutual funds to Merrill's retail clients in the United States. The conclusion of the review was that MLAM needed to expand geographically, provide a broader range of global products, and develop an institutional franchise in order to complement its defined-contribution capabilities.[16]

On the face of it, Mercury seemed the perfect target. Merrill needed to internationalize, and MAM was the leading U.K. independent management company, with clients that included pension funds, corporations, private clients, and charities, both in the United Kingdom and overseas. MAM was also the third-largest investment manager in Japan. Merrill wanted to access local, pan-European, emerging market, and global product capabilities. MAM had all these capabilities, mainly in equity products, however. Merrill was looking for an institutional as well as a retail franchise. MAM was the leading U.K. investment management company, but it did not have much retail brand awareness. Finally, Merrill Lynch was one of the largest providers of defined-contribution plan services in the United States, and Mercury was one of the largest in the United Kingdom.

What did MAM need from ML? Ironically, Mercury had also completed a strategic review in which four broad strategic options had been identified:

- Tackling the U.S. market.
- Concentrating on continental Europe as the savings markets deregulated with the adoption of the euro.

- Growing the U.K. retail and private client businesses. (Mercury had an excellent reputation in the wholesale market, but it was not a retail brand. Would Merrill Lynch be able to distribute Mercury funds to access the retail markets in the United Kingdom?)
- Providing investment products to other distributors. (A deal with Merrill Lynch did not add anything, since ML's brokers were also distributors of other asset managers' products.)

What Were the Synergies Anticipated from the Acquisition?

According to Roy C. Smith and Ingo Walter at NYU's Stern School of Business,

> *Besides gaining access to distributors and fund-management expertise, the underlying economics of M&A deal-flow in asset management presumably have to do with the realization of economies of scale and economies of scope. These can facilitate cost reductions and cross selling of multiple types of funds, banking and insurance services, investment advice, and high-quality research in a one-stop shopping interface for investors."[17]*

Merrill Lynch had undertaken to guarantee the independence of Mercury. However, economies of scale can be found in back-office functions. To exploit economies of scale, it had to merge the back offices, technologies, and risk controls. And, of course, it couldn't merge Mercury's buy-side research with Merrill Lynch's sell-side research! There are simply too many conflicts among the various activities to accommodate economies of scale in a merger between two money management firms.

Then there were expected revenue synergies from economies of scope. The idea was that Merrill Lynch with Mercury would benefit from cross-selling complementary products. Merrill Lynch was strong in U.S. retail and fixed income; Mercury was a U.K. institutional firm and an equity house. The problem was that there are wide differences among countries in how mutual funds are distributed. In the United States, full-service broker-dealers maintain large retail sales forces to market mutual funds to retail investors, whereas in the United Kingdom, independent advisors play an important role. Merrill Lynch could not sell Mercury funds to retail investors in Europe. And how could Mercury have sold Merrill Lynch funds to institutional investors in Europe? Finally, how could Merrill Lynch have helped Mercury to sell into defined-contribution pension products in Europe? (The last never happened anyway.)

Synergies from cost economies of scope were even less impressive. There could have been cost-effective distribution of Mercury services through Merrill Lynch's infrastructure if the two structures had been capable of merging. Merrill could have gained access to fund management consultants through Mercury. But Merrill's investment management processes would have had to change. Mercury followed a disciplined and tightly organized top-down investment process based on a strong commitment to primary research. At Merrill Lynch Asset Management, there was practically anarchy, with separate research being conducted by different portfolio teams. Finally, there were many potential "dis-synergies." There was the usual risk of conflict with investment banking and the need to assure Mercury's institutional clients that the fund manager's decisions were not being unduly influenced by Merrill's investment-banking division.

The Mercury acquisition was supposed to produce economies of scale and economies of scope. According to Smith and Walter, "Empirical evidence of either economies of scale or economies of scope in asset management is lacking although the plausibility of scale economies exceeds that for scope economies. In any event, there has been little evidence so far that M&A activity in this sector has led to lower fees and charges to retail investors."[18]

In spite of all the expected synergies, Merrill Lynch did not significantly grow its assets under management after the Mercury acquisition. While Mercury had grown 16 percent per annum on average between 1993 and 1997, Merrill Lynch had assets under management of only $501 billion at the end of 2004, which was less than in 1996.

It turns out that freestanding mutual fund companies like Fidelity and Vanguard did far better at attracting fund investors than the multifunction firms like Merrill. One reason that the large brokerage firms (including Merrill Lynch) have not done well, says Wharton finance professor Jeremy Siegel, is that "the fees are high and the performance is extremely mediocre."[19]

A Strategic Mistake

In February 2006, eight years after the Mercury acquisition, Merrill Lynch decided to sell its asset management operation to BlackRock, a money manager specializing in fixed-income and risk management products, in exchange for just under 50 percent of BlackRock. BlackRock was one of the largest publicly traded investment management firms in the United States, with nearly $500 billion worth of assets under management. In the negotiations, Merrill's business had been assigned a value of about $8 billion (including MAM, which had been acquired for $5.3 billion). The deal made BlackRock one of the world's biggest money managers, with about $1 trillion in assets and 4,500 employees in eighteen countries.

It seems that one-stop shopping may work for the "Louis Vuittons of finance," but it does not work for the financial equivalents of Wal-Mart. It may work for Goldman Sachs, but not for American Express, Citigroup, or Merrill Lynch. American Express famously tried it in the 1980s and failed, selling its asset management arm in 2004. Citigroup adopted the brokerage-firm supermarket model in the 1990s, only to sell its way out in 2005. Merrill Lynch followed suit shortly thereafter. According to many commentators, the reason for the breakup was to avoid potential conflicts of interest arising from the distribution. Their marketing forces could be accused of favoring in-house products rather than the best products for their clients, particularly when brokers had incentives to push a house brand.

The conclusion seems to be that there are no real synergies in acquiring an asset management firm, but there are a lot of synergies in Goldman Sachs's strategy of being a financier, a market maker, and a principal investor. Until the early 2000s, unlike Goldman, Merrill had no principal investment business. To rectify this, Merrill Lynch participated in the 2005 buyout of Hertz, one of the largest transactions at the time. The following year, the firm took part in the $31.6 billion buyout of the hospital chain HCA, the biggest private-equity deal at the time. The fact that Merrill Lynch was imitating Goldman Sachs was the best compliment to Goldman Sachs's strategy.

Notes

1. Farrell and McKinsey Global Institute, "$118 Trillion and Counting," McKinsey Global Institute, February 2005.
2. Employee Benefit Research Institute, "U.S. Retirement Trends over the Past Quarter-Century," June 21, 2007.
3. Profit Sharing/401(k) Council of America, "49th Annual Survey of Profit Sharing and 401(k) Plans," October 4, 2006.
4. "This survey was carried out in 16 of the world's major industrialized countries, through telephone interviews of 11,590 people, of which half working, half retired. It provides comprehensive and comparative information on beliefs and attitudes of working people, as well as experiences and evaluations of retirees." www.retirement-scope.axa.com.
5. Farrell and McKinsey Global Institute, "$118 Trillion and Counting," op. cit.
6. Goldman's presentation at the Merrill Lynch conference in November 2005.
7. "Goldman Sachs: Behind the Brass Plate," *Economist*, April 29, 2006.
8. Ingo Walter, "Strategies in Financial Services, the Shareholders, and the System: Is Bigger and Broader Better?" *Brookings-Wharton Papers on Financial Services*, 2003.
9. Alternative investments are often defined as a category of funds designed to generate absolute returns, independent of market direction. They include hedge funds, which are discussed in Chapter 18.

10. Andrei Voicu, "Passive versus Active Investment Management Strategies," *Journal of Financial Planning*, July 1, 2004.
11. Bing Cao, Bin Jiang, and Timothy Koller, "Balancing ROIC and Growth to Build Value," *McKinsey on Finance*, no. 19, Spring 2006, pp. 12–16.
12. UBS's core activities are investment banking, institutional fund management, and private banking.
13. Walter, "Strategies in Financial Services."
14. Robert C. Doll, address at the 2005 Lehman Brothers Financial Services conference.
15. Anthony Saunders, *Financial Institutions Management: A Modern Perspective*, 3rd ed. (Burr Ridge, Ill.: Irwin, 2000).
16. Andre F. Perold, Imran Ahmed, and Randy Altschuler, "Merrill Lynch's Acquisition of Mercury Asset Management," HBS case study, July 16, 1999.
17. Roy C. Smith and Ingo Walter, *Global Banking* (New York: Oxford University Press, 1997), p. 259.
18. Ibid.
19. "The Merrill Lynch-BlackRock Deal Signals Major Shift in Financial Services," Knowledge@Wharton, March 8, 2006.

18

Alternative Investments and the Strategy of Investment Banks

There is no universally accepted definition of what constitutes an alternative investment. And what, by the way, are these investment vehicles an alternative to?

In the United States, funds (pooled investment vehicles) are regulated by the Investment Company Act, except when they remain private and are available only to highly sophisticated investors. Regulated funds must register with the SEC and disclose their investment positions. The Investment Company Act places significant restrictions on the types of transactions that registered investment companies may engage in to protect against conflicts of interest and to limit leverage.[1] These companies have little flexibility to change their investment objectives and take alternative investment approaches when market conditions change. Most of the restrictions on registered investment companies are self-imposed, and are designed to assure investors that the fund will be managed in a manner consistent with their expectations.[2] They are precluded from trading on margin, and they cannot take short positions. They cannot invest in real estate or in commodities, and they cannot take on significant debt without their shareholders' approval.

The term *alternative investment funds* (or "alternative funds") generally is used to refer to funds that are not registered as investment companies under the Investment Company Act and are exempt from registering with the SEC.[3] Alternative investment funds include hedge funds, private-equity funds, and venture capital funds. They can use a wide variety of techniques that are not available to more traditional investment funds. Alternative investment funds are typically organized as limited partnerships, where the fund managers are the general partners and investors are the limited partners. The fund managers are typically compensated through a dual fee structure, for example, the "2 and 20" setup, where managers receive 2 percent of the net asset value of the fund and 20 percent of returns in excess of some benchmark. All investment banks sponsor alternative investment funds. As we know, Goldman Sachs Asset Management has about 20 percent of its assets under management invested in alternative investments.

Hedge Funds

According to the staff report to the SEC on hedge funds, "Although there is no universally accepted definition of the term 'hedge fund,' the term generally is used to refer to an entity that holds a pool of securities and perhaps other assets, whose interests are not sold in a registered public offering, and which is not registered as an investment company under the Investment Company Act."[4] Hedge funds, in short, are largely unregulated private pools of capital.

Hedge funds are not restricted in the type of trading strategies and financial instruments they may use. They can take both long and short positions in debt and equity, and they can trade on margin (using money borrowed from a broker for trading purposes). They trade in all sorts of assets, from traditional stocks, bonds, and currencies to more exotic financial derivatives and even nonfinancial assets. Hedge funds often use leverage, whether directly to increase their returns or indirectly through derivatives.

Originally, these funds "hedged" their investments by holding opposing positions, which gave rise to the name. Alfred Winslow

Jones is credited with establishing one of the first hedge funds as a private partnership in 1949. That hedge fund invested in equities and used leverage and short selling to hedge the portfolio's exposure to movements of the corporate equity markets. Another explanation of the name is that hedge funds originated by emulating the strategy of proprietary units of investment banks.[5]

The continued rise of hedge funds has been a major force in finance. They were dominant players in several markets by the end of 2006. By early 2006, their estimated share of credit derivatives trading had increased to 58 percent. Hedge fund assets grew from $500 billion in 2000 to $1.43 trillion by the end of 2006.[6] Much of this growth can be attributed to institutional investors. These investors do not want to pay a fund manager for a broad market exposure that they can obtain more cheaply— through investing in exchange-traded funds (ETFs),[7] for example.

Registered investment companies tend to favor a relative return approach: they attempt to duplicate or exceed the performance of a selected asset class or securities index. Hedge funds generally employ an absolute return approach to investing, seeking to make money in a variety of market environments. Negative returns represent failure for a hedge fund manager, even if the equity market is down. He tends to be opportunistic in seeking positive returns while avoiding loss of principal.

The organizational documents of most hedge funds establish broad objectives and authorize alternative investment approaches to take advantage of changing market conditions. Typically, a hedge fund manager would want to invest the funds entrusted to him to produce a performance close to that of stocks with a volatility close to that of bonds. In reality, absolute-return funds often fail to even match the returns of cash. For instance, every single absolute-return fund rated by Standard & Poor's failed to hit its return targets after fees in 2006.

The strategies implemented by hedge funds are highly varied and are independent of the equity and bond markets, thereby further heightening diversification. Some of these funds take positions in currencies, stocks, bonds, or commodities in accordance with their vision of the future. They make a bet on the future; in fact, they speculate. Other funds instead bet on the reduction of price spreads in the financial markets, and they hedge. In principle, they take only a limited risk.

Hedge funds follow highly varied strategies that read with the brevity of a haiku:

- Directional
- Macro
- Long/short
- Event-driven
- Arbitrage

The SEC study distinguishes three broad categories of strategies: *market trend, event-driven*, and *arbitrage*.

Funds using *market trend* strategies exploit broad market trends in equities, interest rates, or commodity prices. They include macro funds and long/short funds. Macro funds may take positions in currencies (often unhedged) based on their opinion of various countries' macroeconomic fundamentals. For example, in 1990, Britain had decided to join the European Exchange Rate Mechanism (ERM). By 1992, Britain's ability to sustain its exchange rate appeared questionable. Quantum, a group of hedge funds led by George Soros, famously made approximately US$1 billion from shorting the pound.

Long/short funds try to exploit perceived anomalies in the prices of securities. For example, LTCM bought bonds that it believed to be underpriced and sold short bonds that it believed to be overpriced. No matter what happened to overall interest rates, as long as the spread between the two narrowed, the fund would profit. Unfortunately for LTCM, as discussed in Chapter 7, gains quickly turned into losses because spreads widened instead. Long/short equity is the most frequently used strategy among hedge funds. A fund can take a "market neutral" position, meaning that it has equal amounts of long and short positions in trading pairs, for example, buying Total SA but selling BP PLC in the oil industry.

Event-driven funds seek to profit from special situations—events such as a merger, a bankruptcy, or a takeover that may affect a security. They speculate on the future value of the security following the foreseen event. For example, merger arbitrage funds attempt to profit from pending merger transactions by taking a long position in the stock of the company to be acquired in a merger, and simultaneously taking a short position in the stock of the acquiring company.

Arbitrage funds exploit price disparities between neighboring types of assets. For example, a newly issued ("on-the-run") ten-year Treasury bond may trade at a slightly higher price than a similar previously issued ("off-the-run") ten-year Treasury bond. A hedge fund may seek to profit from this disparity by purchasing off-the-run Treasuries and selling on-the-run Treasuries short. It utilizes leverage to amplify these small differences.

The Crisis of 2007

The short history of hedge funds has shown that they know how to manage many risks, but not liquidity risk. This is not something new. The panic of 1907 was the reason for the founding of the Federal Reserve System, as Congress decided that it could not rely on the good will and ability of bankers like J. P. Morgan to coerce cooperation. The liquidity crisis of 2007 was very much a modern version of the 1907 bank run.

There are two types of liquidity:[8] *market liquidity* is the ability to trade without affecting market prices, while *funding liquidity* is the ability to acquire funding. Market-liquidity shocks strain a trader's ability to fund its positions, as additional funds (for instance, to meet the daily offsetting of profits and losses or variation margin calls) can be raised only by selling assets into a falling market.[9] This mutual dependence creates the potential for market instability, which is exactly what happened in 2007.

In the summer of 2007, many hedge funds suffered as a result of concerns about the state of the credit markets in the United States. Hedge funds that had highly leveraged positions based on illiquid assets, such as mortgage-backed securities, and that used short-term funding, lost nearly all of their value. Some hedge fund investors wanted to redeem their shares in the funds. Since defaults on mortgage loans were rising, trading in the securities that were underpinned by those loans seized up. The value of these securities was impossible to guess. Hedge fund managers had to pony up more money or collateral to back up their falling investments.

What happened in 2007 was very similar to the liquidity crisis of 1998, which was initiated by the deleveraging of LTCM. During a liquidity crisis, arbitrage funds may hold opposing positions that unexpectedly move in the same direction all of a sudden. Another fixture of hedge funds is the imbalance between liquid and illiquid assets. All these factors may force hedge funds to sell their assets.

In 1998, liquidity-driven selling by hedge funds to meet margin calls, along with a general deleveraging by global banks, contributed to a downward spiral in prices for debt securities and other investments. In 2007, the wave of deleveraging also precipitated price declines and credit spread, widening across multiple sectors of the credit markets. In turn, this presented serious challenges to many market-value structures with mark-to-market and deleveraging triggers.

The Federal Reserve Bank of New York had described the mechanisms of the 2007 crisis just before it struck:

> *Commercial banks and securities firms are directly linked to hedge funds through their counterparty exposures, for example, short-run financing for leveraged positions, prime brokerage activity, and trading counterparty exposures in over-the-counter and other markets. If a bank has a large exposure to a hedge fund that defaults or operates in markets where prices are falling rapidly, the bank's greater exposure to risk may reduce its ability or willingness to extend credit to worthy borrowers.*[10]

Banks did cut back on their credit lines to other banks around the world in case they might have faced hedge fund exposure. The spreading fears forced the central banks in Europe, the

United States, and Japan to inject billions of dollars into the financial system to help prevent borrowing and lending in credit markets from freezing up.

In another perceptive article written a year before the crisis,[11] two analysts from Fitch explained:

> *The risk to hedge funds and the market as a whole is that a price decline in a particular asset class can result in forced selling of multiple positions that is magnified by the effects of leverage. For example, a hedge fund leveraged at 4.0x could be forced to sell 25 percent of its assets in the event of an initial 5 percent price decline, assuming that prices were not further depressed by one or more sellers acting in concert. An increase in margin requirements, which is not uncommon in times of stress, and/or further selling-driven price erosion, would amplify this effect. In the prior example, a modest increase in the dealer's margin from 20 percent to 25 percent (75 percent advance rate) would require a fund to deleverage as much as 40 percent to meet margin calls and restore leverage to within limits.*

Venture Capital Funds

Venture capital is a source of capital for young and rapidly growing companies. A venture capital fund (VC fund), like a hedge fund, is an unregistered investment vehicle in which investors pool money to invest in the start-up or early stages of companies. A new firm may require substantial capital. The amount that the founder, his friends, and his family have does not suffice, so the founder must seek outside financing. He can't easily find equity, bank loans, or debt financing. Venture capital funds invest equity in such companies to help them finance their growth.

VC funds differ from hedge funds in a number of significant ways. VC investors typically commit to investing a certain amount of money over the life of the fund, and make their contributions in response to "capital calls" from the fund's general partner. VC funds typically do not retain a pool of uninvested capital; instead, their general partners make a capital call when they have identified or expect to identify a portfolio company in which the VC fund will invest. In addition, unlike hedge fund advisors, the general partners of venture capital funds often play an active role in the companies in which the funds invest, either by sitting on the board of directors or by becoming involved in the day-to-day management of these companies. In contrast to a hedge fund, which may hold an investment in a portfolio security for an indefinite period based on market events and conditions, a venture capital fund typically seeks to liquidate its investment once the value of the company increases above the value of the investments.

The first formal venture capital firm was established in 1946 by a naturalized American born in France, a professor at Harvard, and the founder of INSEAD, the graduate business school based in Fontainebleau, near Paris, Georges F. Doriot.[12] Doriot founded ARD (American Research and Development), the first and one of the most successful publicly traded venture capital corporations in the United States. While American R&D funded numerous business entities, Doriot's big success came in 1957 when ARD provided the $70,000 seed money (80 percent of the start-up equity) to Ken Olson, who founded Digital Equipment Corporation.[13]

During the 1960s and 1970s, most private-equity funds were created as venture capital funds. These funds played a prominent role in starting up Internet and related companies before the dot-com bubble burst. Venture capitalists backed high-technology companies like Microsoft, Sun Microsystems, and Google. But investment banks have not been very active in this business, yet.

Private-Equity Funds

Private-equity funds concentrate their investments in unregistered (and typically illiquid) securities. They provide funds to companies that are not listed and that cannot or do not want to raise equity in the public market. In the United States, private-equity funds are firms that seek control of nonlisted enterprises through management buyouts (MBOs), management buy-ins (MBIs), leveraged buyouts (LBOs),[14] or going private transactions. In Europe, private equity also includes venture capital. The two industries are quite different, however, since venture capital involves minority investments in firms at early stages of development (seed, start-up, and development capital), whereas private-equity funds make majority investments in mature companies.

Private-equity funds started developing seriously after 1978, the year when the Employment Retirement Income Security Act (ERISA) guidelines were reformed to allow pension funds to invest in private equity. Numerous funds sprang up during the early 1980s to finance LBOs of companies like Avis, Dr. Pepper, and Beatrice Foods.

For many corporations and their shareholders, a buyout became an alternative to a stock market flotation (IPO) or a trade sale (M&A). Since buyouts were an alternative to their core business, investment banks could not afford to neglect the private-equity industry. According to Goldman Sachs, which has specialized in M&A and advisory services for financial sponsors, private-equity investment grew from $20 billion in 1995 to $315 billion in 2005.[15] According to figures compiled by Thomson Financial, all but four of the twenty largest generators of investment-banking fees in 2005 were private-equity groups.

Private-equity funds are typically structured as limited partnerships, where investors are the limited partners and the general partner is a private group of specialized managers responsible for the day-to-day management of the fund. Often the general partner firms have become household names: Blackstone, Carlyle, Clayton Dubilier & Rice, Kohlberg Kravis Roberts (KKR), and Texas Pacific. The limited partners tend to come from old-line wealthy families, but also (and increasingly so) include large institutional investors like pension funds, high-net-worth individuals and families, endowments, banks, and insurance companies. These private-equity investors typically commit to investing a certain amount of money over the life of the fund, and they make their contributions in response to capital calls from the fund's general partner when it has identified a company in which the fund will invest.

The general partner typically purchases companies using little of the fund's equity capital, instead borrowing a substantial amount of money (from 50 percent up to 70 percent of the enterprise value of a company). A special-purpose vehicle (SPV) is created, often using the company's own assets and future cash flows as collateral. The main feature of a buyout is the use of a lot of debt to acquire a company, backed by the assets of the purchased company, which will be paying the interest with the future cash it generates.

The key, therefore, is to increase the amount of cash generated by the acquired firm. The buyout funds put in place a management team they trust, to improve profitability and ultimately seek an exit strategy for their investment within three to five years. The exit will be either an IPO or a trade sale, often to another buyout firm, but normally at a significant profit.

For example Apollo, Blackstone, and Goldman Sachs's private-equity arm bought Ondeo (today Nalco), a water treatment company, from Suez in November 2003 for $4.3 billion. The funds invested $1 billion in equity and $3.3 billion in debt. They paid back the $1 billion through dividends and from selling 30 percent of the equity in an IPO in November 2004. After the IPO, they were comfortably sitting on a paper gain of almost $1.5 billion.

On the way to the exit, the buyout fund will receive dividend payouts when the firm becomes profitable. The cash-out itself can come about in one of three ways:

- The sale of the company to a corporate buyer and the unwinding of the SPV
- The sale of the SPV to another private-equity fund (called a secondary buyout)
- An IPO of the company (or of the SPV after a reverse takeover)

Investment banks show a lot of imagination in structuring these arrangements. They are also involved in many aspects of these deals. First, they act as placement agents for the general partners. Because these entities rely on an exemption from registration of the offer and sale of their securities, the partners solicit investors either directly or through a registered broker-dealer, rather than through a general solicitation, general advertising, or a public offering of the securities.

Second, most of the investment banks have their own buyout funds and/or "funds of funds." (A fund of funds is one that invests primarily in private-equity funds rather than in operating firms. The major investment banks raised the investments that make up these funds of funds in the late 1990s from their high-net-worth clients.)

Third, they can act as advisor to a buyout firm negotiating the acquisition of a company. The role of an investment bank will be very important in what we call a "going private" deal. This is what happens when a private-equity group purchases the publicly owned stock in a firm. Investment banks can arrange the public offer for the company, which will force shareholders to accept cash for their shares if the offer is successful. After that, the stock will be delisted, hence the phrase "going private."

Then the investment banks can raise debt or mezzanine financing for a buyout. Debt can be provided by commercial banks, but it can also be found in the high-yield corporate bond market, which has now become the territory of investment banks.

An LBO is often financed by banks through bridge loans, which are later repackaged as CDOs (as discussed in Chapter 13). Alternatively, the bridge loan can be restructured as a mezzanine tranche of financing. Later the investment bank can organize the exit of the buyout firm through a trade sale or an IPO.

Let us illustrate the role of investment banks with the example of Kappa Packaging. In October 2004, Cinven and CVC, the U.K.-based private-equity firms that jointly bought the paper and packaging group Kappa Packaging in 1998, appointed Goldman Sachs to "explore strategic options" for a sale.[16] This is the final role that the investment banks played in the private-equity deal.

Investment banks were first involved in the 1993 merger between Buhrmann-Tetterode and KNP of the Netherlands that created Kappa Packaging. In 1998, Kappa Packaging was the object of an auction sale organized by investment banks. The bidders included both strategic acquirers and financial buyers. The financial buyers won, and Kappa Packaging was sold to the management. The MBO was financed by the two private-equity firms, Cinven and CVC. In 2001, investment banks were again involved when Kappa Packaging bought the packaging activities of AssiDomän in a $1 billion deal that doubled its size. In 2004, Goldman Sachs was selected as Kappa's financial advisor after a "beauty contest" that also included UBS and Deutsche Bank. At the end of 2005, Jefferson Smurfit Group and Kappa Packaging announced an agreement to merge to form Smurfit Kappa Group. Once again investment banks were financial advisors.

In an attempt to supplement and enhance this advisory role, the strategy of investment banks has been to create and develop a subordinated debt market for buyouts. We said that the target's value[17] could be financed by up to 70 percent of debt. But this does not mean 70 percent of plain-vanilla secured debt. Secured debt represents only a thin slice, about 10 percent. The other 60 percent comes from mezzanine financing or new types of debt invented by investment banks (see Chapter 12). Therefore, the funds raised in private equity become more and more specialized by asset classes.

Illustration: The Strategy of Goldman Sachs in Alternative Investment Funds

The strategy of investment banks in private equity can best be illustrated by Goldman Sachs, one of the biggest providers of financing and deal-making services to private-equity firms. We saw that within the last five years, the firm has become a leader with hedge funds and private-equity firms. It was around that time that the border between private-equity firms and hedge funds became somewhat indistinct. Some hedge funds were becoming

active in buyouts. And some private-equity firms—for example, Carlyle and Blackstone—were managing not only private equity but also hedge funds, hedge funds of funds, and real estate. Goldman Sachs provided services to both the hedge fund industry and the private-equity industry.

As we saw in Chapter 4, Goldman Sachs began making principal investments in 1982, and it allowed outside investors to participate in private investments with the firm in 1986. The firm formed its Merchant Banking division in 1998 to house its principal investment and real estate activities. Private pools of capital have developed very rapidly since the mid 1990s, from $20 billion in 1995 to $315 billion in 2005.

Goldman Sachs benefited from these inflows, which were principally from its own clients. As of 2005, Goldman Sachs had formed ten private-equity funds aggregating over $17 billion of capital. Almost 80 percent of the money came from clients ($13.3 billion), and the remaining 20 percent ($3.7 billion) came from the bank's own capital (this included corporate and real estate investing). These funds invested primarily in corporate equity securities through the Goldman Sachs Capital Partners series of funds and in mezzanine opportunities through the Goldman Sachs Mezzanine Partners series of funds.

Between 1996 and 2005, Goldman Sachs Capital Partners, which managed two-thirds of the group's private equity, invested $11 billion in equity in 480 companies globally. Goldman Sachs Mezzanine Partners raised more than $5 billion, and it invested over $2.5 billion in mezzanine and associated securities in North America and Europe.

The Triple-Play Strategy

It was the strategy of Goldman Sachs to provide financing for private-equity firms, even if the latter could become competitors to its own private-equity funds. In 2006, the bank was in competition with itself and its customer KKR for the buyout of Univision, the first Spanish-speaking communications group in North America. This "triple-play" strategy can pay off superbly, garnering fees from investing, advising, and financing. In 2005, all Goldman Sachs equity funds paid out $262 million in investment-banking fees (M&A, equity capital markets, debt capital markets, and loans), with some of them going to the investment-banking branch of Goldman Sachs. And the four other equity funds that paid even more fees must have paid some of those fees to Goldman Sachs.[18]

Here's another example of a triple pay. In January 2005, MeadWestvaco Corporation announced that it had sold its papers business and associated assets for $2.3 billion to a new company controlled by Cerberus Capital Management L.P., a private, New York–based investment firm. NewPage Corporation (OpCo) was created as an SPV to effect the acquisition of the papers group from MeadWestvaco while another acquirer purchased the timber business and related assets of MeadWestvaco. Goldman Sachs had helped Cerberus to finance the acquisition with bank debt and mezzanine financing. The acquisition was financed as follows:[19]

- With credit facilities for up to $750 million under a senior secured term loan facility of OpCo
- By borrowings under a $350 million senior secured asset-based revolving facility of OpCo
- With the issuance by OpCo of $100 million of mezzanine notes to MeadWestvaco
- With cash common equity investments of $439.3 million

Finally, Goldman Sachs provided a coated paper basket hedge to mitigate the downside risk to profitability associated with coated paper prices. Hedging solutions are difficult to find because coated paper does not trade on an established exchange or commodities market. The value of the hedge provided by Goldman Sachs was not specific to changes in coated paper prices, but instead was tied to market prices for a mix of commodities and currencies. The design of the contract was such that it was expected to have a response to movements in market pricing that would be equivalent to essentially all of the coated paper sales each year for three years.

Occasionally Goldman has joined forces with other private-equity firms. In July 2005, Goldman Sachs Capital Partners and the private-equity investment firm Kelso & Company acquired Coffeyville Resources LLC, an oil refiner and fertilizer maker based in Kansas City. Again Goldman Sachs provided a hedge to mitigate the risk of refining.

The Subtle Management of Conflicts of Interest

Goldman Sachs's strategy in private equity (as in other fields of investment banking) was to get involved in all aspects of a transaction. "Sometimes we're asked how we could be a private equity investor when we are also an advisor to private equity firms," its then chairman, Henry Paulson, said in 2005. "We do act as an advisor, as a principal, and as a financier in complex transactions."[20] As we saw in Chapter 3, for Paulson, clients do not resent this role as being a conflict of interest, as the bank invests with its clients as partners. Rather than a conflict, it is a partnership of interests.

"Complex transactions demand the spreading of risk and the sharing of expertise. That expertise is why our clients come to us," said Paulson. But there is a fine line to be drawn. In a simple example, if Goldman finds a great investment, does it put its own money into the deal, or does it tell a client about it? This inherent competition is accepted by some ("We're all big boys," says Jim Coulter, a founding partner of the Texas Pacific Group), but not by others. "It drives me nuts," says one client. "I scream at them once a month."[21] The latter's vexation may turn out to be closer to the rule than the exception: many investment banks have found it difficult to manage the conflict well. This is probably why several major investment banks were exiting the private-equity business in 2005.

As I mentioned before, in 2006 JPMorgan Chase spun off its private unit, J.P. Morgan Partners. In July 2004, Morgan Stanley had announced an agreement to establish an independent private-equity firm, "Metalmark Capital LLC," to manage the Morgan Stanley Capital Partners funds, comprising over $3 billion of private-equity investments. Morgan Stanley continued as general partner for the Capital Partners funds, however, and retained its limited partner interests. But it took only two years for Morgan Stanley to be scrambling to rebuild the private-equity business that the firm had spun off.

Sometimes the conflict of interest involves other types of investors. For example, in April 2005, Goldman Sachs Capital Partners and EQT, a satellite of the Swedish family-controlled fund Investor AB, launched a takeover bid for the publicly listed services group ISS (the Danish leader in cleaning and other industrial services). The bid included a 780 million high-yield bond bridge—and it was quite controversial with investors in ISS bonds, whose value fell because of the new capital structure.

Notes

1. See Investment Company Act, Sections 10(f), 17 (conflicts of interest), and 18 (leverage). The Investment Company Act generally allows open-end investment companies to leverage themselves only by borrowing from a bank, and only if the borrowing is subject to 300 percent asset coverage.
2. "Section 13(a)(3) of the Investment Company Act requires registered investment companies to obtain the consent of their shareholders before deviating from their fundamental policies, including concentration in certain industries, but does not require registered investment companies to have policies restricting investments. Similarly, Section 13(a)(2) of the Investment Company Act requires registered investment companies to seek the approval of their shareholders before they deviate from their policies regarding borrowing money, issuing senior securities, underwriting certain securities, purchasing or selling real estate or commodities, and making loans; but does not preclude registered investment companies from having policies permitting all such activities to the extent permitted by law." Staff Report to the United States Securities and Exchange Commission, "Implications of the Growth of Hedge Funds," September 2003.

3. In 2007, however, the SEC adopted a new rule that makes it a fraudulent, deceptive, or manipulative act, practice, or course of business for an investment advisor to a pooled investment vehicle to make false or misleading statements to, or otherwise to defraud, investors or prospective investors in that pool. This rule applies to investment advisors not only of hedge funds, but also of private-equity funds, venture capital funds, and mutual funds.

4. Staff Report to the United States Securities and Exchange Commission, "Implications of the Growth of Hedge Funds."

5. Ibid.

6. John Kambhu, Til Schuermann, and Kevin J. Stiroh, "Hedge Funds, Financial Intermediation, and Systemic Risk," Staff Report 291, Federal Reserve Bank of New York, *FRBNY Economic Policy Review*, 2007.

7. ETFs are baskets of securities that are designed to track indexes and trade like stocks. They provide the market return. ETFs were first introduced by the asset management firm State Street in 1993.

8. Actually there is a third way to look at liquidity, which has to do with overall monetary conditions (money supply, interest rates, and the price of credit).

9. Kambhu, Schuermann, and Stiroh, "Hedge Funds, Financial Intermediation, and Systemic Risk," op. cit.

10. Ibid.

11. Roger W. Meritt and Ian C. Linnell, "Hedge Funds: An Emerging Force in the Global Credit Markets," *Fitch Ratings*, February 28, 2006.

12. Brigadier General Georges F. Doriot was born on September 24, 1899, in Paris, France and died June 2, 1987. He served as an artillery officer with the French Army in World War I, then graduated from the University of Paris in 1920. He came to the United States in 1921 and attended Harvard Business School. In 1926 he became an assistant dean and associate professor of industrial management at Harvard. In 1940, the same year he became a naturalized citizen, General Doriot

was instrumental in creating the Army Industrial College for the U.S. War Department. (Source: Quartermaster Hall of Fame, 1996.)

13. Twentieth Century American Leaders Database; www.hbs.edu/leadership/database/leaders/224/.

14. Technically, an LBO is an acquisition of a firm by a private group using debt financing, while an MBO is led by the firm's own management.

15. From a presentation by Henry Paulson at the Merrill Lynch Financial Services Conference, November 2005.

16. Lina Saigol and Peter Smith, "Goldman to Advise Kappa on Its Options," *Financial Times*, October 6, 2004.

17. Enterprise value = market value + debt – cash

18. Information from Thomson Financial/Freeman & Co, cited in Peter Thal Larsen, "Banks Face Big Test to Keep Clients," *Financial Times*, May 30, 2006.

19. sec.edgar-online.com/2005/10/31/0001047469–05–025639/Section59.asp.

20. From Paulson's presentation to the 2005 Merrill Lynch Financial Services Conference.

21. Quoted by Bethany McLean in "Goldman Sachs: Inside the Money Machine," *Fortune*, September 6, 2004.

Conclusion

I wrote this book to demystify the workings of investment banks. If you are in touch with one side or another of an investment bank—whether you are a customer, supplier, professional, or competitor—I hope that this will enable you to negotiate your way more easily. It has also been my goal to explain how investment banks really function for the many business school students who go into investment banking each year. They will need to be experts in their area, but they also will need to know what the other areas of the bank are doing if they want to be involved in solving the complex financial problems of their clients. This book should also answer the many questions asked by senior executives who are selecting an investment bank. Finally, I hope that my experience in the business will prove useful for my colleagues in any of these institutions who are still wondering what the heck happens here and what course of action they should be taking in light of what investment banks have done in the past and are doing now.

Bibliography

Bessis, J. *Risk Management in Banking*, 2nd ed. New York: Wiley, 2002.

Bloch, E. *Inside Investment Banking*. Illinois: Dow Jones Irwin, 1986.

Blume, M., Jeremy J. Siegel, and D. Rottenberg. *Revolution on Wall Street: The Rise and Decline of the New York Stock Exchange*. New York: Norton, 1993.

Bogaert, R., G. Kurgan-Van Hentenryk, and H. Van der Wee. *History of European Banking*. Antwerp: Fonds Mercator, 1994.

Braudel, Fernand. *Civilisation Matérielle, Economie et Capitalisme, XV–XVIII Siècle, Les Jeux de l'Échange*. Armand Colin, 1979.

Briys, Eric, and François de Varenne. *The Fisherman and the Rhinoceros: How International Finance Shapes Everyday Life*. New York: Wiley, 2000.

Cairncross, A. K. *Home and Foreign Investment, 1870–1913*. Cambridge: Cambridge University Press, 1953.

Crouhy, Michael, Dan Galai, and Robert Mark, *The Essentials of Risk Management*. New York: McGraw-Hill, 2005.

Darwin, Charles. *On the Origin of Species*. London: John Murray, 1859.

Deleuze, Gilles, and F. Guattari. *Mille Plateaux*. Paris: Les Éditions de Minuit, 1980.

Eccles, R. G., and D. B. Crane. *Doing Deals*. Boston: Harvard Business School Press, 1988.

Endlich, Lisa. *Goldman Sachs: The Culture of Success*. New York: Alfred A. Knopf, 1999.

Gasparino, Charles. *Blood on the Street*. New York: Free Press, 2005.

Ghosn, Carlos, and Philippe Riès. *Citoyen du Monde*. Grasset, 2003.

Green, Stephen. *Serving God? Serving Mammon?* Marshall Pickering, 1996.

Gross, D., and the editors of *Forbes* magazine. *Forbes Greatest Business Stories of All Time*. New York: Wiley, 1996.

Hitt, Michael A., R. Duane Ireland, and Robert E. Hoskisson. *Strategic Management: Competitiveness and Globalization,* 4th ed. Cincinnati: South-Western College Publishing, 2001.

Hull, J. C. *Options, Futures & Other Derivatives*, 4th ed. Upper Saddle River, N.J.: Prentice-Hall, 1999.

Jacobs, B. *Capital Ideas and Market Realities*. New York: Blackwell, 1999.

Jacoby, N. H. *Corporate Power and Social Responsibility, a Blueprint for the Future*. New York: Macmillan, 1973.

Kessler, Andy. *Wall Street Meat*. New York: Harper Business, 2003.

Knee, J. A. *The Accidental Investment Banker*. New York: Oxford University Press, 2006.

Levitt, A. *Take On the Street*. New York: Vintage Books, 2003.

Liaw, K. T. *The Business of Investment Banking*. New York: Wiley, 1999.

Maister, D., C. Green, and R. Galford. *The Trusted Advisor.* New York: Free Press, 2001.

Marshall, J. F., and M. E. Ellis. *Investment Banking and Brokerage.* New York: McGraw-Hill, 1993.

Marx, K. *Capital,* www.marxists.org/francais/marx/works/1867/Capital-I/kmcapI-31.htm.

Partnoy, F. *Infectious Greed.* Profile Books, 2003.

Rolfe, J., and P. Troob. *Monkey Business.* New York: Warner Books, 2000.

Ross S., R. Westerfield, and J. Jaffe. *Corporate Finance,* 7th ed. New York: McGraw-Hill, 2005.

Saunders, Anthony. *Financial Institutions Management: A Modern Perspective,* 3rd ed. Burr Ridge, Ill.: Irwin, 2000.

Schilit, H. *Financial Shenanigans,* 2nd ed. New York: McGraw-Hill, 2002.

Smith, Roy C., and Ingo Walter. *Global Banking.* New York: Oxford University Press, 1996.

Sobel, Robert. *Dangerous Dreamers: The Financial Innovators from Charles Merrill to Michael Milken.* New York: Wiley, 1993.

Vlasic B., and B. A. Stertz. *Taken for a Ride: How Daimler-Benz Drove Off with Chrysler.* New York: HarperCollins, 2000.

Index

About the Author

Michel Fleuriet is currently an associate professor at the University of Paris–Dauphine. He is also a visiting professor with international business schools in China (CKGSB), Brazil (FDC), and the United States (Wharton).

Fleuriet spent half of his professional career in the academic world and half as an investment banker. He started his career as a lawyer at the Paris bar. In 1973, he became assistant, assistant professor, and then professor of finance at HEC, one of France's leading business schools, where he taught until 1989. Fleuriet started his M&A boutique in 1980, which was merged into a French investment bank, Worms & Cie. He left Worms & Cie in 1989 to join Chase Manhattan. From 1989 to 1991 he was the president of Chase Manhattan in Paris. In early 1991, he joined Merrill Lynch to develop its investment-banking activities in France. Merrill had two people in Paris in investment banking at that time, and the firm employed 220 people in 2000. In 1997, Fleuriet was appointed chairman of Merrill Lynch France, with responsibility for all activities. In December 1999, he joined HSBC in France as chairman in order to develop the business and to lead the coordination of its investment banking and markets business. He participated in the acquisition of CCF by HSBC in 2000, and he left HSBC CCF in September 2001.

Fleuriet holds a doctorate of law from the University of Paris (summa cum laude) as well as a Ph.D. in finance from the Wharton School of Finance of the University of Pennsylvania. He is a member of the Council of NYSE Euronext Paris and a founding member of the French association of directors, IFA.